MAGISTRATES' COMPANION TO THE ADULT COURT COMPETENCES

By Janet Carter
LL.B (Hons), Barrister, DPMS, MCIPD

Lawtexts,
PO Box 289,
Leeds LS6 3YG

1st edition
ISBN 0-9540636-1-9

CONTENTS

Dedicated to the memory of my mum, dad and aunt Mary

ACKNOWLEDGEMENTS

For their advice and comments I thank Angela Barker, J.P.; Grizelda Collier, J.P.; Sallie Davies, J.P.; Caterina Fagg, West Yorkshire Probation Service; Lesley Gunawan; Jane Hall, Education Leeds; Judith Hartshorne, Department of Work and Pensions; David Jennings; Interfaith Education Centre, Bradford; Clare Lunt, HIT; Sue Marsh, Gita Sisupalan, Lee Davidson, Home Office; Lynne McGechie, Judicial Studies Board; Eleanor Philips; Dr. Sue Rayner Jacobs, Lis Ramsay, Department of Constitutional Affairs; Ann Robinson; Jodie Sheppard; Philip Solity; Dick Weber, Prison Service.

For their support and encouragement, I thank my husband Neil and our sons, John and Andrew.

PREFACE

This book draws together all the essential, up to date, information which the busy, committed magistrate needs to contribute effectively towards high quality decisions, using personal life experience and initiative. There are a few legal building blocks and lots of practical discussion and examples.

There have been numerous statutory changes over the past two years which have increased powers and options to deal with contemporary problems such as anti-social behaviour, drug abuse, truancy and the rise in prison population. During the same period there has been an unprecedented number of government initiatives to improve the criminal justice system to ensure that more defendants are brought to justice, more trials go ahead on the day and more fines are paid as ordered. All are covered in the text.

Rather than simply following the list of MNTI competences which would be disjointed, repetitious and incomplete for the purpose of a comprehensive text, the book begins by discussing the Magistrates' Court in its current context. It then moves through the legal processes from the point of charge through to bail, trial, sentence and enforcement of the penalties. It then considers the individual role under the judicial oath, to maintain and develop awareness and skills, whether as a winger in the team or as a chairman. The final chapter deals with important current issues which impact significantly upon the court and decision-making.

Both MNTI 1 and MNTI 2 competences are summarised and referenced in the appendices to the relevant part of the text. The book may be used as a 'dip in' reference for new magistrates, or as a three hour armchair read to refresh and update existing magistrates. Practical examples, case law outlines and statistics are provided to avoid the necessity of looking up other sources. All you need is here!

The aim is to equip the reader with the basic legal tools to know enough about the law to be able to do enough for the victims. Many 'perfect sentencing cocktails' are only created in the retiring room and a life is turned around. Many ancillary orders are not applied for at all, but on the court's initiative those orders make the most immediate positive changes for the community. An informed magistrate can make all the difference.

Cross-references are made to the Adult Court Bench Book (published for every magistrate by the Judicial Studies Board), and the checklists, sentencing guidelines and pronouncements therein.

Throughout the text I have used the masculine gender purely to avoid tedious reference to both genders - please assume the feminine as equally applicable. I have stated the law to the best of my understanding as at 17th March 2004.

Janet Carter,
Leeds,
March 2004.

CHAPTER 1
The Magistrates' Court in context

This chapter sets out the context of the Magistrates' Court in relation to the higher courts, together with an outline of the types of cases dealt with and the main players both inside and outside of the courtroom.

A basic awareness of the court hierarchy is helpful to understand where the Magistrates' Court sits in the big picture. Whilst the main source of our law is found in legislation e.g. Acts of Parliament and rules, a large body of law is also created by judges in the course of deciding cases. The decisions of the higher courts bind the lower courts - known as the doctrine of binding precedent. Appeal lies generally from the lower courts and up through the higher courts.

1.1. The court hierarchy (in descending order)

1.1.1. **The House of Lords** is the ultimate domestic appeal court and deals with appeals on points of law which involve matters of public importance.

1.1.2. **The Court of Appeal** lies 'below' the House of Lords in the hierarchy. It is made up of two divisions – the Civil Division and the Criminal Division. The hearing is not a rehearing with all the evidence, but merely a review of the lower court's decision. However fresh evidence may be admitted and a retrial may be allowed if it is in the interests of justice to do.

1.1.3. **The High Court** is made up of 3 divisions – Chancery, Family and Queens Bench Division. The Queens Bench Division is the largest of the 3 and the Lord Chief Justice is President of the Division. Its work includes dealing with claims for judicial review, and criminal appeals on points of law either directly from the Magistrates' Court or via the Crown Court. Trials in the High Court are heard either in London or in one of the provincial trial centres.

1.1.4. **The Crown Court** is a single court which can sit anywhere in England and Wales. Sittings are usually confined to the towns designated as court centres (currently 78). When the Crown Court sits in the city of London, it is known as the Central Criminal Court - often referred to as the Old Bailey.

It deals with trials on indictment before a judge and; criminal appeals from Magistrates' Court; cases committed for greater sentence than the magistrates may impose, and it also has a very limited civil jurisdiction.

The decisions of the above courts are binding on the Magistrates' court, provided that they are compatible with the Human Rights Act (see 4.9).

1.1.5. **The County Court** is the lowest tier of court which deals only with civil matters (see 1.2). There are currently 218 county courts in England and Wales and each county court has one or more circuit judges and a number of district judges.

1.1.6. **The Magistrates' Court** is locally based into geographical commission areas which are then subdivided into petty sessions areas, with benches of lay magistrates who must live in, or within 15 miles of the commission area. Each justice is then assigned to a petty sessions area within the commission area. There are about 31,000 lay magistrates, hearing over one million criminal cases a year – 95% of all criminal cases. Additionally there are approximately 182 District Judges (Magistrates' Courts) who are qualified lawyers and sit alone. Normally a lay bench will consist of 2 or 3 members. There are limited exceptions when a lay magistrate may sit alone with limited powers e.g. dealing with a bail application; search warrant application; requesting a pre-sentence report; prohibiting publication and giving directions for conduct of a trial.

Specialist panels of magistrates deal with family and youth cases in family proceedings and youth courts, and procedures are modified to deal with the sensitivities of these types of cases. However, there are circumstances in which youths appear in the adult court and all magistrates must therefore have some knowledge of youth-related law and procedures.

1.2. Types of cases and where they are originally dealt with

1.2.1. Criminal and civil cases - the key differences

Criminal cases	Civil cases
Regulates conduct considered by the state to be prejudicial to the community as a whole.	Regulates relationship between legal persons - individuals and corporations.

Aim is to determine guilt/ innocence and impose appropriate penalties.	Aim is to settle disputes and make formal orders between the parties e.g. to determine claims to property, award compensation, probate matters, grant divorce, make orders for child contact etc.
Terminology: Prosecutor prosecutes the defendant/accused. Defendant is found guilty/convicted	Terminology: Complainant/plaintiff sues (brings an action) against a defendant/respondent. An order is made against the defendant/respondent if the case is proved.
Proceedings are normally instituted by officers of the Crown.	Proceedings are instituted by one of the parties.
The evidential burden of proof is on the prosecutor.	The evidential burden of proof is on the complainant/plaintiff.
Order of evidence and speeches (disputed matter): Prosecutor may address the court. Prosecution evidence. Defendant may address, whether or not he afterwards calls evidence. Prosecutor evidence to rebut defence evidence. Defendant may address if he has not done so already (usually left to this point). Either party may address a 2nd time with leave of the court If both address the court twice, the accused has the last word.	Order of evidence and speeches: Complainant may address the court. Complainant evidence. Defendant may address, whether or not he afterwards calls evidence. Complainant evidence to rebut defence evidence. Defendant may address if he has not done so already. Either party may address a 2nd time with leave of the court. If both address twice, the complainant has the last word.
Standard of proof is to prove beyond reasonable doubt - does not mean beyond a shadow of a doubt.	Standard of proof is to prove on balance of probabilities - being more probable than not.

1.2.2. Civil cases - High Court/County Court/Magistrates' Court

There is a financial limit to the cases which the County Court can deal with, whereas the High Court has unlimited jurisdiction. Victims in Magistrates' Courts' cases may well pursue the civil aspect of their case in the County Court or High Court e.g. compensation claims arising from traffic accidents, disputed or complex compensation claims arising from criminal charges.

The Magistrates' Court does have some civil jurisdiction, predominantly, family law cases which are dealt with by its family proceedings court. The Magistrates' Court currently has jurisdiction for licensing matters. This includes the grant, renewal, revocation, transfer and removal of licenses of licensed premises and extensions of licensing hours for special events and occasional licenses for supply of liquor in unlicensed premises for particular events. The licensing responsibilities will be phased out during 2004/2005, during which time the local authorities will take over the administration of licences and the Magistrates' Court will simply deal with appeals from the local authority.

1.2.3. Criminal cases and legislation - Crown Court/Magistrates Court

Criminal matters involve acts against the rules of the community at large and the state, through the Crown Prosecution Service, who will normally (but not exclusively) take action against the offender.

Criminal cases are classified into three categories in terms of seriousness. Firstly, 'summary only' offences may only be dealt with by the Magistrates' Court e.g. taking a motor vehicle without the owner's consent, common assault, speeding.

Secondly, 'either-way' offences, which offer the defendant a choice to 'elect' to be dealt with by a judge and jury at Crown Court for trial e.g. theft, burglary, assault occasioning actual bodily harm. 'Either-way' offences may also be committed to the Crown Court by the magistrates, for trial or for sentence, if it is considered that the offence merits greater punishment than the Magistrates' Court may impose, i.e. above 6 months imprisonment for a single offence or £5000 fine or compensation.

The third type of case is 'indictable only' and they must be 'sent' on to the Crown Court because they are so serious, e.g. murder, rape, robbery. Normally the case is 'sent' after the first hearing in the Magistrates' Court which is usually a first bail application.

The most common offences are listed below, along with the legislation (Act of Parliament)) which created them:

- Theft Act 1968 – theft, robbery, burglary, handling stolen goods, taking a motor vehicle without consent, going equipped for theft, deception
- Public Order Act 1986 – violent disorder, affray, causing harassment, alarm or distress, threatening behaviour
- Road Traffic Acts – dangerous driving, speeding, no insurance
- Offences against the Person Act 1861 – assault occasioning actual bodily harm, wounding
- Criminal Justice Act 1988 - common assault
- Misuse of Drugs Act 1971 – possession and supply of illegal drugs e.g. ecstasy, heroin, cannabis
- Criminal Damage Act 1971 – criminal damage and arson.

The statute gives the definition of the various offences and the maximum penalties. Rules, regulations and case law from the higher courts further interpret the law.

1.2.4.   Crime statistics - 2002/3

The total number of crimes recorded by the police in 2002/3 = a 3% fall on 2001/2 (after allowing for changes in police recording practices over the reporting period).

British Crime Survey (BCS):

- Crime rate - a 25% fall in the crime measured by the BCS over the last 5 years.
- Clear up rate - 23.5% of crimes recorded in 2002/3.
- Burglary - 39% fall since 1997.
- Vehicle-related theft - 31% fall since 1997.
- Violence - 19% fall since 1999, due to reductions in domestic and acquaintance violence rather than stranger assaults.
- Robberies - 14% fall in 2002/3. (Largely attributed to Street Crime initiative). Two thirds of robberies in 5 police areas - Metropolitan (39%), West Midlands, Greater Manchester, West Yorkshire and Avon and Somerset.

Crime in England and Wales (Home Office Statistical bulletin) uses the BCS and the number of crimes recorded by the police. BCS figures are based on questioning a sample of the population.
See <http://www.crimereduction.gov.uk/statistics28.htm>[accessed 17/01/04])

1.3. Appeal from the Magistrates' Court

1.3.1. Criminal appeals to the Crown Court against conviction and/or sentence

The appeal is based on fact only, ranging from disputed identity through to whether the defendant had the requisite intention to steal the property or not. Dealing with an appeal involves rehearing the case. The parties are not confined to the evidence given in the Magistrates' Court. The sentence may also be increased.

Between 2 and 4 magistrates sit on appeals to the Crown Court, depending upon the type of case, along with the judge or recorder. The decision is that of the majority on the bench and the magistrates carry equal weight with the professional judge, unless a casting vote is required. The judge or recorder presides and his rulings on legal matters bind the magistrates.

The Crown Court will give reasons for the decision and the magistrates involved in the original case are entitled to see the reasons.

> *Example:*
> *Custodial sentence is too severe for this defendant who has never served a custodial penalty before and has taken positive steps to deal with his drug addiction – reduced from 4 months imprisonment to 28 days enabling immediate release to re-commence drug rehabilitation programme.*

1.3.2. Civil appeals - licensing and family on fact

Appeals concerning family proceedings go to the Family Division of the High Court. Appeals on licensing matters are currently heard by the Crown Court, but this will cease when local authorities take responsibility for licensing and appeals will then lie to the Magistrates' Court - anticipated in 2004/5.

1.3.3. Appeal to High Court by way of case stated

This type of appeal relates to a question of law or jurisdiction (as opposed to fact). The proceedings are questioned on the ground that it is wrong in law or in excess of jurisdiction, by requesting the court to state a case for the opinion of the High Court. Never be influenced by solicitors who 'threaten appeal'. There is no discredit in a decision being appealed provided that the bench have taken the advice of the legal adviser and have announced and recorded good reasons for the decision.

The appeal is heard by 2 or 3 judges of the Queens Bench Division of the High Court in respect of criminal matters, who simply hear counsel from each side. The court may confirm, reverse or vary the decision; give the magistrates their opinion on the relevant point of law; or make such other order as it sees fit, which may include ordering a rehearing before a different bench.

1.3.4.   Appeal to High Court by way of application for judicial review

The review is limited to considering whether the Magistrates' Court has failed to exercise its jurisdiction properly or whether it has come to some error of law which appears on the face of the record. It is not focussed on the decision, but on the decision-making process.

The decision may be quashed and remitted back to the magistrates with a direction to reconsider it and reach a decision in accordance with the findings of the High Court or damages and remedies may be ordered by the High Court. Application must be made within 3 months of the date when grounds for the application first arose.

Judicial review is not an appeal as such but a challenge to the decision making process and leave must be obtained from a High Court judge that there is an arguable case.

1.3.5.   Appeal to the Court of Appeal

On a criminal matter, the High Court must first certify that a point of law of general public importance is involved in the decision and leave must be given for the appeal to the Court of Appeal.

1.4.   European Court of Human Rights and The Convention on Human Rights

The European Court of Human Rights sits in Strasbourg and deals with Convention/Human Rights issues. Any individual, non-governmental organisation or group of individuals can petition the court, alleging a violation of Convention rights.

The objective of the European Convention, proclaimed in 1950 was 'the protection of individual Human Rights, and the maintenance and promotion of the ideals and values of a democratic society'. It became incorporated into our domestic law in the Human Rights Act 1998, implemented in October 2000. This entitles individuals to argue Convention rights in the UK courts and places responsibility on all public authorities, including the courts, to apply Convention rights. A summary of the Human Rights Act 1998 appears at 4.9.

1.5. The roles of other agencies

1.5.1. **The Home Office** is responsible for policy and legislation regarding the police, probation service, prisons, national security, and immigration. The current aims of the Home Office include 'to reduce crime and the fear of crime' and 'to deliver effective custodial and community sentences'.

1.5.2. **The Department for Constitutional Affairs (incorporating the Lord Chancellor's Department) (DCA)** was created in June 2003. It is responsible for the administration of the court system, the appointment of judges and magistrates, and policy on human rights and freedom of information. Its current agenda includes the creation of a single, unified courts administration by combining the Court Service, one of the Department's agencies and the 42 Magistrates' Courts Committees by April 2005.

1.5.3. **The Police** are responsible for the detection, investigation, apprehension and institution of criminal proceedings. The primary function of today's police is to uphold the law fairly and firmly; to prevent crime; to pursue and bring to justice those who break the law and to protect, help and reassure the community.

There are 43 police forces in England and Wales. The Home Secretary is responsible for the organisation, administration and operation of the service. Chief Constables are responsible for the 'direction and control' of each police force. In recent years there has been an increase in more civilian staff, including neighbourhood wardens and community support officers.

Police powers are contained within statutory Codes of Practice which include powers to stop and search; search of premises; detention, treatment and questioning; identification; recording of interviews. Breach of the powers may result in disciplinary proceedings and inadmissibility of the relevant evidence.

1.5.4. **The Crown Prosecution Service (CPS),** subject to a few exceptions, is responsible for conducting all police prosecutions. The Service is independent of the police and has been in existence since 1986. The CPS lawyers advise the police, review each file, decide whether or not to prosecute and appear in court to present the prosecution case. A Chief Crown Prosecutor heads each of the areas. The Director of Public Prosecutions heads the Service as a whole.

The Code for Crown Prosecutors highlights the duty to review all files presented by the police. It sets out two stages in the decision to prosecute.

The first stage is the evidential test which requires 'enough evidence to provide a realistic prospect of conviction.' The objective test is whether a properly directed bench or jury is more likely than not to convict. The second stage is the public interest test. The Code gives examples of common factors where a prosecution is less likely to be appropriate. Examples include where the court is likely to impose a nominal penalty; where the prosecution is likely to have a very bad effect on the victim's health; where the defendant is elderly or suffering from significant ill health or where the defendant has put right the loss or harm caused. The Code states that any offence which is motivated by discrimination is likely to require prosecution.

1.5.5. **The National Probation Service (NPS)** is now described as a 'law enforcement agency', and its remit is to protect the public, operate and enforce court orders and prison licences, and rehabilitate offenders. All NPS work includes continuous assessment and management of risk. Each year, courts are assisted in their sentencing decisions through the provision of over 200,000 pre-sentence reports and 20,000 bail information reports.

1.5.6. **The Prison Service** objectives are to protect the public by maintaining a safe, decent and healthy environment for prisoners and to reduce crime by providing constructive regimes in custody. There are 139 prisons in England and Wales ranging from maximum security prisons to open prisons. Currently the service has 47,000 staff looking after a prison population of around 73,000 (March 2004).

1.5.7. **Victim Support** is the national charity which helps people affected by crime, by providing free and confidential support. It also provides a Witness Service in every criminal court in England and Wales. In 2003, local branches contacted nearly 1,500,000 victims and the Witness Service supported over 250,000 witnesses.

1.5.8. **The National Criminal Justice Board (NCJB)** membership includes the Lord Chancellor; Home Office and DCA ministers; Chief Executive of the CPS; Director General of the National Probation Service; President of the Association of Chief Police Officers, and the Chairman of the Youth Justice Board. Its aim is to remove barriers to joint working, and give strategic direction of resources, particularly by identifying and sharing effective local practices. It has specific responsibility for supporting **Local Criminal Justice Boards (LCJBs)** which bring together the chief officers at local level to deliver on the Public Service Agreements e.g. Narrowing the Justice Gap (see 7.1); combating inequality and discrimination in the Criminal Justice Service (CJS) and communication across the CJS. Each of the local boards have a Performance Officer to assist in managing and monitoring performance.

1.5.9.   The Youth Justice Board became operational in September 1998 and maintains oversight of the youth justice system as a whole, including the Youth offending teams (see below). It is sponsored by the Home Office and its principal aim is to prevent offending by children and young people. Responsibilities include setting standards for the provision of youth justice services and custodial accommodation, and commissioning places for secure facilities.

1.5.10.   Youth offending teams (Yots) are local multi-agency teams which include members of the police, probation service, social services, education, health, drugs and alcohol misuse and housing. The wide expertise ensures a comprehensive and swift response to needs and potential reasons for offending.   These are identified through a national questioning and assessment process which ensures a consistency of information for the court, including care history, relationships, education, health, motivators and indicators of vulnerability whenever the child or young person comes to the attention of the authorities.

1.5.11.   Local authorities play an active part in the work of the court. Their role includes bringing care and supervision proceedings in respect of children; applications for anti-social behaviour orders; enforcement of council tax and enforcement of relevant legislation e.g. Food and Environment Protection Act 1985, local parking offences, noise pollution etc.

1.5.12.   Other prosecuting agencies (other than CPS and local authorities):
*   British Transport Police – e.g. trespass on the railway lines, urinating in railway stations.
*   Environment Agency – e.g. water pollution, illegal dumping of waste.
*   Department of Transport – e.g. no vehicle excise licence, fail to notify change of ownership.
*   Health and Safety Executive - e.g. safety of machinery and operation.
*   H.M. Customs and Excise – e.g. fail to pay duty.
*   Trading Standards Department – e.g. breach of Trade Descriptions Act, under-age sales.
*   TV Licensing - using television without a licence (it is now possible to purchase a licence by instalments using the Cash Easy Entry system - prosecution for 'no TV licence' will follow if the payment scheme is not complied with).

- RSPCA – e.g. cruelty to animals.
- Post Office – e.g. theft of postal packages by postmen.

1.5.13. The legal profession is made up of solicitors, barristers, legal executives. There are around 70,000 solicitors and a number specialise in representing defendants in the Magistrates' Court. Barristers appear occasionally in the Magistrates' court upon the instructions of a solicitor as they cannot be approached directly by the defendant. In 1999, provision was made for the prosecution of straightforward guilty plea criminal cases by lay presenters, rather than by solicitors/barristers.

The defence solicitor will essentially take instructions; advise on plea; interview witnesses and conduct the case in court. The professional duties of a solicitor are contained within the Guide to the Professional Conduct of Solicitors which is published by the Law Society. The duties include the following:

- Must promote and protect fearlessly and by all proper and lawful means the client's best interests.
- Must not deceive or mislead the court.
- Must not rehearse, practice or coach witnesses in relation to their evidence.
- Must not accept instructions to act for 2 or more clients where there is a conflict or a significant risk of conflict between the clients e.g. blaming each other.

In general there is no duty upon a solicitor to enquire in every case as to whether his client is telling the truth. The Legal Services Commission grant contracts to firms of solicitors who provide legal services on behalf of the State and provide payment of periodic lump sums conditional upon dealing with an estimated number of cases.

1.5.14. The Community Safety Partnership and legislation hinges on crime prevention, rather than crime processing, and The Crime and Disorder Act 1998 created the responsibility for local authorities and police forces to co-operate in the formulation and implementation of crime reduction strategies for the local authority area. Other agencies are also involved. The purpose is to reduce crime in local communities and this is achieved through local crime audits, local consultation, determination of priorities and responsibilities for necessary actions. The Act also created the Anti Social Behaviour Order (see 7.3) which is a primary tool for making safer communities. The local community strategy must be published and reviewed every three years. It is an interesting and helpful document for magistrates to read and may be obtained from the local authority.

1.5.15. Magistrates Association (MA)

What does the MA do? It promotes uniformity of practice; consults and represents its 29,000 members; has representatives on government working groups; provides information and advice to members; promotes public awareness of the magistracy, and delivers and supports training. A monthly publication, The Magistrate, provides helpful update on legislation and issues.

The 'Magistrate in the Community' (MIC) project involves magistrates going out to community groups and giving presentations, and welcoming visitors to the courts in order to increase awareness of the magistracy and the role of the Magistrates' Court.

1.6.   Local management and administration

1.6.1.   Magistrates' Courts Committee (MCC) →

1.6.2.   Unified Courts Administration (UCA) in April 2005

The Magistrates' Courts are currently managed by 42 Magistrates' Courts Committees (MCCs), with a Justices Chief Executive (JCE) who acts as clerk to the MCC and allocates responsibilities to staff.

The MCC is financed by the local authority with a grant of up to 80% from central funds. Excluding Greater London, it is made up of active magistrates and membership is determined by a selection committee which is made up of representatives of each bench. The general powers and duties of the committee include responsibility for the 'efficient and effective' administration of the Magistrates' Courts for their area.

The Unified Courts Administration, created by the Courts Act 2003 deals with the future administration of all types of courts in order to ensure more effective use of facilities and services. It brings together the current 42 Magistrates' Courts Committees, and the Court Service which is currently responsible for the running of all courts, except the Magistrates' Court and the House of Lords. The administration will be brought into 7 regions within which there will be 42 management areas based upon the criminal justice areas. Each area will have a statutory Courts Board to consider and review plans for the courts in the area and it will include at least one judge and two magistrates. The new agency will exist in shadow form, under the lead of the Chief Executive who took up appointment in March 2004, before launch in April 2005.

1.6.3. Local Advisory Committee

Magistrates are appointed by the Lord Chancellor on behalf of the Crown, on the recommendation of the Lord Chancellor's Advisory Committees or by the Chancellor of the Duchy of Lancaster (Greater Manchester, Merseyside and Lancashire).

The functions of the Committee are as follows:

*   To determine the number of magistrates to be recommended each year.
*   To recruit and recommend for appointment, candidates with the necessary qualities, taking into account the need for benches to be balanced in terms of gender, ethnic origin, occupation, geographical spread and political affiliation.
*   To ensure that benches do not include a disproportionate number of magistrates who are members of any one group or organisation.
*   To ensure that magistrates fulfil their undertaking to sit and undertake training,
*   To draw to the attention of bench chairmen and justices clerks, instances of magistrates sitting too little or too often and to seek explanations.
*   To consider, and where appropriate make recommendations about the conduct and competence of magistrates.

The committee size is not stipulated, but should ensure that there are sufficient members to provide panels of a minimum of two for first stage interviews and three for second stage interviews. So far as practicable, one member of the panel should be a non-magistrate i.e. about one third of the committee membership should be non-magistrates. There is no expectation that every member should see every candidate.

The term of office is for nine years and should only be extended in exceptional circumstances.
(Lord Chancellors Directions for Advisory Committees on Justices of the Peace 1998).

1.6.4. Bench Training and Development Committee (BTDC)

The committee is appointed each year at the annual meeting of the bench, and consists of 3, 6 or 9 members, with one third retiring each year. No magistrate may serve for more than 9 years in total. It is recommended that the committee meets at least once each quarter.

The role of the committee is to:

- Compile and maintain a list of magistrates who are approved to act as chairmen in court and ensure that they are adequately trained to do so. This includes the selection of magistrates to undertake chairmanship training.
- Identify the training needs of the bench and report these to the Magistrates' Courts Committee. Training needs will emerge through appraisals, bench and rota meetings, and panel meetings.
- Assessment by a BTDC representative of individual training needs outside of the appraisal programme when a magistrate is transferred/re-appointed/returns from leave of absence of 6 months or more, or where there has been a complaint about the performance of a magistrate.
- Oversee and manage the panels of mentors and appraisers. A joint panel may be created.
- Ensure a scheme of appraisal is in place which will ensure that every magistrate is appraised at least once every 3 years.
- Decide upon the size of the appraiser panel, with a recommended minimum of 6 appraisals per appraiser.
- Allocation of mentors to new magistrates as soon as possible after the Lord Chancellor has announced the appointments to the bench.
- Recruitment to the mentor and appraiser panels based upon criteria for appointment which should be published to the bench. Appraisers and mentors should have a minimum of 3 years of regular sittings and be appraised as competent to the level at which they are appraising. A magistrate may serve as a mentor and an appraiser, but never to the same individual magistrate.
- Refer an individual magistrate to the Advisory Committee if they are persistently unable to demonstrate competence when appraised following additional training.
- Agree and publish an appeal and grievance procedure.
- Ensure a quality assurance mechanism of the appraisal scheme is in place. The expectation of the Judicial Studies Board is that this will be through a proportion of appraisals being undertaken by appraisers from another bench and that this will include some members of the BTDC.
- Provide feedback to the Judicial Studies Board on the operation of MNTI 2 on an annual basis.

(Judicial Studies Board (2003) Magistrates National Training Initiative Handbook: MNTI 2, p125 - 149).

1.6.5.   Sitting patterns

The Lord Chancellor expects magistrates to sit in court on at least 26 half days per year. The average number of sittings in 2003 was 35 half days. Ideally adult court magistrates should sit for a maximum of 70 half-day sittings and panel members for a maximum of 100 half day sittings. Sitting patterns vary on each bench, and are organised in various ways. They include computerised annual/quarterly/monthly plans by some courts and weekly liaison with the listing office by others. The benches for the various daily courts may be determined on an annual basis or may be determined on the day. Some benches expect magistrates to be available for full days and list cases accordingly; others operate on jig-saws of half day availability.

There are various factors for the listing office to juggle. They include ensuring that a mentor is placed in the same court as his mentee and that there are mixed gender benches in youth and family court. That 'tied benches' return to their cases and that magistrates are not listed to sit on cases they are disqualified from. That a supervised new chairman gets a particular type of list, and also filling in the inevitable unforeseen absences. Never an easy task!

1.6.6.   Specialist panels

The two obligatory specialist panels are the youth panel and the family panel which each service the relevant courts. Members are appointed at the October Annual Meeting and serve for three years. Whilst it is possible to serve on both panels, this may be onerous as the work is specialised and both youth and family law is in a state of constant change. Specialised training is required. Panel members must meet at least twice a year. The number of panel members is fixed to ensure that: -

*   Magistrates are available to sit, with a man and a woman on each bench so far as practicable and
*   Magistrates achieve at least 18 sittings in the adult court and about 13 sittings on a panel in order to maintain continuity of experience in both courts.

Many courts also have a drug treatment and testing order review panel (42% of courts in 2003), and/or a specialist fine enforcement panel. Additionally, consideration is currently being given to the formation of specialist licensing panels to hear appeals from local authority decisions, when the licensing function moves from the court to the local authority.

1.6.7. Clerk to the Justices

They are currently appointed by the MCC with the approval of the Lord Chancellor, and must be solicitors or barristers who have a 5 year Magistrates' Court qualification. The principal function is to advise on law. The Clerk to the Justices is not subject to the direction of the Justices Chief Executive when exercising any legal function.

1.6.8. Legal Adviser

What exactly is the legal adviser required to do? The most straightforward way to describe the role of the legal adviser is to summarise the provisions of the relevant Practice Direction (Justices: Clerk to Court) 2000.

The Justices Clerk has the following responsibilities and powers which are delegated to the legal advisers:

*   To give advice on the following matters, whether or not the justices so request:
    *   ✓ Questions of law, and mixed law and fact.
    *   ✓ Matters of practice and procedure.
    *   ✓ Range of penalties available.
    *   ✓ Relevant decisions of superior courts or other guidelines.
    *   ✓ Other issues relevant to the matter.
    *   ✓ Appropriate decision-making structure.
*   To assist the court, where appropriate, as to the formulation of reasons and the recording of those reasons.
*   To ask questions of witnesses and the parties in order to clarify the evidence and any issues in the case.
*   To ensure that every case is conducted fairly.
*   To play no part in making findings of fact but may assist the bench by reminding them of evidence, using any notes of the proceedings.
*   To assist an un-represented party to present his case, without becoming an advocate for the party.
*   To be allowed in default proceedings, to ask questions to elicit information. The legal adviser must not appear to be adversarial or partisan. Advice may be given upon the various options, but he cannot set out to establish wilful refusal/culpable neglect, or offer opinion on facts, or urge a particular course of action on the bench.

    *   ✓ Any request by the bench for the legal adviser to join the bench in the retiring room should be made in open court, in the presence of the parties.

✓ Any advice given in the retiring room is 'provisional' and should be repeated for representations in open court and then the advice should be confirmed or varied openly.

Local practices may vary slightly, but in practical (rather than legal), terms the legal adviser will normally deal with:

- Identification of the defendant and charge.
- Provision of information to the bench about the history of the case.
- Liaison with the usher, prosecutor, defence solicitors and prison escort services to keep the list running smoothly.
- Liaison with court listing officers to fix adjournment dates.
- Completion of the paperwork e.g. results, notices to defendant (please allow time for this to happen!)
- Grant of legal aid applications.
- 'Filling the gaps' in the proceedings.

CHAPTER 2

Core legal knowledge and structured decision making

This chapter covers the main knowledge-based competences for adult court and describes the criminal process from start to finish – from laying the information through to the bail process, trial and sentence.

2.1. Initiation of criminal prosecutions

2.1.1. By an information

An 'information' is exactly what it says. It sets out brief particulars of the offence, the statutory authority, the name and address of the party charged, and the party laying the information. The informant must sign the information. When a summons is sought, it will normally be written and delivered to court for consideration in a large bundle along with the accompanying summonses.

Alternatively it may be made on oral application in court. This is a regular occurrence when an alternative offence is considered on reflection to be more appropriate than the original charge. When a defendant is arrested and charged at the police station a copy of the charge sheet is delivered to the court and this is treated as the information.

2.1.2. Issuing of a summons

Once the information has been laid for consideration of a summons or warrant, the magistrate or justices' clerk must consider whether this is appropriate. A summons will only be issued if the alleged offence is known to law, and if it is a summary offence, it must be laid within the 6 month time limit from the alleged offence and be within the appropriate local commission area. The summons itself is effectively a directive to attend or at least respond to the court in answer to the allegation on a specific date and time.

2.1.3. Issuing of a warrant

When a warrant is sought the information must be in writing. When issuing a warrant in respect of an offence, the issuing magistrate must be satisfied that the offence is either indictable or imprisonable or that the defendant does not have a fixed address. A summons should always be considered first, particularly for minor offences, as a warrant at this stage is essentially authorising arrest without conviction. The second consideration should be for a warrant with bail. A warrant without bail should only be granted when there is information to suggest that the defendant would not attend court following a bail warrant.

Other types of warrants are discussed in the relevant part of the text e.g. following a failure to surrender to bail (2.2.1), fine default warrants (3.3.1), and search warrants (2.15.1).

2.2.   Bail provisions

In practical terms, it would be unrealistic to expect the police to possess the full information to charge every individual immediately following arrest, or expect the court to finalise every case on the first hearing - adjournments are often inevitable. What happens whilst the necessary information is gathered and considered by the prosecution and defence? The police have the power to bail suspects back to the police station prior to potential charge. After charge, the police may grant bail to attend court at a specific date/time, or may detain the defendant with an application to court that he is remanded in custody if the case is not finalised on first hearing.

2.2.1.   The general right to bail

There is a general right to bail for all unconvicted defendants, and also convicted defendants if the case is adjourned for reports, with one exception. This relates to defendants who are facing a 2nd offence within the list of murder, rape, attempts, or manslaughter, when exceptional circumstances must be found to grant bail. There is therefore no presumption of bail following committal to the Crown Court for sentence, on appeal against conviction or sentence, or in extradition proceedings (i.e. they are convicted but the case is not simply adjourned for reports which does give the right to unconditional bail).

The defendants with the right to bail must be granted unconditional bail unless one or more of the statutory exceptions to bail apply. The only obligation of unconditional bail is to attend court at the time/place given. Failure to comply with this requirement may result in the following:

- Issue of a warrant without bail and arrest
- Refusal of bail and remand in custody until the case is finalised

- Commission of a further offence of failing to attend court which carries a custodial penalty
  +
- Any offences committed whilst on bail are aggravated in seriousness.

2.2.2. Statutory exceptions to bail

Specific statutory exceptions must be found. The court must find substantial grounds (reasons) for finding exceptions, 1 to 4 below. The list below applies to all imprisonable offences and gives examples of reasons.

Exceptions	Reasons
1.Fail to surrender to custody	• Previous failure to answer bail/comply with bail conditions • Character, antecedents, and lack of community ties • Nature and gravity of offence/*or breach of order* and probable sentence + strength of evidence **or** + character, antecedents etc. above
2.Commit offence on bail	• Previous offences committed on bail • Positive drug test on charge + character, antecedents etc.
3.Interfere with witnesses or obstruct the course of justice	• Behaviour/proximity to witnesses
4.Charged with indictable/either-way offence and appears on bail on date of offence	• Character, antecedents, and lack of community ties • Strength of evidence
5. Impracticable to complete inquiries or make the report without keeping defendant in custody	
6. Requires custody for own protection, or welfare(child)	
7. Not practical to obtain sufficient information to make a bail decision	
8. Already serving a sentence of imprisonment	
9. Having been released on bail, has been arrested for breach of bail conditions	

2.2.3.　Conditional bail - conditions relevant to the exceptions to bail

When one or more exceptions apply, the next stage is to consider whether bail conditions would adequately address the exception, or risk. A remand in custody can only be ordered if conditions are properly considered and are considered to be inadequate. The first right is to unconditional bail. The second right is to conditional bail. Conditions may only be added if they are considered to be 'necessary' because of a 'real risk', rather than a 'possible risk'. which every defendant arguably presents to the court.

What exception has been found and can the particular risk be covered adequately by a condition or not? If so, it must be practical, proportionate to the risk and be capable of clear understanding by the defendant, the victim and the arresting police officer if breached. No room for doubt!

Bail information is supplied to the Crown Prosecution Service as part of the probation service function, particularly in respect of accommodation e.g. checking that the postcode given actually relates to the address and it does exist.

(I)　Fail to surrender:

• 　To live and sleep at ...

'Live and sleep' is a stronger condition than mere 'residence' which is basically just a mailing address. The defendant could take a holiday right through to hearing and still comply with the 'residence' requirement provided that he can show that it has remained his usual abode. It may be necessary to check that an address is genuinely available and suitable through the probation service. Placing a night curfew on this condition is not appropriate unless the risk of further offending at night is also found. A belief that a defendant may leave the area simply requires a stable, genuine, 'living at' and 'now' address, and a curfew would be a disproportionate restriction on liberty.

• 　To report to ... police station between ... and ... on ...

Will this realistically prevent this defendant from absconding? It simply demonstrates that the defendant is in the locality for the 5 minutes of reporting time, but with rapid travel, he could be out of the country an hour later. Consider the practical aspect of the defendant who uses the opportunity to identify the unmarked police vehicles, plain clothes officers, being legitimately out and about in his target offending area and listening in to police business as he waits to sign on. Consider the resource implication in prioritising interim arrests. It is not an offence to breach a condition and it simply re-opens the question of bail - often re-granted again by the court! Consider the alternative of an earlier surrender to bail on the day of a trial, particularly for local defendants and if police officers are attending as witnesses. If the defendant has failed to attend, say at 9 a.m., the officers can then make early morning enquiries and either arrest for the court hearing at 10.30 a.m. or proceed in absence if there is no response. When the police ask for a reporting condition through the Crown Prosecution Service they clearly see a value in reporting for this particular defendant and this can be compared to a suggestion which comes instead from the defence.

- To reside at a hostel approved by the Anytown Probation Service and to abide by the rules of the hostel and to reside initially at the ... hostel.

The initial residence aspect allows the probation service to have flexibility to move the defendant without having to come to court to vary the location if this should become necessary subsequently.

The purpose of a Home Office approved hostel is to provide an enhanced level of supervision with the aim of protecting the public by reducing the likelihood of offending. There is 24-hour cover with at least 2 members of staff on duty at any one time. The normal curfew is 11pm to 7am. All bailees are subject to ongoing assessment and support. The bail hostel is an expensive, specialised resource rather than a 'bed for the remand period'. If that is all that your defendant needs, please do not tie the officer's hands to a hostel – leave the suggestions of accommodation open.

- To provide a surety in the sum of ...

The court must consider the financial resources which are actually available, the character of the proposed surety and the residence and relationship proximity. Is it realistic that this person lives near enough and is influential enough towards the defendant to ensure his attendance? It is no longer necessary to find that the defendant may leave the United Kingdom. A warning must be given that the whole sum may be forfeited, dependant upon the culpability of the surety, if the defendant fails to attend.

- To provide a security namely ... cash, passport.

Surrender of passport is now notified immediately by the court by fax to the UK passport office to prevent any application for a duplicate/replacement passport.

(ii) Would commit further offences/charged with further offence whilst on bail:

- To live and sleep at .... and to remain indoors at that address between ... and ...

Curfews should only be imposed where there is evidence to support a genuine concern that further offending will be generated during the curfew period. Adults cannot be electronically tagged as part of their bail condition, but this is open to children and young persons if criteria are satisfied (see 2.2.6).

The court may also make a 'doorstep condition' requiring the defendant to present himself at the door on the request of a police officer during the curfew period. This is a requirement over and above the restriction of movement and must only be imposed as an extra if it is proportionate to the risk.

- Not to enter ... area where crime committed, areas frequented by the witnesses.

Be careful with definitions of areas and the reality of enforcement. Shoplifters may be realistically kept out of named shops, or specific parades of shops but it is usually unrealistic, unnecessary and disproportionate to bar defendants from whole areas of cities where they are likely to travel in their day to day life. On the other hand a defendant who operates in a particular area with a particular group of victims may usefully be excluded from that area, e.g. mobile telephone thefts in the environment of university bars; locker thefts from leisure club; handbag snatches in local market.

- Not to associate with ... (named persons, usually co-accused).

This condition may be appropriate if the defendant is alleged to have acted in unison with others in committing offences and it is considered likely that their continued association may result in further offending.

(iii) Would interfere with witnesses/obstruct the course of justice exceptions:

- Not to contact directly or indirectly .... named witnesses.

Where this is a serious concern it may be worthwhile to stress that arrest may follow upon breach and, in addition, there is also a separate offence of obstructing/perverting the course of justice which carries imprisonment. If the contact has been by e-mail – include it specifically; through a 3rd party – include him by name in the definition and indeed 'any other 3rd party'. In domestic cases, it may be worth reminding the defendant that the condition is there to protect both parties, and if the other party wishes to communicate, they should both come to court for it to be varied or deleted rather than breaking the condition.

- Not to enter ... area where crime committed, areas frequented by witnesses.

This condition can afford some peace of mind to witnesses and may encourage their co-operation. They may be store detectives following a shoplifting charge; victims of burglaries in a particular neighbourhood; licensees of public houses where a disturbance has occurred or victims of domestic violence who simply wish to proceed with their daily life to the local shops and school. Keep the restriction proportionate to the crime and the risk, and seek representations on your suggested exclusion area definition e.g. exception to keep doctor's appointments, to pass directly through by vehicle.

The bench may attach a condition requiring the defendant to attend for interview with his solicitor before the next hearing. This condition is useful for several reasons, even though it is unlikely to be pursued as a breached condition. It encourages progress; provides the court with justification for referral to the duty solicitor if there has been no effort to seek advice during the adjournment, and also to proceed with a trial in absence if instructions have not even been given and there is no explanation for non-attendance.

2.2.4. Implications of Human Rights Act and proportionality (see 4.9)

Most bail conditions, and certainly custody on remand, will engage the Human Rights Act. Care must be taken particularly with Article 8, the right to private and family life (the right to live a peaceful life as we choose) and Article 11, freedom of assembly and association (the right to go where and with whom we want to). Both Articles contain qualified rights.

The 3 questions must therefore be asked in order to ensure that the condition (restriction) is appropriate: -

1. Is the restriction based on law which is clear and accessible? Yes, the Bail Act is available for anyone to refer to.
2. Does the restriction pursue a legitimate aim e.g. to prevent disorder or crime; to protect the rights, freedoms and morals of others? A curfew upon a night-time offender is fair enough if it is specifically designed to prevent further crime.
3. Is it proportionate i.e. is no more than is necessary to deal with the situation? Not a sledgehammer to crack a nut!

Example:

A city-wide exclusion bail condition for a defendant charged with being drunk and disorderly is strictly speaking - legal, and it would certainly help to prevent disorder in the city centre. However it is not a proportionate restriction on liberty for an offence at this level (does not even carry imprisonment on conviction).

The other important Article is Article 7, 'no punishment without law' (no punishment unless we know exactly how and when we are breaking the law) as this requires certainty of restriction e.g. 'not to interfere with prosecution witnesses' – who are they? 'not to enter the city centre' – where are the city limits? Definition and certainty is critical.

2.2.5. Custody

When the bench find exceptions but cannot safely attach conditions to deal with the risks, then the defendant must be remanded into custody. At this stage it is worth checking that the court has sufficient information on which to make a full bail decision, as the proceedings are inquisitorial which means that there is an onus on the court to ask!

A further statutory exception to bail is that 'the court does not have sufficient information on which to make a decision'. When this is the case e.g. address to be checked out, then the remand must be for the shortest possible period e.g. overnight. A remand in custody before conviction is a serious infringement of liberty and it is wrong to rely on the possibility of a 'stronger application next week' if the decision simply rests upon information which can be obtained overnight. Legal representation must always be offered if a remand in custody is being considered.

The exceptions and reasons must be announced and recorded .The initial maximum period of remand is 8 clear days to prison/detention or 3 days to police cells.

A remand to police cells is for the purpose of enquiring into other offences and the defendant must be brought back before the court as soon as that need ceases. In the meantime he must have his detention periodically reviewed under police detention rules.

The period of remand may be extended to 28 days after the 2nd remand in custody. This period is subject to the requirements that the defendant is before the court; that representations are sought from both parties and that care is taken to set a realistic early date for the next stage of the proceedings e.g. for committal.

2.2.6. Bail and children and young people.

Bail applications for children and young people may be made in the adult court. A parent, guardian or, if necessary, a member of the youth offending team (yot) should be present in court with all under 16s, and they may be asked to attend with the 16 and 17 year olds. The Bail Act applies, but there are a few differences.

Firstly, a parental surety of up to £50 may be ordered with the parent's consent to ensure compliance with conditions. The 'live and sleep' bail condition is often defined as 'where directed by the local authority' to allow scope for effective placement and movement if necessary - often away from parent initially and then perhaps with a staged return. A condition may be attached where appropriate to comply with bail supervision and support. This will involve instructions to deal with the particular bail risk, and also the vulnerability of the youth e.g. to use time constructively by attending specific leisure activities and reporting to the supervising officer, rather than committing further offences.

The more serious bail risk may require the more stringent restrictions of the Intensive Supervision and Surveillance Programme (ISSP) as a bail condition provided that they are facing a 5th imprisonable charge in the last 12 months, or they must satisfy the criteria for a secure remand apply (see below). The compliance with ISSP condition includes 25 hours per week of input from the youth offending team and at least 2 surveillance contacts per day.

So far as refusal of bail is concerned, a young person of 17 will be remanded to prison custody as an adult. For the age 10 to 16 group, the most common option is to remand to local authority accommodation which may be a children's home, foster home, or even a return to family if this is considered to be appropriate. Where there is a history of absconding and there is a likelihood of significant harm or injury to the defendant or others, the local authority may apply for a secure accommodation order to be made in a secure children's home. The local authority may apply for this restriction at any time for any youths they are responsible for.

It is important to recognise that the remand 'to local authority accommodation' does not confer any parental responsibility on the local authority. After consultation with the local authority, the court may add any conditions except a condition as to residence, as this would effectively take away the discretion to place the youth as considered appropriate by the local authority. The court may however, specify that the child/young person is not placed with a named individual e.g. co-accused adult.

Provisions for electronic tagging of a curfew condition and remands to secure accommodation/remand centres apply to youths of 12 upwards. The basic criteria is that they have been convicted or charged with a serious offence, or have a history of offending on bail and also present a risk which cannot be met in any other way. The youth offending team (yot) must be consulted to consider alternatives e.g. a bail support or ISSP condition of bail, and also whether such restrictions are necessary.

The detail of the criteria for a secure remand is as follows:

1. Defendant is charged with or convicted of a violent or sexual offence, or an offence which is punishable with imprisonment of 14 years or more, e.g. robbery.

    OR

2. Defendant is charged/convicted of imprisonable offence(s), which, together with any other imprisonable offences of which they have been convicted in any proceedings amount (or would, if convicted of the charges), amount to a recent history of repeatedly committing imprisonable offences whilst remanded on bail or to local authority accommodation.

    AND

3. The court is of the opinion, after considering all the options of the remand, that only remanding him to a remand centre or prison or to secure local authority accommodation would be adequate to protect the public from serious harm from him or prevent the commission by him of imprisonable offences.

The accommodation will be to a secure children's home for girls aged 12 to 16, and for boys aged 12 to 14. Boys of 15 and 16 will be sent to a remand centre or prison, unless they are deemed to be 'vulnerable', physically or emotionally, and then they may be placed in a secure children's home instead.

2.2.7. Bail application procedure

The legal adviser will give details of the bail history, including the results of previous applications and the reasons. The prosecutor will then give details of the allegations, submit previous convictions and make representations about bail. This will be followed by the defence representations and submissions on bail. The extent of information is likely to be limited, particularly if the arrest and charge is recent. Finally, the court may ask any questions necessary to assist in the decision-making process.

Bail information may be provided by the probation service/youth offending team for youths, to assist the court by providing the Crown Prosecution Service and defence with verified information to contribute to the representations on bail e.g. regarding accommodation, employment. Where a risk of serious harm is identified, the information must be copied to the police, social services or health authority as appropriate, e.g. domestic violence risk to children.

2.2.8. A structured approach to bail
(Adult Court Bench Book - 1.17).

A bail decision is critical. The ultimate decision of a remand in custody is available and this is very often based on slim information about a defendant who is not convicted. The decision-making process is about bail risk. It is not about guilt or innocence.

The 'ABC' approach is suggested as a structured approach for the decision and for the reasons.

A. Adjournment (or not!)

Should the case be adjourned? The advocates will be aware of the basis for the adjournment and if they have no objection, they will understandably tend to focus their attention on the bail representations. However, the court must first consider carefully whether the case should be adjourned at all. Can it proceed today? This is particularly relevant when the defendant appears in custody on a warrant, having failed to attend an Early First Hearing. It is likely that the prosecution file will be attached to the court file and the expectation should be for the case to go ahead, at least to plea.

The first question is 'why can't the case proceed?' rather than 'shall we grant bail?' The second question is 'what is the shortest adjournment for progress to be made?' rather than 'what date are we adjourning to?'

In any pronouncement, the word adjourn should normally be followed by the reasons and the focus for the next hearing 'because' ..., 'so that' ... and this aspect is part of the decision-making process.

B. Bail

Following the decision to adjourn, the adult defendant must be bailed if the offence is 'either-way' and he appears on bail or in custody, and bail must apply on adjournment of committal proceedings. In other circumstances, it is a matter for the court. Remember the right to bail for all unconvicted defendants and for those who are adjourned for reports after conviction.

In order to identify whether any of the exceptions to unconditional bail exist, it is helpful to focus on the features of the offence itself, and then the offender.

- Offence

What is alleged by the prosecutor? What is conceded (if anything) by the defence? Is the evidence strong and if so, what is the probable sentence, as this may be relevant to finding the exception of failure to surrender. Is there a pattern of offending which is likely to continue e.g. thefts to fund a drug habit? Is there a reliance on the prosecution witnesses and are they vulnerable - if so, can they be adequately protected by conditions or not? Remember that the issue of guilt or innocence is not an issue for a bail decision. The only concern is whether the facts of the offence suggest that there could be further offending; interference with witnesses; or failure to attend court if there is strong evidence and a lengthy custodial penalty is probable, e.g. drug dealing.

- Offender

Does the defendant have a stable address or family/employment commitments - if not, is there a risk that he will fail to surrender? Does he hold a current passport which should be taken as security? Does he have any supporters in court who are suitable to stand as surety or provide a cash security to the court? Do the previous convictions show any previous failures to surrender to court, or does their absence indicate that he does attend court? What are the explanations/circumstances of any recent failures to attend? Was the defendant on bail at the time of the alleged offence? Was there a positive drug test on charge (currently available in pilot police stations in respect of 'trigger' offences, including theft)? If so, this may be evidence of a likelihood to commit further offences on bail to fund a drug habit.

- Options (bail)

If there are no concerns (exceptions) found, then unconditional bail must be granted.
Where there are exceptions with reasons, can they be allayed by relevant conditions?
Define any conditions carefully so that both the defendant and the arresting officer have the same understanding of what they mean?
Check that any conditions are proportionate to the risk.

C. Custody

If exceptions are found and conditions are inadequate, then custody becomes inevitable. (Check with legal adviser that selected exceptions may be used if the offence is non-imprisonable.)

2.2.9. Bail pronouncement
(Adult Bench Book - Pronouncements 3-18 to 3-32)

The pronouncement must include which specific exceptions to bail have been found, reasons for finding them and details of any conditions. It is often well worth checking that the defendant understands the conditions. Reliance on 'reading the bail form' afterwards is often unrealistic, and results in the unnecessary time and expense of breach arrests which arise purely from a lack of clear understanding. Keep out of where exactly? Stay indoors when? Key points which can understandably be lost to the defendant in the relief of being released on bail! And the bail form? Unread.

Finally, the warnings for the defendants released on bail.

- To comply with the bail conditions and attend on the day, date and time given or risk the following:

✓ Arrest
✓ Remand in custody until the case is finalised
✓ Additional charge of failing to attend court on bail which carries imprisonment

• Increased seriousness and heavier penalty for any offences committed during the bail period.

2.2.10. Failure to surrender to bail

It is an offence to fail to surrender to bail (police or court bail) in criminal proceedings, without reasonable cause. The defence of reasonable cause may, for example be illness or detention elsewhere to 'assist the police with enquiries'. It is not a defence to 'get the dates muddled up' - this is simply mitigation.

Alternatively, if there is reasonable cause for failing to attend on the return date, it is an offence if the defendant fails to surrender 'as soon as reasonably practicable thereafter', i.e. when the medical certificate expired, when he was released from police custody. Both offences carry a maximum of 3 months imprisonment/level 5 fine in the Magistrates' Court and on committal to Crown Court, carry 12 months imprisonment/fine.

• **Procedure**

The procedure is slightly different between police and court bail. Police bail charges are dealt with as for any additional charge and will usually have been charged by the police following arrest on warrant. However, if it is court bail, the prosecutor will consider the matter, often following a brief informal discussion with the defence, and then 'expressly invite' the court to initiate the proceedings. Court bail belongs to the court but it would be inappropriate for the court to both prosecute and adjudicate.

The decision to prosecute rests with the prosecutor effectively, but the court should be vigilant to ensure that the charge is considered by the prosecutor. Whenever the defendant appears in the dock on warrant following a failure to attend on court bail – enquire! This is potentially a very important conviction for future benches to assess the extent of bail risk.

• **Dealing with the failure to surrender conviction**

When a defendant has been convicted of a Bail Act offence, the court will obviously need to review the remand status of the defendant, as the conviction will be a significant factor in weighing against the re-granting of bail. That is the first implication to consider and it may affect whether the court sentences immediately and in isolation for the failure to surrender, or adjourns it to be dealt with alongside the principal offence.

The Sentencing Guideline entry point is a community penalty.

An amendment to the Practice Direction (Bail: Failure to surrender and trials in absence) was issued in January 2004 in relation to sentencing. Automatic deferral of the failure to surrender matter must no longer be followed as a common practice. The conviction should be dealt with as soon as practical and the Direction states that the following matters should be taken into account:

✓ When are the proceedings expected to conclude?
Unless there is a conviction for the original offence and the case is specifically adjourned for reports, there is uncertainty about plea and/or about how long the original offence will remain in the system. It is difficult to identify a good reason to defer. Early resolution is likely to deter further failures to attend during the course of the proceedings. A short, immediate curfew order may well provide the appropriate punitive reminder to attend next time and it may well expire before the original offence is dealt with. If not, it has the advantage that it may run to completion alongside any other community penalty which the court may subsequently impose for the original offence e.g. community rehabilitation, community punishment.

✓ Seriousness of the offence in respect of which bail was granted.
It is surely an aggravating factor to evade justice on a serious assault charge than on a drunk and disorderly charge.

✓ Type of penalty that might be imposed for the failure to surrender.
If all mitigating features are present, e.g. defendant surrenders voluntarily and the court accepts that he genuinely confused the dates, and he has no similar previous convictions, then the court may well consider that a fine or a one day detention for a few hours will finalise the matter immediately. In chaotic lifestyles, the latter may be more appropriate than expecting the discipline to pay the weekly instalments of a fine.

✓ Type of penalty that might be imposed for the original offence.
If custody is foreseen for the original offence, and particularly, if the defendant is remanded in custody in the meantime, it may be appropriate to impose a short immediate custodial penalty immediately to run alongside the remand in custody e.g. 7 days if the offence merits custody.

Full reports may be considered to be unnecessary for such a short sentence, particularly if he has already served custodial sentences. He has already lost his liberty due to the remand in custody in any event and cannot comply with any other penalty. The regime on sentence will be slightly different and he will have added a custodial sentence to his record. However if a longer period is appropriate, then full reports may be required and the Direction encourages a custodial penalty which is consecutive to the original offence. This could be up to 3 months in the Magistrates' Court and up to 12 months in the Crown Court. If the original offence is ultimately discharged, the failure to surrender appropriately remains to be dealt with.

✓   Any other relevant circumstances.

It is suggested that the key relevant circumstance will be the decision on whether bail should be granted during the adjournment or not. If bail is refused because of the evidence of failure to surrender, then the court is effectively limited to a one day detention for a minor failure or a short immediate custodial penalty without reports. If any other penalty is considered to be appropriate e.g. community penalty, lengthy custody, then it will rarely be practicable to sentence immediately. If bail is granted, then the defendant can basically be sentenced to any option and it can be monitored and varied if necessary on sentence of the original offence e.g. if custody is imposed, a fine can be remitted and a community order revoked, otherwise the order can continue on.

Failure to surrender to bail is an offence as any other, and reasons must be given for the choice of penalty, together with an appropriate warning as to the option of custody if a further offence is committed.

2.2.11.   Failing to comply with bail conditions

A defendant may be arrested if a constable has reasonable grounds for believing that the bailee is likely to break any of the conditions of his bail or has reasonable grounds for believing that he has broken any. The defendant must be brought before the court within 24 hours (excluding Sunday etc.) for the breach to be put.

Very importantly, it must be recognised, that the court is not dealing with an offence, there is no proof 'beyond reasonable doubt', no power to adjourn and no penalty (unlike the failure to surrender to court where all aspects apply!).

If the court is simply 'of the opinion' that the defendant has broken or is likely to break a condition, it may remand him in custody or grant bail as before, or with different conditions. Breach of bail effectively re-opens the whole question of bail - that is all.

2.2.12. Time limits relating to bail

1. The maximum period for which someone may be detained without charge or appearance before a court for an arrestable offence is 36 hours, unless a formal extension application is made and granted.

2. A defendant who is charged with an offence and kept in custody must be brought before the Magistrates' Court as soon as practicable after being charged, and in any event not later than the first sitting of the court after being charged. For example, he is charged on Saturday evening and must be brought before court on Monday (no sittings on Sundays).

3. A defendant who is charged and bailed must be bailed to a date which is not later than the first sitting of the court after charge or a later date if the appearance cannot be so accommodated e.g. usually about 4/6 days later depending upon local arrangements.

4. The maximum period for the first two remands in custody is 8 days. Thereafter the maximum period is 21 days after conviction and 28 days before conviction if the next stage is fixed.

5. The maximum period of remand in custody in respect of indictable offences is 70 days between first appearance and commencement of the committal or trial. The maximum period of remand in custody in respect of offences which are triable summarily is 56 days. Application may be made to 'extend the custody time limits' in specified circumstances, provided that the prosecution have acted with all due diligence and expedition, and application must be made to the court.

2.2.13. Final points on bail procedures

1. In January 2004, the police were given the power to grant immediate bail from the scene of arrest rather than taking the defendant to a police station. This is known as 'street bail'. The only condition is that the bailee attends a police station at a later date specified at the time on the street bail notice or by a subsequent notification - normally within 6 weeks. By allowing for file preparation time, this reduces the time in which a suspect is kept in the cells by giving a future date/time for legal representatives and appropriate adults (to accompany youths) to attend at the police station.

2. Specific reasons must be given if bail is granted in respect of murder, manslaughter and rape e.g. the court is satisfied that the general public are not endangered by the release of the defendant, and the victim is sufficiently protected by the bail conditions.

3. A defendant has the right to make 2 applications which may be based on any argument. Thereafter the court may decline to hear arguments as to fact or law which it has heard previously. The question must be asked 'What is the change of circumstances and how does it relate to the exception(s) found?' Application may also be made a judge in chambers.

4. The prosecutor may ask for bail to be reconsidered based upon information which was not available to the court or to the police when the original bail decision was made e.g. a new witness comes forward and the strength of evidence increases substantially.

5. Applications may be made to the court to vary conditions of police and court bail at any time e.g. to change address/time of reporting to the police station. Always ask for a brief outline of the offence and the details of the surrounding conditions. A variation of a single condition in isolation may sound uncontroversial until it is placed in context e.g. the return home to live with mother may place the defendant back into the proximity of vulnerable witnesses.

6. The prosecution may appeal if the court grants bail in respect of offences carrying 5 years or more, and taking a motor vehicle without consent, providing that bail was opposed. Appeal lies to a judge of the Crown Court and oral notice must be given before the defendant is released and written notice must be given within 2 hours. It will usually be necessary to retire for a short time after the oral notice has been given so that the prosecutor can formulate the written notice of appeal. The judge will then hear the case within 48 hours.

2.3. Taking the plea and mode of trial

This process will depend upon the type of offence - indictable only, summary or either-way.

2.3.1. 'Indictable only' matters

These are the most serious offences which may only be dealt with by the Crown Court, e.g. murder, rape, robbery. They are 'sent' from the Magistrates' Court to the Crown Court along with any other qualifying offences. No plea is entered in the Magistrates' Court, but bail must be dealt with for the period between appearance in the Magistrates' Court and the next hearing in the Crown Court.

2.3.2. 'Summary' matters

These are offences which may only be dealt with in the Magistrates' Court, e.g. common assault, taking a motor vehicle without the owner's consent, driving whilst disqualified. The charge is read out by the legal adviser and the defendant is simply asked whether he pleads 'guilty' or 'not guilty'. Following a guilty plea, the prosecutor will outline the circumstances of the offence and produce any offences to be taken into consideration, any previous convictions and also make any applications, e.g. for compensation. The defendant or his solicitor will then give the defence version of events and mitigate. The court will then determine whether to sentence immediately or obtain a probation report to assist in determining penalty.

2.3.3. 'Either-way' matters and 'mode of trial'

These are offences which may be dealt with by the Magistrates' Court or the Crown Court, e.g. theft, burglary, assault occasioning actual bodily harm. The defendant is entitled to receive details of the prosecution case against him before indicating his plea. This is known as 'Advance Disclosure'.

The charge is read out, and the defendant will be asked for indication of his plea, 'guilty' or 'not guilty' or no indication. Additionally, the legal adviser will explain that the magistrates may commit the case to the Crown Court if they consider that their sentencing powers are insufficient, i.e. more than 6 months maximum custody for a single offence.

When a 'guilty' plea is indicated, the matter proceeds as for a summary offence - prosecution outline, followed by defence. The big difference is that the court must decide whether its powers are actually sufficient before moving into sentencing, or adjourning for pre-sentence reports. See examples below where the court should always pause and consider venue before sentencing. The defence must always be given the opportunity to respond if the court considers that the case should be committed for sentence to the Crown Court. Committal to Crown Court 'for sentence' may then follow immediately if appropriate.

When a 'not guilty' plea is indicated, the court will hear representations from the prosecution about the seriousness of the case so that the court can assess whether Magistrates' Court powers are sufficient, and so determine, 'mode of trial'. For this purpose, the court should assume that the prosecution version is correct, e.g. value of goods stolen, that a weapon was used, even though this is the denied.

In order to assist in the decision, the Sentencing Guidelines 2004 in the Adult Court Bench Book set out entry points.

Examples:

- *Burglary (dwelling) - Crown Court, compared to*
- *Burglary (non-dwelling) - Magistrates' Court - community penalty.*

- *Supply of drugs - Crown Court, compared to*
- *Possession of class A drugs, e.g. heroin, ecstasy - Magistrates' Court - community penalty.*

- *Possess indecent photographs - Crown Court.*

- *Theft - Magistrates' Court - community penalty, compared to*
- *Theft in breach of trust - Magistrates' Court - custody (this has been reduced from the previous entry point of committal to Crown Court).*

- *Assault occasioning actual bodily harm - Magistrates' Court - custody (this has been reduced from the previous entry point of committal to Crown Court).*

There is further guidance in the National Mode of Trial Guidelines which are found in Section 2 of the Adult Bench Book.

Example:

Burglary (non-dwelling).
Entry point - Magistrates' Court - community penalty.

Cases should be tried summarily unless the court considers that one or more of the following features is present in the case and that its sentencing powers are insufficient.
1. *Entry of a pharmacy or doctor's surgery.*
2. *Fear is caused or violence is done to anyone lawfully on the premises.*
3. *The offence has professional hallmarks.*
4. *Vandalism on a substantial scale.*
5. *The unrecovered property is of a high value.*

Where cases involve complex questions of fact or difficult questions of law, committal should be considered.

Representations will also be made by the defence and the court will then determine whether the case is suitable for summary trial in the Magistrates' Court or not. If not, the case will normally be adjourned for statements to be prepared for later committal to the Crown Court 'for trial'. The case can only be committed if the statements disclose that there is sufficient evidence to put the defendant on trial - that a 'prima facie' case is made out. This is usually conceded by the defence and the Magistrates' Court is rarely required to consider the evidence. The court commits the defendant, fixes a plea and direction hearing date at Crown Court, and warns him that he must give notice if witnesses are required to give evidence in person.

If the court does accept jurisdiction, the defendant has the right, in any event, to elect trial at Crown Court on his own choice because the offence is 'either-way' e.g. theft of a bar of chocolate can be tried at Crown Court if the defendant so chooses. Where there are 2 or more defendants who are jointly charged, each individual has the right to elect trial by jury. Provided that the court feels that its powers are sufficient, the defendant may equally choose to be tried in the Magistrates' Court.

2.4.   Trial - sequence of events

2.4.1.   Witnesses

Normally witnesses will attend voluntarily and will be paid appropriate expenses. Occasionally it is necessary for a summons or warrant to be issued in order to secure attendance. In such circumstances the issuing magistrate must be satisfied that the witness would not attend or produce a document/exhibit, voluntarily and that they are likely to be able to give material evidence.

Special measures provisions may be used in respect of child witnesses in cases involving sex and violence, which include the facility of video link to avoid the child coming face to face with the alleged perpetrator in court.

Evidence must normally be given on oath or by solemn affirmation. A witness may not be sworn unless he is aged 14 upwards and appreciates the solemnity of the occasion and the responsibility to tell the truth which is involved in taking the oath. The court usher will endeavour to establish the nature of the appropriate holy book or whether the witness wishes to affirm instead, before the witness is called.

The administration of the oath is lawful provided that the oath appears to the court to be binding on the witness's conscience, and is considered by the witness to be binding. The ceremony itself is immaterial for the purpose of perjury provided that the oath has been accepted without objection - it is not for the court to go into the intricacies of the religion or lack of religious persuasion of each witness. The affirmation is regarded in law as being equally binding, valid and renders the witness liable for perjury in exactly the same way as a deliberate lie on religious oath.

At the time set down for trial, the bench should consider calling the witnesses into court, whether or not the case is ready to proceed. There are various purposes. It provides advance awareness of the courtroom - quite different from the empty courtroom which some witnesses may well have seen in advance. It also provides an opportunity to check that the witnesses are aware of the support provided by the Witness Service, the whereabouts of refreshment facilities and also to ensure that prosecution and defence witnesses are separated in the waiting area. Most importantly, it ensures that they are aware of the reason for any delay and what the immediate time-table is likely to be. It also enables the magistrates to identify whether any of the witnesses are personally known to them at the outset and avoids a case having to be re-heard because of potential prejudice, which may only emerge much later in the day when the witness is called. This applies equally to the witness possibly recognising a magistrate, particularly ex-teachers!

Once the oath has been taken, it is becoming increasingly normal practice for witnesses to be asked whether they prefer to sit down to give their evidence. Occasionally this may mean coming out of the witness box to assist vision and hearing. A preliminary instruction to 'speak slowly to allow notes to be taken' may avoid several interruptions throughout the case to 'slow down'.

Throughout a criminal trial, the basic rule is that the witness must give all evidence in the first person, 'I saw/did ...' and he cannot give evidence about what someone else has said to him about the incident. This is known as 'hearsay' evidence. There are a few exceptions and it is preferable to check with the legal adviser before acting on submissions about admissibility of evidence.

2.4.2. Prosecution opening

Before the prosecution begins, all witnesses must be cleared from the court to wait outside the court until called to give their evidence, so that each witness is heard to be giving their own independent recollection, rather than building on what someone else has said. A person is presumed innocent until proved guilty.

The prosecution case in a criminal matter must be proved beyond reasonable doubt and the initial outline will give the basis on which the proof will be given. At this stage the prosecutor will normally describe what is alleged to have happened and how it is intended to prove the various elements of the offence. It is recommended that the magistrates refrain from taking detailed notes at this point so that there is no appearance of the case being decided upon representations rather than on actual evidence. Obviously it is helpful to get a feel for the case and in particular to identify any potential line of defence which is disclosed in interview e.g. mistaken identity, self-defence. This will highlight the evidence which must be noted carefully.

2.4.3. Prosecution case

Undisputed evidence may simply be read from statements.

> *Example:*
>
> *A statement from the owner of a stolen motor car - 'I was the owner of vehicle registered XXX 333. I parked the car in the YY car park, next to the bottle bank at about 7 p.m. on the 1st May. I went into the SS supermarket and when I returned at about 8 p.m. my car was not there. No one else had any right to take my car'.*
> *No dispute, but the facts are material to the case.*

A witness may normally be led through undisputed matters with 'leading questions' which basically suggest the correct answer e.g. Is it correct that at 9 a.m. on the 20th July you were on duty at the Anytown shopping centre? The prosecution and defence will normally agree how far into the evidence, it may be 'led'.

2.4.4. Examination in chief

This is conducted by the party calling the witness, i.e. the prosecutor will examine the witnesses called for the prosecution. The purpose is to assist the witness to put forward his version of what he saw and what he did. The questions must not suggest the answer - this is called 'leading' the witness and can only be done if that part of the evidence is agreed, or in very specific circumstances.

Example:

'Is it correct that on at 6 p.m. on the 1ˢᵗ May, you saw a man with a tattoo on his right arm, strike John Smith, the victim in his face with a clenched fist?'
Not allowed! - leading question!

Instead - examination-in-chief:
- *Where were you at 6 p.m. on the 1ˢᵗ May?*
- *What did you see?*
- *You say that you saw two men shouting at each other and one of them struck the other. Can you describe the man who struck the blow?*
- *Was there anything at all distinctive about his appearance?*
- *Would you describe how the blow was struck?*
- *What happened next?*

2.4.5.   Cross-examination

This is followed by cross-examination by the 'other side', i.e. the defence cross-examine prosecution witnesses and vice versa. The purpose is to probe the version of events and check out the accuracy and truthfulness. Differences between the original statement and the evidence given in court will often form the basis of cross-examination e.g. 'Today you are saying that you were 3 feet away but in your statement you said you were 3 metres - quite a difference - which was it?'

Normally, a witness may only refer to 'contemporaneous' notes in the witness box e.g. a car registration number jotted down at the scene of the accident, police notebooks if the notes were made sufficiently soon after the incident so that the officer had a distinct recollection of the facts. The reality is that the vast majority of witness statements are made some considerable time after the incident. The witness will normally refresh his memory by reading through the statement before the hearing, but cannot refer to it, or check out what he said in the statement, whilst in the witness box.

Cross-examination may include leading questions, and questions which shake his character, or attempt to discredit the evidence, e.g. 'I put it to you that you are mistaken about what happened because you were too far away to see clearly - that is the reality isn't it?'

2.4.6. Re-examination and clarification

The prosecutor may then re-examine on any new matters which have arisen or explain answers which have been given in cross-examination. Finally the magistrates may ask any clarifying questions and should safely begin with 'May we clarify ...' in order to avoid raising any new matters.

All witnesses should be thanked for their attendance and the chairmen will check with the prosecution and defence whether they can safely be released or whether they should remain at the back of the court because they may need to be re-called. Very occasionally, witnesses may be re-called if unforeseen evidence emerges through the case. When witnesses are released, even over the lunch period, they should be warned not to discuss the case until it is concluded.

2.4.7. No case to answer

Once the prosecution case is complete, the court may dismiss the case either on the submission of the defence or on its own initiative. The criteria for finding no case to answer at this stage are:

- There is no evidence to prove an essential element in the alleged offence.

Example: The offence of criminal damage requires proof that the defendant committed the act of damage, but it must also be proved that he intended or was reckless as to whether the damage was caused. Accidental damage is not a criminal offence. If there is no proof of intention or recklessness, there is no case to answer.

- The prosecution evidence is so manifestly unreliable or tenuous that it cannot be relied upon e.g. witnesses giving widely different versions of events, key witness discredited under cross-examination, insubstantial identification evidence.

The court must consider whether a reasonable tribunal could convict at this stage. The prosecution must be given the opportunity to respond before the decision is made, so that comment may be made on the significance of any omissions or contradictions.

2.4.8. Defence case

The defendant is under no obligation to give evidence and he may choose to remain silent. However, he <u>must</u> be warned that if he does choose not to give evidence then the court may draw an 'inference from his silence' i.e. it may understandably come to the conclusion that he has something to hide.

The failure to give evidence cannot be the only factor to justify a conviction, and it is very important to stress in the reasons for the decision, the nature of other supporting evidence. However, the silence may properly <u>contribute</u> to the totality of evidence which proves beyond reasonable doubt that the defendant is guilty.

The same inference applies if the defendant chooses not to answer questions during the course of his evidence e.g. in a case of being drunk and disorderly the defendant chooses not to answer a question asking how much alcohol he had to drink. Marginally better to respond with, 'I can't remember'! Again the court must give an appropriate warning.

Occasionally the prosecution case may include the 'evidence of silence' during the actual investigation. This may be a silence, when asked if he had anything to say at the time of arrest/charge; when asked why he happened to be at the scene of the crime; when asked why he had stolen property in his possession and blood on his sleeve. Account should be given as to whereabouts and evidence, otherwise inferences may be drawn from such silences in the same way.

The defendant will normally give evidence first, followed by his witnesses, following the same order of questioning as for the prosecution witnesses:

- Examination in chief by the party calling the witness i.e. the defence - the open questions.
- Cross examination by the other party, i.e. the prosecutor - the challenging questions.
- Re-examination by the defence - any new matters.
- Clarification by the bench - clarifying only!

2.4.9.   Defence closing address

The defendant is given the right to address the court at the end of the evidence and may summarise his case and draw out any particular points which have been given for and against his case. The prosecutor may reply on legal points only. Any advice from the legal adviser should be given in open court for comment by the advocates if appropriate.

See also 6.3.6. Chairman's guide through a trial.

2.5. Structured approach to verdict
(Adult Bench Book - 1-31)

The decision-making following a trial will normally be conducted in the retiring room and the following process is based upon the structure recommended by the Judicial Studies Board, which provides a clear framework for recording and announcing reasons.

Verdict reasons – example

Charge of criminal damage.

1) What are the elements of the offence charged?

There are 2 elements to the criminal damage charge - (i) that damage was caused by the defendant and (ii) that this was either intentional or reckless.

2) What is the burden of proof and where does it fall?

The prosecutor must prove the offence beyond reasonable doubt.

3) Identify what facts are agreed.

It is agreed that the defendant caused damage to the window valued at £200.

4) Identify what facts are disputed.

It is disputed that it was an intentional kick or reckless kick. It is said by the defence that it was caused by an accidental fall.

5) Exclude any evidence which is not admissible.

We exclude the hearsay evidence given by one of the witnesses that her friend heard the defendant bragging about the incident.

6) Any inferences to be drawn from silence during trial/investigation?

We note that the defendant failed to account for glass splinters inside his shoe when interviewed in the presence of his solicitor and he did not reply to the prosecutor's question "You did kick the window, didn't you? The question was repeated after a warning about the implication of his silence was given by the legal adviser and again he failed to answer. We add this to the clear evidence given by the prosecution witnesses.

7) What is found to be fact with reasons? Preferred evidence.

We find that the damage was caused by an intentional kick. The 2 prosecution witnesses give consistent eye-witness evidence of a deliberate 'kung-fu' kick' and we find them to be reliable witnesses. The defendant gave a confused and improbable version of events that he tripped and fell backwards and damaged the window purely with his body weight. No other witnesses were called by the defendant.

8) Has the burden of proof been discharged in respect of all elements of the offence?

We find that the prosecution have proved beyond reasonable doubt that the criminal damage was caused by the defendant intentionally.

Reasons should not normally take up more than half a side to a side of A4 paper unless there are separate issues surrounding numerous witnesses or arguments in law to be determined. It is important to recognise that the Practice Direction 2000 states that 'it shall be the legal adviser's responsibility to assist the court, where appropriate, as to the formulation of reasons and the recording of those reasons'. Furthermore, the legal adviser has the responsibility to advise on 'the appropriate decision making structure to be applied in any given case', 'whether or not the justices have requested that advice'. Use the legal adviser!

2.5.1. A few 'rules' of evidence

Evidence is a specialised subject and is potentially complex. It is most likely to be an issue during a trial and reasons must include any determinations which are made about any evidential issues. Evidence which is able to be considered by the court is referred to as 'admissible' and evidence which cannot be considered is referred to as 'inadmissible'. Sometimes statements are made which are 'inadmissible' and they must be struck out from any notes and disregarded.

Most 'rules' of evidence have exceptions to them in certain circumstances so it is always worth checking with the legal adviser. Subject to those exceptions, the general rules are as follows. N.B. virtually every one carries exceptions!:

- Criminal cases must be proved beyond reasonable doubt. Civil cases must be proved on the balance of probabilities.
- The burden lies on the prosecutor in criminal cases and on the complainant in civil cases.
- The test for all evidence is that it is 'relevant'. It must either aim to prove or disprove some matter which requires to be proved.
- Evidence is generally admissible if it relates to the facts in issue e.g. the quantity of alcohol in an offence of driving over the prescribed limit.
- It may be admissible of other facts, often referred to as 'circumstantial evidence' which render the facts in issue probable or improbable.
- Hearsay evidence of a statement made by someone else is not admissible in criminal proceedings because the person who actually made the statement is not present to be cross-examined e.g. Mrs. X told me that the defendant hit the victim. Note that hearsay is admissible in civil proceedings e.g. an application for an Anti Social Behaviour Order, family proceedings.
- Leading questions which suggest the answer cannot be asked by advocates when questioning their own witness e.g. Mr. Client, I put it to you that you were not present at the scene of the crime. That is correct isn't it?
- The magistrates may only ask questions which clarify issues already raised in a trial.
- Evidence of previous convictions or character are not admissible because it is dangerous to assume that facts will repeat themselves.
- A witness cannot be asked questions which tend to show that he has been charged or convicted of any other offence.
- Inferences may be drawn from silence in court and also from failing to answer particular questions from the point of charge and throughout the trial, but silence can never be the sole basis for a conviction.
- Identification evidence based on brief sightings must always be considered carefully. The court must consider the period of the sighting, whether the person was already known to the witness, the lighting, any special reason for remembering the accused, the period between observing and the subsequent identification to the police, and any material discrepancy between the description and the actual appearance. These are known as the Turnbull guidelines.
- Special measures may be used so that children under 17 may give evidence by video link in sexual/violence cases, and vulnerable witnesses may give evidence from behind a screen in court.

2.6. Information to be considered for sentencing purposes

During the course of a trial, there are currently very limited circumstances in which previous convictions may be disclosed e.g. to attack the character of a witness, to prove system. However, following conviction, whether following a guilty plea, or on a finding of guilt after trial, the bench will always be made aware of previous convictions, which will be supplied by the prosecutor. This may well affect sentence in two different ways. Firstly, the record may make the present offence more serious because the defendant has already committed a similar offence and has gone on to do again. Secondly, the response to previous sentences can be assessed and this may affect both seriousness and also choice of penalty.

Which previous convictions may be taken into account to increase seriousness? The first consideration is whether there is any similarity. Offences basically fall into the categories of violence and disorder, dishonesty, and traffic offences. An offender charged with assault could reasonably expect that any previous convictions showing a propensity to violence or disorder could make the current offence of greater concern to the bench, and therefore, it would be considered to be a more serious matter, requiring a greater punishment.

There are safeguards. The defence must be given the opportunity both to check that the record is correct, and also to comment upon any convictions which are likely to increase seriousness e.g. to distinguish the current matter on its facts from those on record. The age of the convictions will also be relevant. The Rehabilitation of Offenders Act 1974 allows convictions to become 'spent' after a specific period without offending further. Whilst the Act does not strictly apply to criminal proceedings, it is recommended by Practice Direction, that the court should 'give effect to the general intention of parliament' and the spirit should normally be applied. The rehabilitation periods are as follows:

Offences punished by:

6 months – 30 months custody/detention   = 10 years
Up to 6 months custody/detention   = 7 years
Community orders and fines   = 5 years
The periods must be entirely clear of offending, otherwise the clock begins again.

2.6.1. Aggravating and mitigating features of offence

There are two general aggravating features which the court must always be made aware of and consider. These are statutory requirements. Firstly, if an offence was committed whilst on bail, the court 'shall treat the fact that it was committed in those circumstances as an aggravating factor'. It does not matter whether it is the same type of offence or not and it does not matter whether the bailed offence is ultimately discharged. Secondly, if an offence is racially or religiously aggravated (other than those specifically charged as such), again, the court 'shall treat the fact as an aggravating factor'.

Other aggravating and mitigating features will be specific to the offence itself and the most common specific features are listed in the Magistrates Court Sentencing Guidelines.

Example:

p.60 Theft
Sentencing Guideline entry point = community penalty.

Aggravating Features	Mitigating Features
High value	*Low value*
Planned	*Impulsive action*
Sophisticated	
Adult involving children	
Organised team	
Related damage	
Vulnerable victim	

2.6.2. Victim personal statement

It is entirely a matter for the victim as to whether or not they make such a statement. The court may take into account, so far as it considers appropriate, the consequences to the victim as set out in the statement. It must be served on the defence in advance. Opinions as to appropriate sentence by the victim are irrelevant - only the consequences of the offence may be considered e.g. 'Since the assault, I am frightened whenever I see X and I feel too frightened to go into the club because he might be there'.

2.6.3. Offender mitigation

Perusal of the record will be followed by mitigation which is given either by the defendant himself (prompted by the chairman) or by his solicitor.

This will include information about the offender's view of the offence; relevant previous convictions which could increase seriousness; home background, employment, financial situation, mental and physical health, and his attitude towards offending.

It will also focus upon the extent of co-operation with the police and the court, and any hard evidence of genuine remorse.

The court must, by statute, take into account the stage in the proceedings when the defendant indicated his intention to plead guilty and the circumstances. It must be stated in open court if the punishment is therefore less severe. The notion of giving credit is to encourage swift admission and outcome and the accepted guideline is a credit of up to one third for a 'timely' guilty plea. 'Timely' is a little different to 'early' as the defendant is entitled to be made aware of the case against him and have the opportunity to take legal advice, which may occasionally not be possible on a first listing. Thereafter, credit will erode as time goes by. Very little credit is appropriate if the guilty plea takes place at the door of a trial hearing when witnesses have had the trauma of attending, albeit they have avoided the trauma of actually giving evidence.

The issue of co-operation with the police must not be overlooked in computing sentence. The defendant who gives a false name and address, even following a minor traffic offence, causes an enormous amount of additional time and effort, and has attempted to avoid prosecution.

Finally, the most obvious expression of remorse is an early guilty plea and this, in itself, will normally bring a reduction in the amount of the selected penalty. Other 'hard evidence' of remorse is an apology to the victim and/or voluntary compensation. Expressions of regret in court, particularly through a solicitor, show respect for the court but, alone, will rarely constitute the 'hard evidence' required to further reduce sentence.

The court may feel that further information is required and the services of the probation service may be called upon at this stage. The nature of the involvement will depend upon the information required and the sentence(s) which the court has in mind.

2.6.4.   Probation reports

There are two types of probation report. The first type is a full written 'pre-sentence report' (PSR) which requires an adjournment, normally of 15 days, for an interview to make a risk assessment and sentence proposal. A PSR is not read aloud in court. The alternative is a 'specific sentence report' (SSR).

This is normally delivered in court verbally by the officer after an interview in the court probation office prior to return to court, either later in the day or earliest listing e.g. next day, if it is impractical to stand the case down and return on the day.

(i)   A pre-sentence report (PSR) must always be considered if the court intends to impose a custodial sentence unless the court considers this to be 'unnecessary.' The Court of Appeal has given guidance that it should be the 'inevitable practice' that a pre-sentence report should be obtained if the court is contemplating a prison sentence for a defendant for the first time, other than for a 'very short period indeed' (R v. Gillette 1999). However, a report was deemed to be unnecessary where 'the judge had assumed every point in the defendant's favour and there was nothing extra that could have assisted the judge in imposing the sentence that was inevitable for the offences before her' (R v. Armsaramah 2000). Sometimes a recent PSR may be available and this may render a new report 'unnecessary' unless the defence can persuade the court that there have been substantial, relevant changes since the last report.

Although local practices vary slightly, a pre-sentence report will normally be also required in the following circumstances, where there are either assessment processes, or complexities which cannot realistically be covered in a court 'stand down' report:
- Assessment for drug treatment and testing order; intensive control and change programme and condition of residence.
- Cases involving sex offences, domestic violence, mental health.

The report must be in writing and copies must be provided to the court, the defence, the defendant, CPS and some other specified prosecutors, within a maximum of 15 days. It will be based on the Offender Assessment System (OASys) which provides a systematic assessment of the nature and causes of the offender's behaviour, the risk of harm the offender poses to the public and the action which can be taken to reduce the likelihood of re-offending.

It must include the following sections and information:

- Offence analysis – nature and circumstances of offence; assessment of culpability and level of premeditation; assessment of consequences and impact on any victim from CPS papers or from a victim statement. An indication of whether or not any positive action has been taken to make reparation or address offending behaviour since the offence was committed.

- Offender assessment – status in relation to literacy/numeracy; accommodation; employment; special circumstances e.g. family crisis; evaluate any patterns of offending; details of any substance misuse; relevant personal background.

- Assessment of the risk of harm to the public, self-harm and the likelihood of re-offending.

- Conclusion – evaluates the offender's motivation and ability to change; explicitly states whether offender is suitable for a community sentence; makes a clear and realistic proposal designed to protect the public and reduce offending, including custody where this is necessary. If a community rehabilitation order - desired outcomes of sentence; methods and interventions and level of supervision envisaged; precise requirements. If curfew - suitability of address and likely effect on other occupants. If custody – any anticipated effects on offender and family.

(National Standards for Supervision of Offenders in the Community 2000 - revised 2002).

Much debate has taken place over the years about what the court should say when adjourning for a pre-sentence report. The most important point is that the court should be guarded about binding a future bench. An adjournment 'for a pre-sentence report to consider suitability for a community punishment order' effectively leaves the next bench with no other option if the defendant is suitable. Case law is very clear that once the expectation of a particular community penalty is created, the next bench certainly cannot impose custody if the defendant is suitable for the identified penalty. Their hands are tied. Similarly, an adjournment within the Magistrates' Court for report carries the expectation that the defendant will finally be sentenced by the Magistrates' Court. The powers are arguably limited to a maximum of 6 months imprisonment for a single offence even if the case is committed to Crown Court for sentence by the next bench.

Whilst the PSR author requires as much guidance as possible as to the type of penalty to be explored, the bench should also consider whether to add a clear statement that the sentencing court may well consider custody and/or committal to the Crown Court for sentence. This avoids the next bench being fettered with a community option, if their view is that the case is so serious that it should be a custodial penalty - possibly even at the Crown Court level.

On a lesser note, it is almost always helpful to specifically seek means information in addition, if only to consider the level of compensation and costs – so much easier than awaiting instructions after the principal sentence is determined on the report.

(ii) A specific sentence report (SSR) provides information about the offender and offence so as to assist the sentencing court to determine the offender's suitability for a specific sentence. It is written, usually in note form, but is usually presented orally to the court. It is used to speed up the provision of information to the court to allow sentencing without delay on the day, following a short stand-down of the case. National Standards are clear that the officer may recommend a full PSR if he believes that further investigation is required, particularly if risk of serious harm, or concern has been identified e.g. previous convictions include sexual offences, discussion creates a concern about mental health. The national target is to reach 20% of community penalties being imposed following a SSR rather than PSR. Some courts are already exceeding this figure.

Whilst the initiative originally required the bench to identify a 'specific' sentence to be considered, e.g. community punishment order, some areas are now offering the alternative facility of reporting on the defendant's suitability for 'all community options', namely community rehabilitation (possibly with a relevant programme), community punishment, and curfew. On the limited information available from the prosecution and defence mitigation, it is often abundantly clear that the level of seriousness is within the community band, but it is less clear which particular penalty is likely to be the most effective. The temptation to adjourn for a 'full picture' through a full pre-sentence report is avoided simply by identifying the level of seriousness and then seeking assistance on likely effectiveness of the various community penalties.

Even if time or resources are not available to return to court later on the same day, a short adjournment to the next day, or within the week, back to the familiar venue of the courthouse for a short interview and sentence, has much to commend it.

2.7. Structured approach to sentence
(Adult Court Bench Book 1-35)

Having gathered all of the information it is necessary to process it in a structured manner. The '4 O' approach is recommended. This provides a dual function of providing a useful and simple agenda for discussion and also provides a useful checklist for reasons.

1. **O**ffence
2. **O**ffender
3. **O**bjective
4. **O**ptions

2.7.1. Offence

- What is the Sentencing Guideline entry point? e.g. community penalty
- What is the nature and extent of criminal intent?
  A pre-meditated offence is more serious than a spontaneous offence.
- What is the nature and extent of any injury or damage to the victim?
  Personal injury is more serious than financial damage.
- What are the aggravating features?
  - ✓ Matters specific to the offence as listed in the guidelines e.g. high value, planned.
  - ✓ Relevant previous convictions - similar type and sufficiently recent (see 2.6)
  - ✓ Was offence committed on bail? - <u>must</u> increase.
  - ✓ Is the offence racially/religiously aggravated? - <u>must</u> increase.
  - ✓ Any failures to respond to previous sentences? - <u>may</u> increase, and may affect choice of penalty.
  - ✓ Victim personal statement - so far as court considers appropriate.
- What are the mitigating features?
  - ✓ Matters specific to the offence as listed in the guidelines. e.g. low value, provocation, spontaneity.

What is the level of seriousness at this stage? e.g. custody.

2.7.2. Offender

- Positive good character e.g. no relevant previous convictions, solid employment record, faithful discharge of family duties.
- Co-operation with the police is highly relevant. Giving the correct name and address is a start! Failure to do so surely cannot be overlooked in the final sentence.
- Hard evidence of genuine remorse e.g. apology to the victim. This is a step further than the solicitor simply conveying his client's remorse in court.
- If the offence is fuelled by drink or drugs – a genuine self-motivated determination to address the addiction. Again, this is rather more than a general expression of future intention.
- Youth/immaturity would often justify a less rigorous penalty than for an adult.

(R v Howells 1998).

What is the level of seriousness at this stage?

Check – Are magistrates' courts powers sufficient? If not, it may be appropriate to return to court and indicate that the court is minded to commit to the Crown Court for sentence and seek representations on this course of action.

2.7.3.   Objectives

What sentencing objectives are necessary and/or likely to be most effective? At this stage, it may well emerge that there are one or more objectives and therefore, one or more, penalties are necessary. Each objective may be achieved potentially by a range of penalties.

- Punishment - where basic 'pay-back' to the community is required to emphasise that rules exist and must be kept - crime does not pay, e.g. fine, compensation, community punishment, curfew to restrict liberty.
- Protection of the public and prevention - where a penalty is required to create a greater protection for the specific victim or the community, from this defendant, e.g. custody, curfew during hours of offending, anti-social behaviour order, binding over order, licensed premises exclusion order, football banning order, restraining order.
- Reform and rehabilitation - where there is realistic optimism for a positive change of behaviour e.g. community rehabilitation order, possibly with an accredited programme; enhanced community punishment order to increase employability.
- Reparation - compensation to the victim: community punishment.
- Deterrence to others - in the occasional situation where it is necessary to deter particular types of offending and it is essential for the safety of the community, that the court send out a clear message that custody can be expected, e.g. local riots.

The purposes of sentencing are actually identified for the first time in the Criminal Justice Act 2003 as punishment, public protection, reform and rehabilitation, crime reduction and reparation.

2.7.4.   Options

- What is the most suitable option to satisfy both the level of seriousness and the identified objective(s)?
- Is a full pre-sentence report required, or a specific sentence report as a stand-down from the list for a verbal report on suitability?
- How much or how long, so that any restriction is proportionate to the offence? This is particularly relevant if a number of penalties are being combined - some pruning may be necessary!

- How much credit should be given for a guilty plea? The starting point is up to one third of the penalty selected. The extent will depend upon the circumstances and whether the guilty plea was entered at the earliest realistic opportunity. The fact that credit, (i.e. a reduction of penalty), has been given must always be stated in the pronouncement. Sometimes it may be practical to actually specify the extent of reduction, e.g. offence merits 6 months custody, but because of the timely guilty plea and co-operation with the court, it is reduced to 4 months. Guilty pleas from the guilty need to be encouraged. We need to 'market' the 'credit' so that more guilty pleas are entered at the earliest stage.
- Compensation must always be considered where appropriate - whether formally applied for or not, particularly compensation for terror and distress. Reasons must be given if it is not ordered.
- Costs?

Check – is the totality of the sentence commensurate to the seriousness of the offence?

Examples:

A perfectly calculated fine on several offences on the basis of net income and band may well result in a total which will take well over 12 months to pay. Overall, the fine needs to be reduced.

A cocktail of options which perfectly covers the necessary objectives of rehabilitation and prevention may well result in a restriction of liberty which is not commensurate to the seriousness of the actual offence. The community rehabilitation order may need to be reduced in length with the curfew requirement reduced to perhaps only 3 nights per week and the bind over reduced to run alongside the period of the rehabilitation order.

2.7.5. Sentencing reasons

The Human Rights Act, Article 6, states that 'judgement shall be pronounced publicly', subject to exceptions which principally concern youth and family cases. This is understandably considered to be part and parcel of a fair trial.

Convention case law is clear that the giving of reasons is a part of the right to a fair trial, with two main purposes:

- To ensure that justice is done and is seen to be done by the person to whom the decision is addressed and by the community at large.
- To enable an aggrieved party to consider whether to exercise his right of appeal against the decision.

The tests for adequacy of reasons are:

- Would a reasonable person with notice of all the facts and representations made to the court be able to understand the decision itself and the basis of that decision including the conclusions reached by the justices on disputed facts or contentious submissions, and why such conclusions had been reached?

- Would a reasonable person with notice of all the facts and representations made to the court be able to properly consider whether to exercise his right of appeal in respect of either a finding against him or the decision made by the court?

Purely and simply, it shows 'where the decision came from'. It is not expected be a House of Lords judgement – just a few meaningful comments. By completing a written reasons form in preparation for the pronouncement, the bench also have the advantage of a valuable aid to reaching a structured decision. The 'pro-forma' below is based upon the example provided in the Sentencing Guidelines (p.103), but adds in the fact that the guidelines have been used and states the 'normal' penalty as a prelude to the individual reasons. It assures the defendant and solicitor that the decision emerges from the Magistrates Court Sentencing Guidelines which can be obtained by any member of the public, and it also covers all necessary aspects of the structured process - not all will be relevant in every case.

Sentencing reasons pro-forma

1. We are dealing with an offence of ...

2. We have used the Magistrates' Court Sentencing Guidelines in this case and the normal penalty for this offence is ...

3. We have taken into account these features which make the offence more serious:

The following features of the offence itself ... (consult guidelines)

Where relevant:
- *Your previous record, specifically the offences of ... and your failure to respond to the sentences of ...*
- *It was committed whilst on bail for another offence.*
- *It was racially or religiously aggravated*
- *We have also considered the impact on the victim which was ...*

4. We have taken into account these features which make the offence less serious and what we have heard about you:

The following features of the offence itself ... (consult guidelines)

The following information about you ...

Where relevant:
And your net income of ...

(*Consider sentencing objective(s) at this stage
in order to create an effective total penalty 2.7.3.*)

5. We have taken into account the fact that you pleaded guilty at an early stage (or not until ...) and we have therefore reduced the sentence accordingly/by ...

6. As a result we have decided that the most appropriate sentence for you is ...

7. *Where relevant:*
We have decided not to award compensation because:

Finally, to emphasise that the Practice Direction requires the legal adviser to advise on the appropriate structured decision making approach (whether requested or not) and it is the legal adviser's responsibility to assist the court, where appropriate, in the formulation of reasons and the recording of those reasons (see 1.6.8.).

2.8.   Sentencing options

Sentencing powers are built on a hierarchy of seriousness with an increasing restriction on liberty as set out in the table below.

Increase of seriousness and restriction of liberty ➜				
Inexpedient to punish		'Serious enough'	'So serious'	Too serious
Discharge	Compensation Fine Disqualify 1 day detention	* Community penalties: • Attendance Centre • Community Punishment • Community Rehabilitation • Community Punishment <u>and</u> Rehabilitation • Curfew • Drug Treatment and Testing	Custody	Commit to Crown Court

Ancillary orders which may be added to the penalty:

Anti-social behaviour order
Binding over
Compensation
Costs
Disqualification (also available as a separate penalty from January 2004)
Endorsement
Re-test
Exclusion from licensed premises
Forfeiture
Football banning order
Parenting order
Restraining order
Sexual Offences Prevention Order (from May 2004)

* Each community penalty is not exclusive, and a fine may also be added if commensurate with seriousness. The only combination which is prohibited by law is community punishment and community rehabilitation which cannot be imposed as 2 separate penalties for a single offence - it must be the combined order, which carries different duration limits.

See Appendix 5 for more detailed handy court sentencing reference chart.

2.8.1.   Absolute discharge

The court must be of the opinion that 'it is inexpedient to inflict punishment'. When is it 'inexpedient' to punish? On the one hand, where a conviction is sought but there is extremely strong mitigation such as driving through a red traffic light to an emergency. On the other hand, a defendant may already be sentenced on other offences and it is either inappropriate or impractical to impose any additional penalty e.g. defendant is serving a lengthy custodial sentence and could not comply with any other penalty.

2.8.2.   Conditional discharge

The criteria are the same as for an absolute discharge - 'inexpedient to inflict punishment'. The difference is that the court feels that a condition of committing no further offences must be attached e.g. discharged for a period of 12 months on the condition that no further offences are committed. If a further offence is committed within the specified period then the court may sentence for the original offence in addition to the new matter.

It is an order which does not anticipate any further offending and so reaches the conclusion that punishment is 'inexpedient,' which in itself carries a message on the previous convictions to the next bench as to its low level of seriousness. This option must be distinguished from the notion of requiring 'something to hang over' a defendant, because further offending is expected. In such circumstances, a greater punishment may be more appropriate to the level of seriousness e.g. a fine or community penalty, possibly with a binding over order.

The order must be explained to the defendant.

✓   Minimum period – none.   Maximum – 3 years.

2.8.3.   Fines

'The amount of any fine fixed by a court shall be such as, in the opinion of the court, reflects the seriousness of the offence'. 'In fixing the amount of any fine to be imposed on an offender, a court shall take into account the circumstances of the case including, among other things, the financial circumstances of the offender so far as they are known, or appear to the court.'

- Minimum – none.
- Maximum – depends upon the amount fixed by law for the particular offence. The maximum fines are described as 'levels 1 to 5' rather than fixing specific amounts in every piece of legislation. This enables the various levels to be adjusted from time to time. As at March 2004, the levels are as follows:-

Level 1 = £200
Level 2 = £500
Level 3 = £1,000 e.g. disorderly behaviour
Level 4 = £2,500 e.g. racially or religiously aggravated disorderly behaviour
Level 5 = £5,000 e.g. driving with excess alcohol

A very small number of offences carry higher maxima e.g. some health and safety offences.

In practical terms, the amount of the fine is fixed after considering 5 aspects which are each considered below: -

(i) Sentencing guideline band.
(ii) Net income.
(iii) Aggravating/mitigating features.
(iv) Credit for guilty plea.
(v) Outgoings and limitation of 12 month repayment period.
(vi) Order to pay.

(i)   Sentencing guideline band

All offences which have an entry point of 'fine' in the sentencing guidelines are given an entry band as follows: -

Band A = 50% of net income e.g. drunk and disorderly.
Band B = 100% of net income e.g. no insurance.
Band C = 150% of net income e.g. criminal damage.

This ensures a starting point figure which is individual to each defendant – not a range, but an actual figure for the individual.

(ii)   Net income

This will normally be gleaned either from a completed means form or directly from the defendant in court. Debate continues after the introduction of the Guidelines as to what fairly constitutes the 'net income', which is described as 'weekly take home pay or benefit'. Whilst it is no doubt agreed that income tax and national insurance should be properly deducted before arriving at the net income, there are other aspects.

Arguably, child benefit should be ignored as this is specifically allocated to the children. By ignoring the allowance, it ensures that the larger family has a higher protected income, bearing in mind that a net income of say, £200 will be the band B fine, whether the defendant is a single person or a defendant with a family to support.

A more complex aspect is the comparison between a defendant in receipt of benefits with no rent/mortgage or council tax to pay out of that income, as compared to a waged defendant who has roof costs and council tax to pay out of his income. Some benches have therefore taken the view that roof costs and council tax should be deducted from a waged income so that the 'net figure' is then fairly equated with that of the defendant on benefits i.e. both are fined from 'the money left to actually live on'. A defendant paying board – deduction of ½ as his notional roof cost contribution.

Example:

Defendant A is working and after tax/insurance, he receives £150 per week. Defendant B is in receipt of job-seekers allowance and receives £150 benefits.

Defendant A		Defendant B	
Take home pay (after tax/insurance)	*= £150*	*Job seekers allowance*	*= £150*
Less:			
Rent	*= £40*	*Rent and council tax are covered by the state*	*= £0*
Council tax	*= £10*		
Money for ordinary living expenses	*= £100*	*Money for ordinary living expenses*	*= £150*

This is a relatively straightforward calculation and ensures that the fine is fixed on the 'money in pocket' for food/clothes/entertainment for each defendant, and the 'roof costs' which cause substantial differences between those who pay and those who do not, are taken out of the calculation. Additionally the defendant on state benefits will normally have the privilege of other monetary passport benefits e.g. free school meals, community care grants, whilst the working defendant will have the expense of travelling to work, but these modifications would be too complex to work through. Rent/mortgage and council tax are the big ones!

Obviously it is relevant as to whether the defendant is solely responsible for paying out expenses. The actual income and domestic financial arrangements with other members of the household is irrelevant, but the question as to expenses should be clearly raised, 'how much do you personally pay towards rent/mortgage etc.?'

What if the defendant fails to supply evidence of means? There are 2 approaches to this problem - either using pressure to obtain the information, or alternatively going ahead without the information.

From April 2004, it becomes an offence to fail to furnish a statement of financial circumstances in response to an official request by the Justices Chief Executive - this applies particularly to cases where the defendant may well chose not to attend court. A means form is sent with the summons, containing the appropriate request and warning about the offence, but the defendant fails to supply means information to the court. The offence is not about failing to complete the form (useful as that would be!). The offence is that he fails to 'furnish a statement of financial circumstances' 'for the purpose of determining the amount of any fine ... and how it should be paid', i.e. at the very least, income and outgoings are required. The penalty is a maximum level 2 fine.

When the defendant does attend court, the failure to supply a statement of financial circumstances on the order of the court carries a level 3 fine on failure. Knowingly false or reckless information carries imprisonment.

The 2nd option is to go ahead without the information if there is no co-operation to provide it, and 'make such determination as it thinks fit'. There are local variations in approaching this determination. In West Yorkshire the figure is based upon an assumption that a defendant is in receipt of the local average net income deducting the average rent/mortgage and council tax figures. These are readily accessible using the New Earnings survey/ Regional Trends and local authority figures. In West Yorkshire the relevant figures in 2000 gave £270pw net income across both genders as an average from the various petty sessions divisions, with an average rent/mortgage of £45pw and council tax of £5 (rounded down).

This creates a fine in absence of £220 (£270 less rent/council tax) for a 100% band B offence, e.g. no insurance, and £110 for a 50% band A offence, e.g. no television licence.

(iii)   Aggravating/mitigating circumstances

Using a structured approach, the aggravating and mitigating features of the offence must be considered, followed by offender mitigation, when considering quantum. If any of these factors come into play, then they should be announced in the reasons as explanation for deviation from the guideline figures. In many situations, particularly traffic document offences dealt with in the absence of the defendant, there will be no information before the court apart from the fact that documents were not held. In those circumstances it will be difficult to justify an increase or decrease from the guideline.

It cannot be emphasised enough that deviation may well be perfectly appropriate, provided there is a clear reason which a reasonable person could understand.

Examples:

> *Aggravating features.*
> * *Drunk and disorderly - band A, i.e. half net income.*
> *Abusive language to fellow passengers on a public bus. Had to be ejected by the driver; police assistance had to be sought, and the bus was delayed. Protracted incident with inconvenience and discomfort to others. Previous similar convictions. Fine increased.*
>
> *Mitigating features.*
> * *No insurance - band B, i.e. full net income.*
> *Genuine oversight that insurance had not been renewed. Documents produced to the court to explain how oversight occurred, together with current certificate. Good character. Fine reduced.*

(iv)   Credit for guilty plea

A deduction of up to one third should normally be deducted for a timely guilty plea, e.g. a net income of £60 for a band B offence would carry an entry point fine of £40.

An easy reference fines calculator is available at Appendix 6. This gives net weekly/monthly/annual incomes for each band together with the one third credit starting point figure. Remember this is a starting point only and can quite properly go up and down.

(v)   Outgoings and limitation of the 12 month rule

Case law and the Sentencing Guidelines are clear that fines should normally be payable within a 12 month maximum period. The logic is that a fine penalty lies below the community penalties which usually carry restrictions for up to 12 months only e.g. curfews up to 6 months, community punishment should be complete within 12 months, most community rehabilitation orders and custody is 12 months. It would be disproportionate for the 'lesser offender' to be penalised for longer, with the very real threat of custody for non-compliance.

Outgoings are therefore relevant to check just how much can realistically be paid within 12 months if instalments are necessary. If the appropriate instalment rate is £4 per week, then effectively the maximum fine is £4 x 50 weeks = £200. This final aspect of fixing the fine can result in re-visiting the guideline fines for a multiple offender so that the total fine falls within the guideline period.

(vi)   Order to pay

- The whole amount is due immediately and the first question must be 'Can it be paid in full now?', possibly by credit card.
- If not, how much can be paid now? There is the positive psychological commitment of 'paying a deposit' and the practical experience of getting things moving.
- If not, how quickly can it be paid? Far easier to enforce a single payment within 14 days than instalment options if they are not really necessary.
- What is a fair and realistic instalment rate? This should have been considered when checking the 12 month capability. A period to coincide with income is helpful e.g. weekly, but consider the hidden costs of lengthy weekly orders e.g. postal orders. However this is irrelevant if the court operates a free card payment system, except insofar as stressing that the payment is still due, whether or not the card materialises.
- From April 2004 a defendant in receipt of Job Seekers Allowance or Income Support may consent voluntarily to deductions from benefits at the point of imposition. Similarly a working defendant may consent to an attachment of earnings order with deductions fixed at a national percentage rate. If there is already default on an existing fine, the attachment must be made unless it is inappropriate or impractical. An

application to attach benefits would be inappropriate if there are already the maximum of 3 debt deductions. An attachment of earnings order would be inappropriate if the wage is below £55 per week, if there are already 2 attachments or if the job is insecure. An existing fine attachment does not prevent application being made for the current offence to follow on. See 3.2.3.

- State the date (and the day of the week) for payment(s) to be made.
- Warn the defendant that missed payments render the whole amount due immediately and default may result in imprisonment.

A careful, reasoned assessment and a clear warning can reduce the number of defaulters on the fine default list and the cost of pursuing payments. It is well worth the extra minute or two whilst the defendant is there in court.

See fines calculator at Appendix 6 for easy calculation of net weekly income within each band and with one third credit.

See Pronouncements - 3-50.

2.8.4. Compensation

Compensation 'wears two hats' - as a sentence in its own right, or ancillary to another penalty, e.g. in addition to a community order. It relates to any personal injury, loss or damage, occasioned by an offence. The amount is such as the court considers 'appropriate' having regard to any evidence, including victim personal statements, and to any representations made on behalf of the parties. When there is a challenge and real issues are raised, evidence must be received, and complex/substantial matters should be left to the County Court.

- Maximum = £5000.
- Where means are limited, compensation must always take precedence over a fine and costs.
- 'Injury' includes 'terror and distress' e.g. to a frightened victim in the house when a window was smashed. Seek representations before determining the extent of the penalty e.g. provocation may reduce seriousness.
- The Sentencing Guidelines set out guideline figures for injuries (page 90) e.g. £125 for a black eye.
- The Criminal Injuries Compensation Board do not make awards in a sum less than £1000 and it is therefore important for the court to explore the possibility of compensation for such personal injuries e.g. loss of non-front tooth falls within range of £500 to £1000.

- Limitations apply to damage in respect of motor accidents unless the vehicle is stolen or if the defendant is uninsured. The Motor Insurance Bureau do not pay the first £300 (October 2000) in such circumstances and the court should therefore consider ordering the defendant to pay this amount, if appropriate, to the victim if the 'bad driving' element is proved along with the 'no insurance'. Additionally, the court should consider an award for loss of 'no claims' bonus and insurance excess payments by the victim – figures will be required.
- Reasons must be given if compensation is not granted in full e.g. insufficient evidence of loss, insufficient means to pay in full.
- ✓ Maximum payment period dependant upon means = 2 years or exceptionally 3 years. Note that this is longer than the 12 month limit for fines.

2.8.5. One day detention

A flexible friend. Distinguish this option from 'imprisonment'! It is available for imprisonable offences and enables the court to detain within the precincts of the court or at any police station until 8pm as a primary sentence, or in default of paying a fine (including the 18 to 21 age group). Custody criteria do not apply. Nevertheless it is a restriction on liberty and if a lengthy period is considered, it may be appropriate to allow consultation with the duty solicitor.

Examples:

- *Detention in the court room 'until the court rises' for an offence at a 'fine entry point' where there is an inability to pay but some punishment is expedient.*
- *Detention 'deemed already served' in respect of defendants/defaulters who have already spent a night in the cells and this meets the seriousness of the situation.*
- *Detention until 8 p.m. in police cells in respect of a failure to surrender to bail for a defendant who surrenders voluntarily to a warrant with substantial mitigation as the likelihood of compliance with any court order, especially a fine may well be very low.*
- *Detention with release after the conclusion of the case as a method of wiping out outstanding costs/excise penalties which cannot be remitted.*

2.8.6. Disqualification from driving

Another flexible friend, which is now available as a penalty in its own right for any offence. For example, it may be used as a sole penalty for the traffic offender who already has substantial fines which are going to take another 12 months to pay. It may also be a method of dealing effectively with a kerb crawler or indeed anyone who is driving a motor vehicle as part and parcel of his means of offending.

OFFENCE IS 'SERIOUS ENOUGH' - COMMUNITY PENALTIES

The following offences are examples of offences which are considered to be 'serious enough' to carry an entry point of community penalty in the Sentencing Guidelines: -

Burglary of non-dwelling; common assault; possess class A drugs; cultivation of cannabis; failure to surrender to bail; going equipped for theft; obtaining by deception; false representation to obtain benefit; taking motor vehicle without owner's consent; theft; vehicle interference; drive whilst disqualified; driving with breach/alcohol limit over 86m.

2.8.7.   Attendance Centre Order

- Imprisonable, 'serious enough' offences only.
- 18 - 20 year old males (under 25 limit for fine defaulters only).
- A reasonably accessible centre, having regard to age, means of access and any other circumstances.
- Regime 'shall include a programme of group activities designed to assist offenders to acquire or develop personal responsibility, self-discipline, skills and interests'.
- Breach - see 2.8.14.
- ✓ Minimum = 12 hours. Maximum = 36 hours (usually 3 hours per occasion).

2.8.8.   Community Punishment Order (CPO)

Since October 2003, all community punishment orders became 'enhanced' community punishment orders, which maximise the opportunities for learning in order to change the offenders' behaviour. An element of rehabilitation has entered into the traditional 'punishment' order. The enhancement is upon employment-related skills and problem-solving with practical learning in real situations. Supervisors have high contact time with offenders and it is recognised that positive role-modelling can encourage positive attitudes and challenge anti-social attitudes.

- Imprisonable,' serious enough' offences only.
- Defendant carries out unpaid work in the community under supervision.
- Defendant must be suitable e.g. does not exhibit high risk of harm, and suitable work must be available.
- Must keep in touch with the officer, notify change of address and perform work as directed.
- Order may be reviewed on the application of the defendant or officer.
- Up to 10% of hours for completing associated basic literacy/qualifications e.g. certified awards for health and safety at work.
- Breach - see 2.8.14.
- ✓ Minimum = 40 hours (5 hours + per week).
- ✓ Maximum = 240 hours (21 hours per week) within 12 months.

(Average order length in 2003 was 113 hours).

2.8.9. Community Rehabilitation Order (CRO)

- 'Serious enough' offence - no requirement of being imprisonable.
- Aims – rehabilitation, or protecting the public from harm, or preventing further offences.
- Supervision plan to be drawn up within 15 days of making the order and include individual and/or group supervision and be related to tangible outcomes.
- Defendant must keep out of trouble, keep in touch with the probation officer and notify any change of address.
- At least 12 appointments should be made within the first 12 weeks, including a home visit. 6 appointments in the second 12 weeks and thereafter, monthly.
- Additional requirements may be included in the order e.g. residence at a specific address or in a hostel; electronic curfew; activities for up to 60 days; treatment for drug or alcohol dependency, or attendance on nationally accredited offending programmes. Programmes include General Offending Programme, Drink Impaired Drivers, Addressing Substance Relating Offending (ASRO), sex offenders, One to One, Enhanced Thinking Skills, Domestic Violence - see below.
- Order may be reviewed on the application of the defendant or officer.
- Breach - see 2.8.14.
- ✓ Minimum = 6 months. Maximum = 3 years.

Nationally accredited offending programmes to include within CRO

These programmes are based upon the Probation Service's 'What Works' initiative, which aims to reduce reconviction rates by providing types of supervision for offenders which are based on research evidence of success.

Examples:

General Offending Programme /'Think First'/ 'Enhanced Thinking Skills'.

22 intensive groupwork sessions. This is a cognitive skills programme, based on the premise that thinking is the basis of all behaviour, so in order to affect or change criminal behaviour, the underlying thoughts and attitudes of offenders must be addressed. This will develop thinking skills to see things from other people's point of view, e.g. the victim; develop a sense of values; consider alternatives to solve problems; resist pressure from others; avoid acting on impulse.

The Enhanced Thinking Skills programme was originally developed by the Prison Service and evidenced a 15% reduction in re-convictions. Psychometric tests are undertaken, before and after the programme to measure change.

Drink Impaired Drivers (DIDs)

14 weekly groupwork sessions followed by individual sessions. The objectives include increasing factual knowledge about the effects of alcohol; encouraging a constructive change in attitude; developing awareness of strategies to resist undue pressure to drink more than they wish; enabling them to recognise implications of drinking on selves and others and effect on essential driving skills. Many drivers chose to attend a voluntary course offered by the court so that their disqualification period is reduced (see 2.14.2). The reality is that when the time comes to attend the course, many are either unwilling to pay the fee, or find that they have managed without a licence and await the natural end of the disqualification instead of attending. Statistics of course attendance/completion vary across the country (approximately 51% in West Yorkshire in 2002/3). This course is court ordered and can result in breach proceedings. No harm in attending both!

2.8.10. Community Punishment and Rehabilitation Order (Combination Order)

- Imprisonable, 'serious enough' offences only.

- Reserved for offences which are at the 'top end' of the community band as the restriction on liberty is so high.
- A special Combination Order for 18-20 year olds also includes curfew and mentoring - the Intensive Change and Control Programme (see below).
- Breach - see 2.8.14.
- ✓ Probation element = 12 months to 3 years.
- ✓ Community punishment element = 40 hours to 100 hours.

2.8.11. Curfew Order with electronic monitoring

- 'Serious enough' offence - no requirement of being imprisonable.
- Must remain indoors at specified place or places e.g. 2 addresses may be used, during the curfew period.
- Approved person responsible for monitoring defendant's whereabouts e.g. security company contract.
- Usual, additional requirement is for electronic monitoring i.e. 'tagging' during the curfew. The local designated contractor will visit, usually during the first curfew period to place the electronic tag on the defendant and install the monitoring equipment.
- May be used simply to restrict liberty as punishment, or to prevent offending during high risk periods e.g. school hours for sex offenders; Thursday to Saturday for city centre alcohol-related offences (same number of total days as a 7 day week order).
- May combine with other community penalties for single offence e.g. curfew + community punishment, or may be placed as a requirement within a community rehabilitation order.
- The most common offences for curfew order in 2003 - theft/handling = 23%: driving whilst disqualified = 15%: burglary = 10%.
- Breach - see 2.8.14.
- ✓ Minimum = 2 hours per day. Maximum = 12 hours per day up to 6 months maximum.

2.8.12. Intensive Control and Change Programme

- A Community Punishment and Rehabilitation Order with special 'frills' for a special group.
- 18-20 year old males and females at risk of custody - the age group which accounts for 20% of re-convictions, particularly after short periods of custody.
- Control element:
  Curfew with tagging - up to 12 hours per day, up to 6 months.
  Intelligence-led police surveillance.
  Community Punishment Order - up to 100 hours.

- Change element:
  1st 3 months - 25 hours per week of structured activity, including supervision, attendance on programmes, community punishment work, access to education/training and mentoring. Partnership arrangements with key agencies, e.g. Connexions, Jobcentre Plus. Reduction to a minimum of 12 hours per week for next 3 months.
- Similar to the Intensive Supervision and Support Programme in youth court - the adult version.
- Breach - see 2.8.14.

2.8.13. Drug Treatment and Testing Order

- 'Serious enough' offence.
- This is not a community rehabilitation order with a drug programme included. It is a completely separate type of order with a high restriction on liberty.
- Aim - to break the link between drug use and crime e.g. reduce acquisitive crime to pay for drugs. It is not the expectation of the order 'to get clean, quick'. At this level of offending/punishment, it is simply not realistic and a reduction in drug use is usually the initial target. This in turn will reduce drug spending and the extent of acquisitive crime to fund the habit.
- Defendant is dependant on or has propensity to misuse drugs and he requires and may be susceptible to treatment.
- Treatment requirement – by specified person, at specified institution at specified intervals if non-resident. This may include authorised provision of drug substitutes e.g. methadone prescription for heroin users.
- Testing requirement – at least 2 urine samples per week for the 1st 13 weeks. Persistent negative results which indicate failing to engage with the order or unsatisfactory progress will lead to breach proceedings.
- Supervision by a probation officer - must keep in touch; notify change of address and comply with instructions e.g. attend relevant programmes. 20 + hours of activities for the 1st 13 weeks. The officer will be informed of the test results and report to the court.
- Order will be periodically reviewed by the court at least monthly and progress will be encouraged and monitored e.g. reduction in positive samples, moving to accommodation away from drug-users, taking up constructive leisure activities, buying an alarm clock and getting into a daytime routine, training for employment. Requirements may be amended as appropriate.
- Consent essential – may revoke and re-sentence if consent is withdrawn.

- Breach - see 2.8.14.
- ✓ Minimum = 6 months. Maximum = 3 years.

(See also 7.4 Drugs and Crime).

2.8.14. Community orders: enforcement, amendment, revocation

Conviction for breach occurs if it is proved that the defendant has failed without reasonable excuse to comply with the requirements of a relevant order. Action may be taken after one unacceptable failure to comply with instructions, and must, under National Standards, be taken after 2 unacceptable failures. All absences are deemed unacceptable unless an acceptable explanation is given, and this must be given within 7 days of the absence e.g. production of medical certificate. A warning letter will be sent within 2 days which states that the evidence must be provided, and that any further absence could lead to breach. Only one warning may be issued within a 12 month period.

Most breach proceedings concern either failing to attend appointments or failing to notify a change of address. The remainder involve failing to comply with particular instructions, e.g. failing to provide a medical certificate within 7 days of a failure to attend an appointment, as this is required to prove that the absence is acceptable; being disruptive in a group session.

The options for failure 'without reasonable excuse' to comply with the requirements of the relevant order are as follows: -

- No action – all punitive options are discretionary and a clear warning from the court as to other possible outcomes of breach, including re-sentence, may well have the desired effect. This is rare, but may well be encouraged by the responsible probation officer who is obliged to bring the case to court because of 2 breaches under National Standards guidance. The officer may feel confident that the defendant will comply in future and a disciplinary fine may exacerbate the very problem which the order is trying to address.
- Fine not exceeding £1000 (Guideline entry point is band B).
- Community punishment order for up to 60 hours (max aggregate 240 hours).
- Attendance centre order for breach of community rehabilitation order only.
- Loss of benefits – pilot areas only.
- Revoke and re-sentence - custody may be imposed if there has been wilful and persistent refusal to comply with a Magistrates' Court order (provided that the original offence carries imprisonment), but

committal to Crown Court would be necessary for a Crown Court order to be revoked. Details of the original offence will be required and the court may well deem it 'unnecessary' to require a pre-sentence report as the defendant clearly cannot comply with community orders.

The court must take into consideration the extent to which the offender has complied with the order in determining the breach penalty.

If the court decides to re-sentence on a combination of community orders, all should normally be revoked, even if the court then decides to include a constituent part of the original sentence in the new sentence.

An application may be made by the defendant or supervisor for amendment/ revocation if circumstances change e.g. revocation of community punishment order due to ill health. An alternative penalty is imposed which reflects the level of compliance so far on the order, e.g.. a reduced community rehabilitation order period to take account of the hours completed on the community punishment order.

OFFENCE IS 'SO SERIOUS' - CUSTODY

The following offences are examples of 'custody' entry points in the sentencing guidelines: -

Affray; aggravated vehicle-taking; assault occasioning actual bodily harm; assault on police officer; breach of anti-social behaviour order; harassment causing fear of violence; indecent assault; possess offensive weapon; theft in breach of trust; dangerous driving; driving with breath/alcohol limit over 116m.

Note that more serious offences are designated as an entry point of committal to Crown Court.

2.9.   Custody

Defendants aged 21 and over will serve the custodial sentence as imprisonment in a prison. Defendants aged 18 to 21 will serve their sentence as detention in a Young Offenders Institution.

(i) Criteria :

- Offence, or combination of offence and associated offence is 'so serious' that only such a sentence can be justified, or
- Violent or sexual offence and only a custodial sentence would be adequate to protect the public from serious harm (i.e. death or serious personal injury), or
- Wilful and persistent refusal to comply with community order, or
- Refusal to comply with proposed requirements of drug treatment and testing order, or a condition of a community rehabilitation order which requires consent, e.g. mental health treatment.

(ii) Requirements :

- Pre-sentence report required unless considered 'unnecessary' e.g. a recent report is available; short period and defendant has previously served custodial sentences; defendant has already served the period on remand in custody.
- Reasons must be announced and recorded on the commitment and court register.

Example:

" We believe that this offence of assault is so serious because it was unprovoked, it caused serious injury to a vulnerable victim and you have failed to respond to a community rehabilitation order made last June for a similar offence."

- Practical effects must be explained i.e. remission of a half of the sentence subject to good behaviour; account to be taken of any period in custody on remand and the power to order a return to custody if a further offence is committed during the balance of the sentence.
- Licence provisions do not apply to full-time sentences which are less than 12 months.
- ✓ Minimum = 5 days imprisonment (7 days for fine defaulters) / 21 days detention for offenders aged 18 to 21.
- ✓ Maximum = 6 months (or statutory maximum if less) for single offence/12 months for 2+ either-way offences.
- ✓ Remission at half way through the sentence, subject to good behaviour.
- ✓ Release prior to remission period, on Home Detention Curfew (HDC) after serving 30 days minimum in custody, or thereafter, at one quarter of the sentence, subject to grant by prison governor e.g. only in exceptional circumstances for sexual offences; presumption of

unsuitability for cruelty to children and racially aggravated offences. Maximum home detention curfew period is 4 and a half months.

Examples:

- *3 months prison sentence - serve 30 days (minimum for curfew) + 15 days on HDC to half way point.*

- *4 months prison sentence - serve 30 days (quarter point) + 30 days on HDC to half way point.*

- *12 months prison sentence - serve 3 months (quarter point) + 3 months on HDC to 6 month half way point. Period in custody on remand prior to sentence will be deducted e.g. 3 months so immediate release?!*

2.9.1. Intermittent custody (pilot areas only as at March 2004)

Under the Criminal Justice Act 2003, custodial sentences of less than 12 months will be replaced by a new sentence of 'custody plus'. This will always involve a period of at least 26 weeks post-release supervision in the community. Sentences of over 12 months will be served as half in custody and half in the community. This will make a big difference to the approach to custodial sentences and the provisions are expected to come into force in 2006.

In the meantime, the provisions in relation to 'intermittent custody', based upon the same philosophy became effective in pilot areas in January 2004. Some custody and some community life interspersed through the period fixed by the court for the total sentence.

The adapted prisons are HMP Morton Hall, Lincoln for women and HMP Kirkham, Preston for men. Basically the intention is for the defendant to be punished with a restriction of liberty of up to 4 days per week, alongside keeping and developing their life in the community, as a family member, employee etc. for the remainder of the week. Throughout the overall sentence they will be subject to licence conditions, which will normally be suggested in the essential pre-sentence report.

- Imprisonment criteria are satisfied.
- ✓ Overall sentence period - 14 to 26 weeks (To 52 weeks if 2+ offences).
- ✓ Overall custody period - 14 to 45 days (To 90 days if 2+ offences).
- ✓ Monday to Thursday (4 days): Tuesday to Friday (4 days): Friday evening to Sunday (3 days) depending upon individual circumstances.

- ✓ Home Detention Curfew (HDC) applies for sentences of at least 42 custody days, after serving at least 28 days. At 56 custody days, HDC will apply at the half way point thereafter.
- No remission - unlike full-time custody. HDC applies right to the end of the custodial period, rather than to the half way point. It is served 'intermittently' and applies only on those days when the offender would otherwise have been in custody.
- Custodial period will include unpaid work, performed by release on temporary licence (ROTL).
- Licence applies throughout the order and may include supervision (normally included), curfew/electronic monitoring, unpaid work, activities, accredited programmes, prohibited activities, exclusion from a place, attendance centre (males to 25 years).
- Approved travelling expenses are paid to and from prison.
- Breach for unacceptable behaviour, or failure to arrive may result in application to court to vary to full-time custody.

2.9.2. Facts and figures on custody

- Prison sentences are not succeeding in turning the majority of offenders away from crime. 58% of prisoners released in 1997, committed another crime within 2 years and 36% returned to custody. The figures for the 18-20 age group rise to 72% of those released committed another crime within 2 years and 47% returned to custody.
- The reconviction rate rose in the 1990s and remains high. At a conservative estimate, released prisoners are responsible for at least 18% of recorded, notifiable crimes.
- The costs of actually keeping prisoners within prison vary significantly, but average, £37,500 per year.
- 80% of prisoners have the writing skills, and 65% have the numeracy skills at or below those of an 11 year old child.
- 60% to 70% of prisoners were using drugs before imprisonment.
- Over 70% suffer from at least 2 mental disorders.
- One third lose their house while in prison: two thirds lose their job and over two fifths lose contact with their family.

(McInerney and Keating v. R (see below), from the report of the social exclusion unit dated July 2002).

2.9.3. General guidance on imposition of custodial sentences

There are 3 major guidance cases which cover important general principles.

R v. Kefford 2002

The Lord Chief Justice, Lord Woolf said:

'Nothing that we say in this judgement is intended to deter courts from sending to prison for the appropriate period those who commit offences involving <u>violence or intimidation or other</u> <u>grave crimes</u>. Offences of this nature, particularly if they are committed against vulnerable members of the community undermine the public's sense of safety and the courts must play their part in protecting the public from these categories of offences. There are, however, other categories of offences where a community punishment or a fine can be sometimes a more appropriate form of sentence than imprisonment'.

In the case of economic crimes, for example, obtaining undue credit by fraud, prison is not necessarily the only appropriate form of punishment. Particularly in the case of those who have no record of previous offending, the very fact of having to appear before a court can be a significant punishment. Certainly, having to perform a form of community punishment can be a very salutary way of making it clear that crime does not pay, particularly if a community punishment order is combined with a curfew order'.

R v. Ollerenshaw 1998

'When a court is imposing a comparatively short period of custody that is about 12 months or less, it should generally ask itself, particularly where the defendant has not previously been sentenced to custody, whether an even shorter period might be equally effective in protecting the interests of the public and punishing and deterring the criminal. For example there will be cases where for these purposes, 6 months may be just as effective as 9, or 2 months may be just as effective as 4'.

R v. Howells 1998

The Lord Chief Justice, Lord Bingham gave the following checklist guidance to courts required to decide in borderline cases whether an offence is 'so serious' that only a custodial sentence is justified for it:

- Nature and extent of criminal intention.
- Nature and extent of injury or damage caused to victim.
- Deliberate and pre-meditated is more serious than one which is spontaneous and unpremeditated or excessive response to provocation.

- An offence which inflicts personal injury or mental trauma, is more serious than one which inflicts financial loss only.
- An admission of responsibility, particularly when combined with a timely guilty plea and by hard evidence of genuine remorse e.g. offer of compensation, is mitigation.
- Where offending is fuelled by addiction to drink or drugs, the court will look more favourably on an offender who has demonstrated by practical steps and genuine self-motivated determination to address his addiction.
- Youth and immaturity will often justify a less rigorous penalty than would be appropriate for an adult.
- Some measure of leniency to offenders of previous good character, the more so if there is evidence of positive good character, such as solid employment record or faithful discharge of family duties, as opposed to a mere absence of previous convictions.
- Sometimes appropriate to take account of family responsibilities or physical or mental disability.
- Greater reluctance to impose a custodial sentence on an offender who has never before served such a sentence.

2.9.4.   Specific offences - guidelines on custody

- **Assault occasioning actual bodily harm - Guideline entry point - custody**

R v. Wallage 2002 - Victim chased defendant following minor traffic incident, and slapped and scratched him. He responded by punching her in the mouth, causing a cut and damage to a tooth. Taking account of provocation, reduced from 6 months to 3 months.

R v. Nolan 2002 - Defendant used a pan to beat his boyfriend. A sustained attack, causing lacerations which required stitches. Mitigation included alcohol problems and suicidal tendencies. Guilty plea on the day of trial. 21 months upheld (i.e. commit this type of attack/level of injuries to Crown Court).

(Sentencing Guidelines - page 14).

- **Burglary of dwelling - Guideline entry point - Committal to Crown Court**

R v. McInerney and Keating 2002 (+ Sentencing Advisory Panel guidance).

The table below summarises the guidance from the case which also referred to the Sentencing Advisory Panel details as set out, and it identifies clearly the type of case which could be dealt with in the Magistrates' Court

Low level (a)	Standard (b)	Medium aggravation (c)	High aggravation (d)
1st time offender. No damage to property. No property or only low value taken. Type includes - low value theft from garage or vacant property.	1+ features: Repeat offender. Theft electricals e.g. TV, video. Damage by break in. Some turmoil e.g. upturned drawers. No injury or violence, but some trauma.	1+ features: Vulnerable but not deliberate target. Victim at home (day or night). Goods high value (economic or sentimental). Burglars in group. On bail at the time. Spiteful.	1+ features: Force used or threatened v. victim. Victim injured. Especially traumatic effect. Professional planning/execution e.g. no. of offences. Vandalism beyond standard. Racially aggravated. Deliberate target of vulnerable.
Sentencing Advisory Panel advice on penalty as amended by case decision at ✓ (see over)			
1st – community penalty.	✓1st – 9 months (see below). ✓2nd – 18 months (after trial). If 2+ convictions after November1999 = 3 years minimum (must commit).	✓1st – 12 months (see below) 2nd – 2 years 2+ - 3 years	1st – 18 months 2nd – 3 years 2+ - 4 years (higher for more than 1 feature)

	✓ Impose community sentence subject to conditions to ensure that sentence is (a) effective punishment and (b) action tackles criminal behaviour and (c) when appropriate, tackles underlying problems e.g. drugs. Only if offender has demonstrated by behaviour that punishment in community is not practicable, should court resort to custody e.g. failure to comply with community penalties, effect on victim, nature of offence, record.	

Mitigating features: First offence; Nothing taken, or low value; Offender only played minor role; No damage or disturbance to property; On impulse; Timely guilty plea; Offender's state of health, physical and mental; Evidence of genuine remorse; Efforts to rehabilitate himself – real effort to break addiction, even if irregular; Response to previous sentences; Ready co-operation with police.

The sentence must reflect the degree of harm done, including the impact of the burglary upon the victim and whether or not the offender foresaw that result or the extent of the impact. The guidance is intended to reduce use of imprisonment but only if consistent with protection of the public.

The Sentencing Guidelines have interpreted this guidance that all cases of burglary of dwelling should be committed to Crown Court unless one or more of the features in the 'low level' exist and none of the listed aggravating features exist. A community order which is made at the Crown Court may well carry the same programme as in the Magistrates' Court, but the powers on breach extend beyond 6 months to 14 years which is necessary to fit the periods suggested by the Sentencing Advisory Panel.

Sentencing Guidelines - page 18.

- **Harassment causing fear of violence - Guideline entry point - custody**

R v. Liddle 1999 - 2nd offence and was also in breach of an existing restraining order. Consider the history, seriousness, effect on the victim, the victim's views, guilty plea and remorse.15 months.

Sentencing Guidelines - page 39.

- **Racially aggravated assault occasioning actual bodily harm - Guideline entry point - Committal**

R v. Saunders 1999

Lord Justice Rose said that racially aggravated assaults:

...'cannot co-exist with fairness and justice. It is incompatible with democratic civilisation. The courts must do all they can, in accordance with Parliament's recently expressed intention to convey that message clearly, by the sentences which they pass in relation to racially aggravated offences. Those who indulge in racially aggravated violence must expect to be punished severely, in order to discourage the repetition of that behaviour by them or others'.

Following a trial, up to 2 years should be added to the sentence. The court must first determine what the sentence would be without the racial aggravation and then add that factor, which could take it over the custody threshold. Relevant factors included, the nature of the hostility shown (such as language and weapons); length of the incident; location (public or private); number of people involved. 3 and a half years upheld for prolonged attack which did not involve serious injury.

A racially or religiously aggravated common assault (as opposed to the more serious charge of occasioning actual bodily harm) carries an entry point of custody.

R v. Salihu 2001 - defendant convicted of racially aggravated assault. He swore and used racist abuse and grabbed the shoulder of the victim, a traffic warden. Traffic wardens had a right to protection against assaults and against racists. 6 months upheld.

Sentencing Guidelines - pages 48 and 49.

- **Supply/being concerned in the supply of drugs - Guideline entry point - Committal to Crown Court**

The maximum sentence for supply of class A drugs, which include heroin, ecstasy, cocaine, morphine and methodone, is life imprisonment.

R v. Thompson 1997 - Defendant sold 4 ecstasy tablets in a night club to 2 undercover police officers for £10 per tablet. 4 years.

Sentencing Guidelines - page 25.

- **Indecent photographs - Guideline entry point - Committal to Crown Court**

The maximum sentence for offences involving the taking or making of indecent photographs of children committed after January 2001, is 10 years. The table below sets out the case law guidance which refers to current accepted definitions of the various activities, and identifies the type of cases which can be dealt with in the Magistrates' Court.

R v. Oliver and others 2002 - Two principal facts affect seriousness, namely the nature of the material and the extent of the defendant's involvement with it. The descriptions of the various levels of activity below are determined by the COPINE project (Combating Paedophile Information Networks in Europe Project). Seriousness increases in proportion to the defendant's proximity and responsibility for the original abuse. Any element of commercial gain increases seriousness. Any swapping of images could be regarded as commercial activity, even without gain, because the activity fuels demand for the material.

Possession and downloading of artificially created pseudo photos is less serious than cases involving images of real children, unless particularly grotesque. The levels of sentence are for adult offenders after a contested trial, and a guilty plea would be a mitigating factor.

Level	Nature of activity	Penalty	Circumstances
1	Images depicting erotic posing with no sexual activity	Fine	D merely in possession solely for own use, including cases where material downloaded but not distributed, and where material consisted entirely of pseudo-photos. Not large amount.

		Community Sentence	Large amount
		Custody to 6 months	Shown, distributed or exchanged on small scale without financial gain
2	Sexual activity between children or solo masturbation	Community sentence	D in possession and no distribution
		Custody up to 6 months	Large amount or Material shown or distributed to others on small scale without financial gain
		Custody 6 to 12 months	Showing or distributing on large scale without financial gain
3	Non-penetrative sex between adults and children	Custody up to 6 months	Possess small amount
		Custody 6 to 12 months	Showing or distributing small amount
		Custody 12 months to 3 years	Showing or distributing large amount or Producing or trading in levels 1-3
4	Penetrative sexual activity between adults and children	Custody 6 to 12 months	Possess small amount
		Custody 12 months to 3 years	Possess large amount

4		Custody 3 years +	Showing or distributing, involvement in production or commissioning or encouraging the production
5	Sadism or bestiality	Custody 6 to 12 months	Possess small amount
		Custody 12 months to 3 years	Possess large amount
		Custody 3 years +	Showing or distributing, involvement in production, or commissioning or encouraging production of images

Factors which aggravate:
- Images are shown or distributed to a child.
- So much material that impossible to quantify.
- Organisation and sophistication of the collection of the images.
- Images posted in public areas of the internet.
- Where defendant was responsible for the original production of the images and the child. was a member of his family, or defendant had abused a position of trust.
- Age of the children especially if they are babies or very young children.

2.9.5.   Suspended sentence of imprisonment

- Imprisonment criteria is satisfied.
- Period of imprisonment is fixed as if order were to be made forthwith.
- Suspension can only be justified by the exceptional circumstances of the case. Not simply youth, good character or early guilty plea, but e.g. offender is sole carer of dependants; stolen money has been repaid; significant provocation. A defendant who is aware of his serious medical condition at the time of committing a further offence cannot successfully argue for 'exceptional circumstances (R v. Wickens 2000).
- A fine and compensation may be imposed at the same time, but not a community penalty.
- Commission of a further offence during the period – court may activate fully, or substitute a lesser term, or vary to a new period of

suspension expiring no later than 2 years from the present date; or make no order and allow the order to continue.

- Crown Court suspended sentence breach - either commit to Crown Court to deal with, or simply notify Crown Court of the conviction.
- ✓ Minimum = 1 year from the date of the order. Maximum = 2 years.

2.10   Committal for sentence

The following offences are examples of 'Committal to Crown Court' entry points in the Sentencing Guidelines: -

Burglary of dwelling; Supply of drugs - all classes; Racially or religiously aggravated assault occasioning actual bodily harm; Violent disorder; Wounding - grievous bodily harm.

Effectively the guideline is stating that the offence is likely to merit more than 6 months imprisonment and would therefore be beyond the powers of the Magistrates' Court.

It is important to be particularly vigilant about the limitation of sentencing powers in these types of cases so that they are properly committed to Crown Court for sentence if appropriate. In most cases this can be identified after the prosecution outline e.g. serious domestic burglary. Discussion should always take place on the bench as to appropriate venue where the entry point is committal, particularly before adjourning for pre-sentence reports. The defence must be allowed to address the court following the bench's indication that it is minded to commit to Crown Court. Occasionally there may be sufficient mitigation to bring the case down to Magistrates' Court powers. In such cases it is important to consider adding a rider to any adjournment for pre-sentence reports that the next bench may commit the case to the Crown Court. If the rider is not added, the court has effectively given a binding indication that the maximum penalty will be 6 months imprisonment. If the next bench were to disagree and commit, the Crown Court will struggle to justify a longer penalty after that indication has been given, unless there is new information.

The National Mode of Trial guidelines (section 2 of Adult Court Bench Book), provide helpful indicators of aggravating features for specific offences which assist in the determination of whether a case lies outside the magistrates' powers. This may occur at the point of considering committal for trial or at consideration of committal for sentence. These are helpful for 'either-way' offences which do not carry a Guideline entry point of Committal to Crown Court.

Example:

> *p.2-8. Dangerous driving - Entry point - Custody.*
>
> *Consider Committal to Crown Court if one or more of the following features are present and sentencing powers are insufficient:*
>
> 1. *Alcohol or drugs contributing to the dangerous driving.*
> 2. *Grossly excessive speed.*
> 3. *Racing.*
> 4. *Prolonged course of dangerous driving.*
> 5. *Significant injury or damage sustained.*
> 6. *Other related offences.*

2.11. Sentences on mentally disordered defendants

Community Rehabilitation Order + treatment requirement

- Defendant pleads guilty or is found guilty.
- Evidence of approved medical practitioner that condition requires and may be susceptible to treatment, but is not such as to warrant detention under a hospital order.
- Court is satisfied that arrangements have already been made for the treatment.
- Specify place and treatment as resident/non-resident patient in a hospital or mental nursing home, or treatment under direction of duly qualified medical practitioner as specified.
- Defendant must express willingness to comply.
- ✓ Treatment may last up to the full period of order.
- ✓ 6 months to 3 years.

Hospital or Guardianship order

Same criteria apply to both:

- Pleads guilty, found guilty, or court is satisfied that defendant committed the act or made the omission charged without conviction.
- Imprisonable offence.
- Consider all circumstances and other available options.
- Written or oral evidence of 2 registered medical practitioners as to mental condition and recommendation is made.
- Hospital order - arrangements already made for reception into hospital within 28 days of order or

- Guardianship order - local social services authority or specified person willing to receive offender into guardianship i.e. care and protection rather than treatment.
- Cannot combine with imprisonment, fine or community rehabilitation order.
- ✓ Interim Hospital Order may be made for 12 weeks initially and then renewed in periods of 28 days up to 12 months.
- ✓ Hospital order is only authority for the patient's detention for 6 months in the first instance. Hospital managers/responsible medical officer/mental health tribunal may discharge at any time. Once discharged there is no recall.

(It may be appropriate to commit to the Crown Court for the making of a Restriction Order in addition to the Hospital Order. It has a fixed duration, subject only to the discretion of the Secretary of State for early discharge, and this may be conditional upon recall if necessary).
- ✓ Guardianship order is indeterminate but subject to regular reviews.

2.12. SENTENCES ON YOUTHS APPEARING IN THE ADULT COURT (with adult defendant)

A parent/guardian should be present with the youth in order for the case to proceed, particularly if sentence is to be considered, so that they can contribute towards identifying the most effective option to prevent further offending. It is the parent/guardian who may be made responsible for paying any monetary orders, and the court must always consider binding over the parent and making a parenting order. If a parent/guardian is not present, enquiries should be made to identify why parent is not present and it may be appropriate to adjourn the case and possibly issue a summons requiring attendance. At the very least an appropriate adult should be present, e.g. a relative, and failing this, a member of the youth offending team should be present with the youth in court to assist.

Whilst the youth will normally be remitted to the youth court to be sentenced following a guilty plea in the adult court, there are limited sentencing options which may be imposed by the adult court, alongside most of the available ancillary penalties, e.g. endorsement, disqualification, compensation.

2.12.1. Compulsory Referral Order

This order basically replaces the option of conditional discharge/fine/ community penalty for youths who are before the court on their first guilty plea for an imprisonable offence. The only alternatives to a compulsory referral order for an imprisonable offence are at the extremes of absolute discharge or custody (or a hospital order if appropriate). Where the offence is not imprisonable, the referral order is discretionary and in the adult court a fine or discharge may be imposed, e.g. driving without insurance.

The referral order has a specific intention of preventing further offending. A local youth offending panel, which includes a yot (youth offending team) officer and 2 members of the local community will agree a contract with the youth and parent, which will include some reparation (community payback), intervention to address risk factors and a guidance/monitoring element. Any breach is referred back to the youth court to consider re-sentencing.

- Youth aged 10 to 17.
- Guilty plea to an imprisonable offence + any associated offence(s)/optional if non-imprisonable.
- No previous convictions or bind overs.
- Court is not considering a custodial sentence, hospital order or absolute discharge.
- Parent/guardian must be ordered to attend the meeting of the Panel (youth aged10-16) and may be ordered to attend if the youth is 17.
- Cannot be combined with parental bind over.
- A parenting order may now be made in addition to the referral order - report required.
- ✓ 3 months to 12 months from the date of signing the contract.

2.12.2. Absolute or Conditional Discharge

Provisions as for an adult. Where a youth has received a Final Warning, and is convicted of an offence within 2 years of the warning, the court must not impose a conditional discharge unless there are exceptional circumstances relating to the offence or the offender.

2.12.3. Fine

- Youth aged 10 -13 = Maximum of £250.
- Youth aged 14 -17 = Maximum of £1000.

A proportionate reduction of fine as compared to adult maximum of £5000 is anticipated, and this may well be reflected by ensuring that the fine is payable within 3 months rather than the maximum of the 12 month period for an adult. This argument is also supported by the fact that most orders made in the youth court for low seriousness do not extend beyond 3 months. The parent/guardian of 10 - 15 year old must pay, unless they cannot be found, or it would be unreasonable to so order, e.g. youth is in local authority care and has no contact with either parent. The parent/guardian of a 16 - 17 year old may be ordered to pay.

If the youth is ordered to pay, the fine cannot exceed the amount of any costs.

2.12.4. Parental bind over

A parent/guardian of a youth aged 10 - 15 must be bound over to take proper care and exercise proper control over a convicted youth if it would be desirable in the interests of preventing the commission of further offences. Reasons must be given if the order is not made, e.g. parent has taken all reasonable steps to control and the court does not foresee any further offending. The order becomes discretionary if the youth is aged 16 -17.

- Consent is required, and unreasonable refusal may result in fine up to £1000.
- ✓ Maximum sum of £1000.
- ✓ Maximum period of 3 years or to age 18.

2.12.5. Parenting order

A parenting order must be made following conviction of any offence in respect of parents of youths aged 10 - 15, if it is considered desirable in the interests of preventing further offending. Reasons must be given if an order is not made, e.g. parenting is being addressed voluntarily or through another court order. The order becomes discretionary if the youth is aged 16 - 17.

The order involves two aspects:
(i)   To comply with specific requirements for up to 12 months, and
(ii)   To attend for a concurrent period not exceeding 3 months, a counselling and guidance programme (2 or more sessions) as may be specified by the responsible officer (usually a yot officer).

Failure to comply with the order carries a sanction of a fine up to level 3.

2.13   ANCILLARY ('ADD ON') ORDERS

2.13.1.   Anti-Social Behaviour Order - 'bolt-on' to a criminal conviction

- The order can be made on application <u>or</u> effectively as an ancillary order (strictly speaking the order is not described in the legislation as an ASBO if it is made following conviction but in common court parlance the term 'bolt-on ASBO' has been adopted).
- In criminal proceedings, it may be added to any sentence, or a conditional discharge.
- Defendant has acted in a manner that caused or was likely to cause harassment, alarm or distress to one or more persons not of the same household as himself, <u>and</u> the order is necessary to protect persons in any place in England and Wales from further anti-social behaviour by him.
- Prohibits defendant from doing anything described in the order - all negatives.
- No provision for an interim order (unlike the order on complaint).
- Note that since January 2004, there are no automatic press restrictions for youth 'bolt-on' ASBOs. In youth court, consider whether to 'impose' restrictions, rather than the 'norm' of 'whether to lift' in youth court.
- Breach is 'either-way' offence and carries 5 years custody. Conditional discharge is not available for breach.
- May apply for variation, and after 2 years, may apply for discharge.
- ✓ Not less than 2 years. No maximum.
- ✓ Effective from the day it is made, but may suspend requirements during period in custody e.g. not to contact co-accused if both are committed potentially to same custodial institution.

A 'bolt-on' ASBO may be an easier to prove and equally effective order than the sexual offences prevention order, exclusion order or football banning orders described below.

See 7.3 for full discussion.

2.13.2.   Sexual offences prevention order (from May 2004)

- The order can be made on application <u>or</u> as an ancillary penalty.
- Court is satisfied that it is necessary to make such an order for the purpose of protecting the public or any particular members of the public from serious sexual harm.
- Prohibition from doing anything described in the order.
- Breach is either-way offence and carries 5 years custody.
- ✓ Period of not less than 5 years as specified, or until further order.

2.13.3. Bind over

- The order can be made on application <u>or</u> as an ancillary penalty.
- The court has grounds for believing that there is a possibility of a future breach of the peace. This is based upon the circumstances of the offence and/or any relevant previous convictions.
- Order is to enter into a recognisance in terms chosen by the court as to duration and amount e.g. 'bind over to keep the peace for 12 months in the sum of £500'. All or part of which may be forfeited if the bind over is breached. Means information is therefore required.
- In order to ensure clarity and certainty under the Human Rights Act, it is important to specify the behaviour which will be punished on breach, so far as it can be defined. For example, to 'keep the peace' and/or 'to be of good behaviour and in particular not to assault/molest/interfere with XX or repeat the following behaviour, namely ... (JCS and MA guidance 2000).
- Refusal to enter into the recognisance may result in imprisonment up to 6 months (defendants over 21 only), or up to the point of agreement to enter the recognisance, if the order is made upon complaint. However, consent is not required if the order is made as an ancillary penalty - simply seek representations and then make the order (R v. Crown Court at Lincoln ex.p Jude 1997).
- This is a highly valuable, deterrent order and should arguably be considered on the court's own initiative whenever dealing with offences of violence and disorder as an additional penalty. The defence must be given the opportunity to make representations if the court indicates that it is minded to add a bind over.
- ✓ No maximum or minimum periods.
- ✓ No maximum amount, but it should reflect the means of the individual and the type of behaviour it is intended to deter. 'Drunk and disorderly' behaviour should arguably reflect the band A fine guidance, whilst an assault, carrying fear of future violence could justify an amount which would extend to the full 12 month repayment period if taken in full.

2.13.4. Exclusion Order (licensed premises)

- Convicted of offence on licensed premises and resorted to violence or threatened to do so.
- Prohibits defendant from entering specified licensed premises without licensee's consent. This may extend to other specified licensed premises if considered necessary.
- Licensee may expel a defendant who enters in breach of an exclusion order and police must help on request.

- Licensee may also consent to allow defendant to enter (profits have slumped?!).
- Breach penalty = level 3 fine/1 month imprisonment.
- ✓ Minimum = 3 months. Maximum = 2 years.

2.13.5. Football banning order

- Order may be made following a conviction <u>or</u> on complaint by the police.
- Offender convicted of a 'relevant offence' e.g. vandalism in the ground, threats of violence on journey to match <u>or</u>
  Order on complaint - court satisfied that respondent has at any time caused or contributed to any violence or disorder in the UK or elsewhere. 'Violence' may be against persons or property, and includes threatening violence. It need not necessarily be in connection with football.
- Reasonable grounds to believe that banning order will help to prevent violence or disorder at or in connection with any regulated football matches. Reasons must be given if order is not made.
- Prohibits subject from entering a football ground to attend a 'regulated match' e.g. Premier League, Football League, UEFA Cup.
- Must report to a specified police station within 5 days of order (unless in custody) - a copy order is sent by the court. A requirement may be included for his photograph to be taken.
- Must surrender passport when regulated matches are played outside the UK unless there are exceptional circumstances reasons for not doing so e.g. pre-booked business trip.
- Order may be varied on application. Application for early termination may be made two-thirds of the way through the order.
- Since January 2004, it is immaterial whether evidence would have been admissible in the proceedings leading to the offence conviction.
- Breach penalty = 6 months/£5,000.
- Note that minimum period is for 3 years – consider 'proportionality' of order for minor offence.
- ✓ Criminal order following conviction: Min = 3 years. Max = 5 years. (6 years to 10 years if custodial sentence imposed). On complaint: Min = 2 years. Max = 3 years.

2.13.6. Parenting Order

- Available as an ancillary penalty whenever a child or young person is convicted of a criminal offence, or the following orders are made on the child - Anti-Social Behaviour Order, Sex Offender Order, Sexual

Offences Prevention Order. Also available upon conviction of parent for failing to ensure school attendance.

- Order is considered to be desirable to prevent repetition of behaviour which led to order, or commission of a further offence.
- Parent is required to comply with such requirements as are specified in the order for up to 12 months <u>and</u>
- Attend guidance/counselling programme for up to 3 months unless previously attended. The programme will be tailored to the individual. It may well be a couple of sessions, a weekly parent craft course over several weeks, or even a residential course.

Example:

Requirement - To comply with directions of education welfare officer and take all reasonable steps to ensure that child, Y, attends school for the next 12 months, commencing on .....

<u>And</u> to attend 3 guidance/counselling sessions at X offices on ..... and .... and ...

- Order must be explained to the parent, along with the proposed requirements.
- Parent or responsible officer may apply to discharge or vary.
- Breach = level 3 fine.
- ✓ Requirements up to 12 months
- ✓ Sessions up to 3 months.

2.13.7.   Restraining order

- Offender is convicted of an offence contrary to the Protection from Harassment Act 1997 – causing harassment (s.2) or conduct causing fear of violence (s.4).
- Order to protect victim from further harassment or fear of violence.
- Definition may be similar to a bail condition and may contain specific exclusions and restrictions e.g. not to approach or communicate in any way with X, not to use 3rd parties to communicate with X, not to go within half a mile of X's home or place of work.
- The order should identify the protected parties e.g. 'prohibit from conduct which amounts to harassment of X and Y', rather than simply must not 'contact or communicate with hostel staff' (R v Mann 2000).
- Breach = 6 months/£5,000 or 5 years/fine at crown court. If in conjunction with new offence, consider committal to Crown Court for sentence (R v Liddle 1999).

✓ No maximum or minimum order; 'until further order' may be appropriate.

2.13.8. Compensation

- The order can be made as a penalty in its own right (see 2.8.4.), or ancillary to another penalty.
- Always consider – is there a victim? Is there evidence that they have suffered any damage, loss or injury, including terror and distress?
- Reasons are required if an order is not made.

2.13.9. Deprivation Order and forfeiture

- Convicted of offence.
- Whether or not the court deals with the defendant in another way.
- Court is satisfied that any lawfully seized property in defendant's possession or control at the time when he was apprehended has been used to commit an offence, or he intended to so use it, or the offence consists of unlawful possession.
- Regard to the value, likely financial and other effect on defendant.
- Cannot make an order to secure payment of fines and compensation.
- Only in simple cases where it will not be difficult to implement.
- Property is placed in police possession and subsequent application for possession may be made - court does not determine ownership on making the order.

2.13.10. Prosecution costs on conviction

- Order must be specified and the court must determine a 'just and reasonable' amount. May include costs of investigation.
- Prosecution must serve on the defence, full details of the costs, to give proper opportunity to consider and make representations.
- If defendant has means to pay it is not wrong in principle to make order for costs which exceed the amount of the fine, but the amounts should not be grossly disproportionate e.g. costs are in the thousands and fine is in the hundreds.
- Unlawful to make order which defendant has no realistic prospect of paying or in the hope that it will be paid by a 3rd party.
- Recoverable as a fine.
- ✓ Normal maximum repayment period = 12 months.

2.13.11. Sex Offender registration → notification requirements (from May 2004)

- Convicted of relevant offence e.g. intercourse with a girl under 13, intercourse with girl aged 13-16/ offender is over 20, possessing indecent photographs.
- Register with local police within 3 days.
- Disclose all names used, address, date of birth, national insurance number and subsequently notify the police of any change of address.
- Where notification is given, police may take fingerprints and/or take photographs of the offender to verify identity.
- Failure to comply = up to 5 years imprisonment.
- ✓ Maximum period of notification varies with the outcome e.g. indefinite if sentenced to 30 months or more imprisonment; 7 years for 6 months or less; 5 years for a community order; or the period of conditional discharge.

2.14   TRAFFIC PENALTIES

2.14.1.   Endorsement and penalty points

Endorsement is obligatory for specified offences e.g. failing to comply with a red traffic light, using a vehicle without insurance, speeding, unless there is disqualification instead. The only exception to mandatory endorsement or disqualification is when special reasons apply (see 2.14.4. below). Every endorseable offence carries penalty points, whether fixed e.g. 3 penalty points for failing to comply with a red traffic light, or variable e.g. 6-8 for no insurance, 3-6 for speeding. The more serious the offence, the higher the points where there is a variable range. Details are endorsed on the driving licence (if held) and also recorded at Driver and Vehicle Licensing Authority (DVLA) at Swansea. The DVLA record can be accessed by the courts and is produced as a computer 'print-out' for court reference.

Where there are 2 or more offences on the same occasion, statute says that 'the total number of penalty points to be attributed to them is the number or highest number that would be attributed to the offence …', but .. 'the court may if it thinks fit determine' that this does not apply and reasons must be given.

Example:

The 'norm'

Date of offence	Offence	Points available	Final decision
1.4.04	No insurance	Variable 6 - 8	8 POINTS
1.4.04	Drive other than in accordance with provisional licence e.g. no 'L' plates, qualified passenger	Fixed 3	No points awarded

The provision regarding allocation of separate points is rarely used. This is because where the scenario exists to distinguish the offences as being worthy of separate allocation, the reality is that the court will most likely be considering a short discretionary disqualification.

Example:

The 'exception' (very much so!)

Date of offence	Offence	Points available	Final decision
1.4.04	Drive otherwise than in accordance with provisional licence	Fixed 3	3 POINTS
1.4.04	Defective tyre	Fixed 3	3 POINTS
1.4.04	Fail comply with red traffic light	Fixed 3	3 POINTS
Reasons for awarding separate points - offences are entirely different types of offences which require a different culpability - a document offence; a driving offence and a defect offence, and this is marked by awarding points on all matters. *Reality? Such a combination would be more likely to warrant a discretionary disqualification as the offences all aggravate each other.*			

2.14.2. Disqualification

This is an immediate order and disqualifies the defendant from driving any motor vehicle on a public road. The Sentencing Guidelines entry point for driving whilst disqualified is a community penalty and the offence carries imprisonment. The minimum period is fixed for the mandatory disqualification offences and for the 'points' disqualification. The maximum period in all cases is 'life' disqualification if appropriate, but it is accepted that generally there should be 'light at the end of the tunnel' and lengthy periods may be counter-productive, particularly for the young offender. It is available as an ancillary penalty and additionally, from January 2004 disqualification became available as a penalty in its own right.

(a) Obligatory

A minimum period of 12 months disqualification applies to the following offences unless special reasons apply:

(i) Driving or attempting to drive whilst unfit through drink/drugs.
(ii) Driving or attempting to drive with excess alcohol.
(iii) Driving and failing to provide a specimen without reasonable excuse.
(iv) Dangerous driving.
(v) Aggravated taking without consent (even the passenger!).

In respect of offences (i)(ii)(iii) the period of 12 months is increased to 3 years if the offender has already been convicted within the past 10 years. It is increased to 2 years if the offender has been disqualified for 56 days or more on 2 or more occasions in the 3 years preceding the offence. This may sound complicated but the legal adviser will draw this to your attention as necessary, but it is well worth being broadly aware that the minimum periods can increase if there is a previous disqualification.

It is not possible to reduce a mandatory disqualification period on the basis that there is substantial mitigation e.g. defendant drank a relatively small amount of alcohol on the night before, had very little to eat, and honestly believed that he would no longer be over the prescribed limit. The only exception is when special reasons are successfully argued (See 2.14.4.).

Since 1.1.2000 the disqualification period for the alcohol-related offences may however be reduced if the offender satisfactorily completes a specified approved course under the Drink Drive Rehabilitation Scheme (DDRS).

The reduced period is not less than 3 months and cannot exceed one quarter of the unreduced period e.g. a 12 month ban may be reduced to 9 months. The course fee is income-related and is payable by the defendant to the course organiser, rather than the court. Consent is required on the day of sentence and the full period and potential reduced period are announced. Appropriate warnings must be given that the course fee must be paid <u>and</u> the course must be satisfactorily completed at least 2 calendar months prior to the end of the disqualification if the reduced period is to be effective. In West Yorkshire around one half of the defendants who say that they intend to do the course, actually do pay the fee and attend the course.

(b) Discretionary

A discretionary disqualification may be imposed for any endorseable offence, and also for taking a motor vehicle without consent (although not endorseable). Basically, it is saying 'too serious for mere points - off the road!' Discretionary disqualification and discretionary period - no lower or upper limit.

Examples:

> *The Sentencing Guidelines give an entry point of discretionary disqualification of up to 42 days for exceeding the 70mph limit by 21 - 30 mph, i.e. over 90 mph.*

> *Speeding and driving without insurance as a combination - 8 points + 3 points does not reflect seriousness - 3 months disqualification.*

> *A serious case of driving without due care - the 9 point maximum points does not reflect the seriousness of the case - 6 months disqualification + re-test (see (e)).*

Any previous points will remain on the licence for 3 years for the purpose of 'points disqualification' (see below). A discretionary disqualification does not wipe the slate clean of points - only a 'points disqualification' does that.

Always seek representations before imposing a discretionary disqualification.

(c) 'Points' disqualification (also known as 'totting')

When 12 penalty points are accumulated by offences committed within the 3 year period, before or after the current offence, the court must disqualify for a minimum of 6 months unless 'exceptional hardship' is proved. The minimum of 6 months is increased to 12 months if there has been 1 other disqualification of 56 days or more within the 3 year period, and to 2 years if there has been 2 such disqualification periods.

It is desirable to hear sworn evidence as to the exceptional hardship. This is about the particular defendant before the court and his personal circumstances. It is not about the offence - no matter how trivial it is - the endorsement and appropriate points must be applied. The court may decide either not to disqualify at all or may reduce the period if satisfied that there is 'exceptional hardship' e.g. reduction from 6 months to 28 days (points are cleared), or no disqualification at all (points remain). 'Exceptional' hardship is a greater burden than simply proving hardship which is virtually inevitable to some extent for every defendant.

Example:

Questions regarding potential loss of employment will normally include:

- *What exactly is the job and what does the job description require in respect of driving?*
- *When exactly does the defendant have to drive in his employment? Occasionally?*
- *Could anyone else drive instead?*
- *What inconvenience/cost would this actually create?*
- *May the defendant be moved to a non-driving role for a period of time?*
- *How long has he been employed in the current driving role?*
- *What other skills does he have for employment?*
- *What is his current wage?*
- *What would the alternative income be in different employment, or on state benefit (when eligible)?*
- *Is there satisfactory proof that the defendant would actually be dismissed if the licence is lost?*

It will usually be necessary for the defendant to produce written evidence that he requires a driving licence to continue his employment e.g. contract, letter from employer, along with details of his current financial situation. Similarly evidence should be sought to prove that any onerous family transport responsibilities must inevitably fall upon the defendant. Alternative employment arrangements and alternative modes of transport should be explored. It is relevant that the hardship may well fall upon the defendant's family or employees.

A 'points' disqualification is the only type of disqualification which 'wipes the slate clean' and points are removed. However, the same reason cannot be put forward for 'exceptional hardship' if a further offence is committed during the 3 year period. It may well be that a 'delayed' ban would justifiably be for more than the 6 month minimum as the points would obviously be higher than 12.

(d) Discretionary disqualification or 'points disqualification??

It is now permissible to consider a discretionary disqualification 'in parallel' with the possibility of imposing points and reaching a 'points disqualification' situation (Jones v. Chief Constable of West Mercia 2000). However, the nature of the record must be carefully considered before imposing a short disqualification for the current offence.

The 2 scenarios are quite dramatically different and the 'pros and cons' need to be weighed. Take an offence of speeding. A discretionary disqualification for 6 weeks for the isolated offence of speeding is very different to endorsing the licence and awarding 6 points which take the defendant into a 12 'points disqualification' of 6 months.

What is the court trying to achieve with this defendant? Deterrence or punishment? By imposing the discretionary disqualification, on the one hand, he will lose his licence for 6 weeks and then be driving (carefully?) with the 6 previous points intact and effective. By imposing a points disqualification, on the other hand, he will lose his licence for the full 6 months, or a lesser period if 'exceptional hardship' is found, but the pre-existing 6 points will be wiped clear. Not an easy decision.

It is important to recognise the benefit to the defendant of reducing a points disqualification down to 7 days on the basis of exceptional hardship - 7 days and then a clear licence and no mandatory increase if the 12 points accrue again!

Remember that the 6 months increases to 12 months 'points disqualification' if there is a previous disqualification of 56+ days in the last 3 years. Watch out for the disqualification periods in the last 3 years as they are just as important as penalty points for calculation of current disqualification period.

(e) Interim disqualification

Disqualification may be ordered on an interim basis when a case is adjourned following conviction e.g. for pre-sentence reports; defendant is committed to the Crown Court for sentence; remitted to another Magistrates' Court, or subjected to deferment of sentence.

The disqualification will lapse if the defendant is not sentenced before the expiry of 6 months, and the one interim disqualification allowed, will usually be for '6 months or until the case is dealt with if sooner'. This will ensure that a disqualified defendant who fails to attend the next hearing, will at least be disqualified for up to 6 months, unless he is arrested in the meantime.

The final disqualification will take into account the interim period e.g. an obligatory 12 month disqualification will effectively be back-dated to the commencement of the interim ban. This is a useful power which ensures that the public are protected immediately, albeit there are further issues to pursue before final sentence.

(e) Disqualification until test is passed - Re-test or first test

The court *must* disqualify an offender until he passes an extended driving test if he is convicted of dangerous driving. The court *may* disqualify until a test is passed in any case involving obligatory endorsement if there is concern about the safety of other road users e.g. serious careless driving; record of 'bad driving'; lengthy disqualification so that driving skills will be stale. The extended test will apply if the defendant is convicted of an offence involving obligatory disqualification or a points disqualification. The ordinary test applies to the remainder.

The defendant is effectively reduced to, or remains as provisional driver status and must display 'L' plates and carry a qualified passenger. Failure to do so constitutes an offence of driving whilst disqualified.

The question effectively is whether this defendant should be on the road without 'L' plates and a qualified passenger. A concern by the bench that he will simply get back in a car and drive without any warning to others following a serious incident and/or after the end of his disqualification! If he does, he is committing the more serious offence of driving whilst disqualified. This is significant when the defendant has never passed a driving test as the offence is far more serious than simply not complying with his provisional licence by driving without the 'L' plates and passenger - he is driving whilst disqualified under the test provision.

2.14.3. Revocation of licence by DVLA, Swansea

A new 'probationary' driver who has passed the relevant test e.g. motor cycle, motor car within the past 2 years and acquires 6 penalty points will be subject to revocation of his full licence by Swansea. Effectively he will revert to provisional licence status. Whilst this is not an order of the court, account should be taken of the implication. In a recent case, the sentencing court awarded 6 points and declared that it would not disqualify as the defendant lived in a rural area and required a full licence to get to work. The Court of Appeal substituted 5 points as it was considered that the sentencing court had effectively disqualified him, by rendering him liable to revocation and the requirement to drive with (find!) a qualified passenger at all times (Re: Damien Edwards 2000).

2.14.4. Special reasons

Endorsement and/or disqualification may be avoided if the court is satisfied that a special reason exists. The main point is that the reason relates to the offence itself, rather than to the offender - all the offender mitigation in the world cannot avoid a mandatory disqualification. It is completely different from the 'exceptional hardship' argument when 12 points are reached, which relates to the offender. For special reasons to apply, the question is what was so special about this particular offence? The reason must satisfy 4 criteria: -

(i)   It must be a mitigating or extenuating circumstance about the offence.

(ii)   It does not constitute a legal defence e.g. that the defendant was not actually 'driving' the car, or the scene of the incident was not a 'road'.

(iii)   It must be directly connected to offence e.g. emergency situation; soft drink had been laced by alcohol without the defendant's knowledge and he had driven 'innocently unaware' of the high alcohol level. It is not a factor which relates to the offender e.g. hardship to individual if disqualified.

(iv)   It must be a factor which the court ought properly to take into consideration such as whether the defendant acted responsibly and reasonably e.g. was it appropriate to drive to the hospital in an intoxicated state rather than ringing for an ambulance or a taxi?

The court must then consider whether to exercise its discretion. This will depend upon various factors e.g. in what manner was the vehicle driven, the reason for the car being driven, level of danger to others.

There are numerous cases involving special reasons and the legal adviser's advice should always be sought before making a determination in this complex area.

Example:

A frequent special reason put forward is 'shortness of distance driven.' Recent guidance has been given that the court must look not only at what the defendant had actually achieved but at what he intended – in the case concerned he fully intended to drive home and special reasons were not made out (CPS v. Dean Humphries 2000).

Procedures

2.14.5. 'Speed camera offences'

A Notice of Intended Prosecution (NIP) is sent to the registered keeper stating where and when the speeding vehicle has been 'captured' on camera. The keeper may then acknowledge that he was the driver and pay the conditional fixed penalty ticket for speeding within 28 days, and submit his driving licence for endorsement and 3 penalty points. Alternatively he may disclose the name and address of the driver on the occasion of the incident, and the driver will then be sent a Notice of Intended Prosecution and be given the opportunity to pay and submit his driving licence in the same way.

If the keeper fails to disclose the name and address of the driver, he is committing an offence and the Sentencing Guideline entry point is a band C fine and 3 penalty points.

2.14.6. Uncontested road traffic matters

Most summary traffic matters are dealt with by way of summons. The majority of defendants choose not to attend and either enter a guilty plea by post based upon a summary of the prosecution facts which are sent to them, or alternatively the case can be proved without their response if full statements are sent to them at least 10 days before the hearing. In the latter scenario it is open to the defendant to ask for the case to be re-opened if he did not receive the summons and statements e.g. he was on holiday or had moved from the address given to the officer at the time. The court will obtain a print out of the driver's record from DVLC Swansea in readiness for the case to proceed – with or without a licence in court.

2.15 SPECIFIC APPLICATIONS TO THE COURT

2.15.1. Search warrants

Whilst search warrants play a vital part in many major criminal investigations, it should always be remembered that the court is effectively giving the police the right to break into someone's house possibly in the early hours of the morning if necessary. The decision should be taken with great care. Although the list of enquiries appears to be lengthy, they are brief checks and brief questions which may occasionally prevent the possibility of lifetime trauma for innocent people. A warrant may be considered for anywhere in England or Wales. It is a discretionary decision and the application is dealt with in private. Notes should always be taken.

(a) Legal requirements

The magistrate must have reasonable grounds for believing that:

- A serious arrestable offence has been committed.
- There is material on the premises, specified in the application, which is likely to be of substantial value to the investigation.
- The material is likely to be relevant and is not in an excluded/special procedure category.
- Entry will not be granted without a warrant, or the purpose of search may be frustrated or seriously prejudiced unless a constable arriving at the premises can secure immediate entry, or it is not practicable to communicate with any person entitled to grant entry/access to the premises.

(b) Checking the applicant and the application

- Check officer's warrant card/identity.
- Check that the application has been authorised by an Inspector, or other senior officer if urgent.
- Check that the legal basis for the application is identified e.g. drugs (Misuse of Drugs Act 1971), stolen goods (s.26 Theft Act 1968), material of 'substantial value to the investigation of a 'serious arrestable offence' (s.8 Police and Criminal Evidence Act 1984).
- Written information is required.
- Separate paperwork and separate consideration for each application.
- The applicant officer must be sworn or affirm.

- Check that the premises to be searched are clearly defined e.g. garage at rear of ...., flat number ...
- Identify the articles being sought e.g. heroin.

Questions to ask

The occupiers

- Who is the anticipated occupier of the property?
- What is known about him?
- Has he got any previous convictions?
- Is he currently the subject of criminal proceedings?
- Are there any young children or other vulnerable occupants?
- If so, what arrangements are in place to care for them during the search and in the event of arrests? e.g. officer to accompany for specific purpose and local social services office are informed.

The information source

- What is the nature of any police surveillance of the property?
- When was the information received?
- Is the informant registered?
- Has the informant previously been used and found to be reliable?
- If anonymous source, what steps have been taken to corroborate the information?

The area

- Is the area ethnically sensitive?
- If so, what steps have been taken to try and diffuse any problems? e.g. police to be accompanied by police community liaison officer.
- When is the warrant to be executed? If any delay is expected, why is this? If during the night, why is this necessary?

Before granting the warrant, the magistrate should have a picture of the property involved and the probable people inside. Is it reasonable to issue a search warrant in all the circumstances? It is appropriate to ask whether a previous application has been made and refused. If so, there should be additional grounds for a second application.

On granting the application, the date and time of grant must be noted on the information and both the information and the warrant must be signed. The information is retained by the court and the police must forward the search warrant after 1 month at the latest, executed or not, endorsed as to whether the articles were found and whether any other articles were seized.

The police are a public authority and in terms of practical execution they also have responsibility for ensuring compliance with the Human Rights Act. Operational issues should be left to the police e.g. when to execute the warrant.

2.15.2.   Utility warrants - gas and electricity - right to enter

Applications may be made for warrants of entry to premises for various purposes, for example for entry to read a meter or to cut off a power supply following non-payment of the bill. Gas and electricity supplies may be cut off where the customer has not paid following a demand in writing, and after notice of the intention to cut off the supply. This power is not available if there is a dispute as to the amount owed.

After appropriate notice, an officer of the supplier may at all reasonable times enter the property for the purpose of cutting off the supply. The right of entry may only be exercised with the consent of the occupier or by warrant.

The court may grant a warrant on sworn information in writing and the magistrate must be satisfied that: -

*   Notice of the application has been given to the occupier (right to fair trial).
*   Admission is reasonably required for the specified purpose.
*   The applicant has a statutory right of entry to the premises.
*   The requirements of any enactment have been complied with e.g. a code of practice exists to avoid cutting off vulnerable people during the winter months if at all possible.
*   That relevant notices have been given.

Premises must be left secure following entry and any damage must be made good.

2.15.3.   Sex Offender Order → Sexual Offences Prevention Order (SOPO - May 2004)

A SOPO may also be made as an ancillary penalty - see 2.13.2.

*   Application by chief officer of police.
*   Civil order with criminal sanctions.

- Defendant is a qualifying offender.
- Sex Offender Order - defendant has acted in a way which gives reasonable cause to believe an order is necessary to protect public from serious harm.
- Sexual Offences Prevention Order - defendant's behaviour makes it necessary to make such an order for purpose of protecting the public from serious *sexual* harm.
- Interim order may be made pending a full hearing.
- Defendant becomes subject to registration with local police (if not already).
- May prohibit from doing anything prescribed by order e.g. keep away from named school(s); swimming baths outside of school hours.
- Breach – summarily (6 months/£5000) or on indictment (fine/5years).
- ✓ Minimum = 5 years. Maximum = until further order.

Three other new orders will occasionally be sought under the Sexual Offences Act 2003.

Notification Orders - requiring registration of offenders who have been convicted abroad, with the local police.

Risk of Serious Harm Orders - evidence of sexual activity/communication on least 2 occasions with a child. The order would prohibit the activity for not less than 2 years, e.g. sexually explicit text messaging.

Foreign Travel Orders - qualifying offender is prohibited from travelling outside the United Kingdom or to any country named in the order for a fixed period up to 6 months.

2.15.4. Anti Social Behaviour Order (ASBO)

Order may also be made as an ancillary penalty - see 2.13.1.
See 7.3 Current Issues for full discussion of the application on complaint.

2.15.5. Parenting order (from February 2004)

Order may also be made as an ancillary penalty - see 2.13.6.
- Application by local education authority or by member of youth offending team.

Education cases:
- Pupil has been excluded on disciplinary grounds from a relevant school for a fixed period or permanently, and regulations are complied with.
- And order would be desirable in the interests of improving the behaviour of the pupil.

Youth offending team cases:

- Child or young person has engaged in criminal conduct or anti-social behaviour.
- And order would be desirable in the interests of preventing further criminal conduct or further anti-social behaviour.

- Court must obtain and consider information about the family circumstances and likely effect of order, and any refusal to sign or comply with voluntary parenting contract between local education authority/youth offending team and parent.
- Breach = level 3 fine.
- ✓ Specified requirements up to 12 months.
- ✓ Counselling or guidance programme up to 3 months.

2.15.6. Statutory declaration

Statutory declarations are a regular feature of Magistrates' Court work and are frequently made particularly in order to declare that the maker was unaware of criminal proceedings. This is often the case when fixed penalty tickets have been registered as a fine but the person making the declaration sold the vehicle long ago and is not responsible for the parking, speeding offence etc. The practical outcome is that the fine is quashed, DVLA are notified if there has been an endorsement, and the prosecutor can determine whether to pursue the true offender or not.

Statutory declarations may also be used for a multitude of other reasons. These include a statement that educational qualifications have been attained but certificates have been lost; that pawn tickets have been lost rather than sold on and also to change the name of the person making the declaration.

The concluding words for a statutory declaration are as follows: -

"I, ... do solemnly and sincerely declare and affirm that the contents of this declaration are true to the best of my knowledge and belief, and I make this solemn declaration conscientiously believing the same to be true and by virtue of the provisions of the Statutory Declarations Act 1835."

The person making the statement must sign the declaration. The magistrate need not consider whether he believes what is said or not and should not be asking questions which indicate disbelief or enquiry to establish the truth e.g. are you sure that you have a degree? The magistrate's role is simply to sign that he is present and hears the maker declare that the contents of the document are true. An untrue statement will render the maker liable for prosecution.

2.15.7. Passport endorsements

A magistrate may countersign an application for a passport and certify the photograph as a true likeness if he has known the applicant personally for at least 2 years. When this is not the case, the applicant should be referred on to a signatory who has known the applicant personally.

CHAPTER 3
Money order enforcement

3.1. Introduction

- In 2002, three quarters of all cases sentenced in the Magistrates' Court resulted in a fine being imposed. In 2002-3, an average of 45% were not paid. In some areas the level of default was as high as 60% (http://www.dca.gov.uk/risk/enforcria.htm accessed 6/2/04).
- On a sample of cases drawn from 20 Magistrates' Courts, only 26% of offenders paid without enforcement action of any kind, 37% paid after enforcement action and the remainder paid nothing (see Mackie, Raine & Burrows, August 2002).
- The national target is a 75% payment rate and there are court budget implications in ensuring that payments are made as ordered and arrears are kept to a minimum.
- Fines are usually the first penalty which an offender experiences. A message that 'the court means business' in making the penalty actually happen can go a long way to demonstrating that crime does not pay. 'Getting away with it' does not promote a positive image of the justice system.
- In 2001, a total of 1,455 defaulters were imprisoned.

The 'teeth' are there, bringing a serious need to tread carefully, but not necessarily, slowly! Effective enforcement is essential in order to build, and maintain credibility and authority.

3.2. Effective imposition

3.2.1. Amount and payment rate

Effective enforcement begins at the point of imposition. A fair, enforceable amount must be fixed with clear and realistic payment instructions.

- Consider individual financial circumstances to ascertain net income - from April 5th 2004 all courts will pilot a standardised means form published by the Department of Constitutional Affairs. The aim is for all defendants and defaulters to either complete the form or provide the information verbally in court so that there is an accurate and consistent assessment of income and outgoings to determine net income and a fair payment rate.

- Use the Magistrates Court Sentencing Guidelines - most offences which normally carry a fine will have a clear entry point of band A (half net income), band B (full net income) or band C (one and a half times net income). When the guidelines are not used, e.g. the figure 'seems too low', the higher amount will be incomprehensible to a court dealing with default (unless reasons are recorded), and it is likely to be remitted to the appropriate figure. This type of 'enforcement action' doesn't help credibility and authority and can build in delay in moving to 'real action'.
- Collection on the day so far as possible - payment in full e.g. by credit card or cash, or at least obtain a part payment, or
- Collection in full as soon as possible - e.g. pay in 14 days - one payment is easier to remember to pay and easier to enforce than instalments. Always try for this option before moving into long term payment plans, or
- Realistic instalments within 12 months maximum repayment period e.g. by bank direct debit. Whilst an offer of an amount by the defendant is a helpful indicator, it is the less experienced defendant who is likely to offer a figure which cannot be sustained. The more experienced are well aware of the local 'norm'!
- Consideration of court payment card facilities if available, particularly for long term instalment payments as it will avoid the additional cost of postal orders etc. In such cases it must be emphasised that the first instalment is due whether or not the card materialises, and a contact telephone number should be given in court so that any delay in delivery can be notified by the defendant.
- Clear warnings - defendant should be told that he must notify any change of circumstances/address to the court and that missed instalments render the whole amount due, and prison can be imposed in default.

See Adult Court Bench Book pronouncement No.19.

When the defendant does not attend and means information is either not provided at all, or there is insufficient information to make a proper determination of the financial circumstances of the offender, then the court must make 'such determination as it thinks fit'. The calculation of a 'fit' amount is determined locally e.g. may be assessed on the average net income for the area. The payment rate will normally require payment either 'forthwith' on receipt of the notice, or within a short period, e.g. 7 days, so that payment, arrangement or enforcement is triggered quickly.

3.2.2   Means information - getting it and using it effectively

What is the incentive for a defendant to provide full means information? If the defendant fails to respond, the court can go ahead and fix a 'fit' amount in any event. If and when there are default proceedings, it can be rectified to a fair figure after a full enquiry. An alternative scenario is the defendant who attends court and has a high income. He may express remorse by stating that he will pay 'any fine' immediately and if he is lucky, the court may well impose a 'fit' figure which is well below his net income calculation. Another defendant may be totally unco-operative and simply refuse point blank to give any details and then state that he cannot possibly pay the 'fit' amount immediately. Neither situation should happen. We aim for fair amounts fixed on individual means on the day of imposition.

This has been addressed by amending previous legislation, and as from 5th April 2004, it becomes an offence to fail to furnish a statement of financial circumstances in response to an official request by the Justices' Chief Executive, or by the court. This is punishable by a level 2 fine (£500). The offence is not specifically about a defendant or defaulter failing to fill in the new means form as such. They may be genuinely incapable of doing so. The responsibility is to provide 'a statement of financial circumstances' - income (to determine the amount of the fine) and outgoings (to determine how it should be paid). The prosecution would follow the normal route through the Crown Prosecution Service who would proceed with the normal decision making process as to strength of evidence and public interest. The likelihood is that there will be few actual prosecutions but some exemplary cases will attract sufficient publicity to demonstrate that information should be given or there will be an additional fine to pay.

Interestingly, the greater incentive to provide means may well come from the court making it clear to a defendant in court that it will otherwise have to fix an amount as 'fit' and then state the maximum figure, e.g. £5,000! Provision of means at this point will be in the interests of the 'low income' defendant, and will also enable a fair figure to be assessed for the defendant who states that he will be paying on the day in any event.

If a statement is made which is knowingly or recklessly false, or knowingly omits a material fact, the penalty is 3 months imprisonment and/or a level 4 fine.

Apart from income and outgoings, the new form also seeks information to identify whether an attachment of earnings or attachment of benefit is likely to be appropriate, i.e. full benefit details, name/address/telephone number of employer and payroll number. It also seeks information to assist in tracing the defendant if he should default, e.g. National insurance number, mobile and home telephone number. The first steps towards a successful distress warrant are taken by asking for vehicle registration number. The form states that proof of financial circumstances should be provided e.g. benefit book, utility bills.

The form is available in 12 different languages and in large print. The success of the enquiries and requests will largely depend upon the form being sent out and also returned on summons cases, and rather more difficult, being given out at police stations on charge and then being completed and brought to court. Forms will obviously be available in the court waiting areas but by this stage, the request to bring evidence or supply some aspects of information will be too late. Some defendants will be unable to read the form and/or complete it.

3.2.3   Enforcement options at imposition

• **Attachment of benefits and Attachment of earnings (see 3.4.2 and 3.4.3)**

Either option is open to the court on the day of imposition with the consent of the defendant.

However, so far as defaulters are concerned, there is a major change from 5th April 2004, as the court must impose an attachment of earnings or of benefits (as appropriate) if:

✓ Payment is not made immediately.
✓ The defendant is already an existing defaulter.
✓ The default cannot be disregarded e.g it is not simply a missed payment with an acceptable excuse during an otherwise good payment record.
✓ It is not impracticable or inappropriate to make the order.

Examples of 'impracticable or inappropriate':

Attachment of earnings - self-employed; temporary employment; employment is at risk; already has 2 attachment of earnings order; net earnings are less than £55 per week/£220 per month.

Attachment of benefits - not in receipt of the qualifying benefits namely income support, jobseeker's allowance or pension credit e.g. total benefit is incapacity benefit; already has 3 debt deductions.

- **Money payment supervision order (see 3.4.4)**

This may be appropriate at imposition, for instance in the scenario of the defendant who already has 3 debt deductions and an attachment is not therefore practicable. Equally as significantly it is apparent that there are difficulties in managing finances and this can be addressed from the outset.

- **Fixing a date for a means enquiry if payments are not made as ordered**

This may be an appropriate avenue if for instance, an employed defendant has just been disqualified from driving and it is highly likely that he will lose his employment as a result. The fine is fixed on current income but an attachment of earnings would be inappropriate. A fixed hearing in a short time can be used to re-assess the order if necessary, rather than awaiting default and warrant.

3.3.   Default process

3.3.1.   Administrative action

Following non-payment e.g. 14 days after due payment date, or 2 missed instalments, procedures vary on a court by court basis. The common starting point is to send a reminder letter which requires payment in full or alternatively the defaulter must contact the enforcement office to make arrangements to pay, usually within 14 days of the letter. The Clerk to the Justices may delegate powers to the court officers so that they are able to determine means and vary payment terms, e.g. £5 per week instead of payment within 7 days. Note that it is only the court who may vary the actual imposition amount, e.g. if the defaulter's circumstances change to the extent that the fine cannot be paid within 12 months.
(In pilot areas, Fines Officers have powers at this pre-court stage to enforce the sum imposed (see 5)).

Failure to respond to the reminder letter will result in an application for a distress warrant, or the issue of a summons or warrant for the defendant to attend a means enquiry.

The warrant may be with or without bail. Arrest may be by court enforcement officers and/or the police. In practical terms, the court enforcement officer may inform the defaulter that there is an outstanding warrant and the defaulter will voluntarily surrender to the next fine default court.

3.3.2. Means enquiry on default

A structured means enquiry is the lynchpin of effective enforcement. The purpose of the enquiry is to reach a fair order which the particular defaulter will obey – whether by encouragement or threat depending upon the individual's likely response. Firstly, the actual amount properly due must be ascertained. Fines have often been fixed in absence and the means enquiry is the first time that the court is able to ascertain actual means and fix a fair amount. Sometimes financial circumstances have changed or fines have accumulated to an unrealistic figure and adjustments need to be made.

Secondly, arrangements must then be made for the 'fair amount' to be paid. There are a wide variety of options which aim to deal with individual ability and attitude. The responses to the means enquiry must therefore be used as evidence of character and motivation as well as a list of figures.

A request will normally be made for the defaulter to complete the means questionnaire before coming into default court. This will assist in the enquiry. A specimen list of questions/possible responses is produced at the end of the chapter (see 6) following the discussion of the various options and so identifying the significance of the various questions. Essentially the enquiry is aimed at establishing why payment has not been made as ordered, identifying the financial situation of the defaulter by using the new means form and determining the most productive disposal.

A means enquiry must take place before the imposition of custody in default.

The Practice Direction (Justices: Clerk to Court) 2000 emphasises that the role of the legal adviser is to assist the court in the means enquiry and we must not act in an adversarial or partisan manner. With the agreement of the justices, the legal adviser may ask questions of the defaulter to elicit information and may advise on the available options. However, it is inappropriate for the legal adviser to set out to establish wilful refusal or culpable neglect, to offer an opinion on the facts or to urge a particular course of action upon the justices. The spirit of this direction applies equally to the bench, and magistrates must not cross the line from objective enquiry into prosecution mode.

3.3.3. 'Getting the bill right' - remission, rectification, review and 1 day detention

(a) Remission.

The court may remit the whole or any part of a fine it thinks 'just' to do so, 'having regard to a change of circumstances.'

Example of remission:

> *Fine was fixed on a net income of £200 per week at level B (full net income) = £200, but defendant subsequently becomes unemployed and is now in receipt of £60 per week benefits. It would be appropriate to remit the fine down to £60.*

Remission may also be appropriate if it subsequently transpires that the defendant has multiple outstanding fines. What is a reasonable global figure which can realistically be paid in a reasonable period, bearing in mind that imposed fines should not normally extend beyond 12 months? If the other fines have not been paid as ordered, then the remission will undoubtedly be accompanied by an enforcement option on the resulting balance.

(b) Rectification

Where a defendant has been convicted in absence or, has otherwise failed to co-operate with the court in respect of providing means information, the court 'may make such determination as it thinks 'fit'. In West Yorkshire this is determined on the basis of the average county net income figure of £220 per week in the absence of any other information.

If, on subsequently inquiring into means at a means enquiry, the court determines that it would have fixed a smaller amount or would not have fined the defendant at all, then it may remit the whole or part of the fine. This type of remission effectively 'rectifies' the fine.

Examples of rectification:

1. 'No insurance' offence fined at £220 (band B = average weekly net income) as there was no response to the court.
Defendant attends for means enquiry and income is in fact £60 per week.
Fine rectified/remitted to £60.

2. A defaulter attends default court and indicates that he was unaware of the proceedings because he has changed address and did not receive the original

124

summons. He does not wish to re-open the case as he states that he would plead guilty and wishes to finalise the matter today. He is in receipt of benefits. The figure could be adjusted to the appropriate net income band with appropriate credit.

(c) Review of compensation orders

The court may discharge or reduce compensation orders on limited statutory grounds. The most frequently used ground is that 'the defendant has suffered a substantial reduction of his means which was unexpected at the time when the order was made and that his means seem unlikely to increase for a considerable period'.

It must be remembered that the maximum period for repayment of a compensation order is 2 years, or exceptionally 3 years, as opposed to the 12 months maximum for a fine. The difference with altering fines is that the review cannot normally go ahead immediately.

The compensatee must be notified and allowed to make representations at the review hearing as to the proposed discharge or reduction. Representations may be made in writing and the compensatee is entitled to dispute the basis of the reduction, e.g. that the defendant is now unemployed and has insufficient means to pay the full amount or that the defendant is serving a custodial sentence and has no income. It is important to explain the basis of the application clearly to the compensatee and also give some guidance as to the criteria for review e.g. maximum repayment period which will fix the fair amount. It will also be helpful to inform them of the right to pursue any balance through the county court.

(d) One day detention

It is not possible to 'remit' costs, excise penalties, or Crown Court fines (except with the consent of the Crown Court), but the situation may well be that the amounts simply cannot be paid in the circumstances. The use of one day detention (possibly with immediate release) as a notional or small final outcome is often required to 'clear the books' in such cases in 'the interests of justice.'

One day detention may be served either in court or in a police station until 8pm at the latest. The only criterion is that it is in the 'interests of justice' to impose one day detention as an alternative to the money order. It is also a useful device for finalising Magistrates' Court fines where there is no change of circumstances to justify remission, but the fine is simply not going to be paid and the defaulter is incapable of being culpable to justify custody. This may result in a short period in the cells to 'wipe out' the fine.

The one day detention is a flexible tool. On the one hand it can be used as a legal mechanism to 'wipe out' orders which the court does not choose to enforce for good reason e.g. fine/back duty/costs for no excise licence when there are already fines which will take 12 months to pay. It can also be used as a punitive 'one off' option with detention up to 8 p.m. where other options are unsuitable.

Example - 1 day detention

A single parent has failed to comply fully with a money payment supervision order and already has attachments to benefits. The only remaining option is custody. However it may be considered to be disproportionate to the offence. A punitive element is nevertheless required. Detention to 3 p.m. prior to collecting the children from school would finalise the matter without affecting the children's right to family life under the Human Rights Act.

Distinguish from the order of overnight detention until 8 a.m. the following day with earlier release to enable the defendant to attend work. This is rarely used.

3.3.4. Order to pay - Attachment of benefits and earnings as first option

An 'order to pay' is not really an enforcement option as such - it is a concession. The starting point now is that an attachment of benefit or attachment of earnings is imposed on the first default hearing if it was not imposed at imposition, unless it is impracticable or inappropriate. Some cases will have been in the system long before the requirement to consider the order on defaulters at imposition. In some cases, circumstances will have changed since imposition e.g. 3 deductions have now reduced to 2 deductions of benefit or employment has now commenced so attachments can be made.

Recent statistics in Leeds - of 380 'further orders to pay' in October 2003 - 80%+ were in default after 6 weeks. An option really needs to be attached to collect or cajole.

3.4. Default options

3.4.1 Distress warrant

Legal

A distress warrant may be issued before or after court default proceedings. It may issue forthwith or be postponed upon payment terms e.g. distress warrant postponed upon payment of £5 per week. The warrant authorises entry and removal by the bailiffs of money and goods to the value of the financial penalty + the bailiff's costs. The distress warrant may be issued by a single justice or delegated court officer.

The defaulter must be given the opportunity to make representations about the proposed distress warrant e.g. to tell the court that the car is essential for employment and therefore ability to pay the fine.

The court must be satisfied that there are likely to be distrainable goods e.g. the defaulter admits that he is the sole owner of a car and it is not subject to any hire purchase arrangement.

The bailiffs may only enter property lawfully and they cannot break into property. They may not take clothes, bedding or tools of trade of the defaulter or his family. Six days must pass before any goods are sold and household goods must not be removed until the day of sale. It is an offence for the defaulter to remove or sell goods which have been distrained upon.

The distress warrant will be cancelled upon payment to the bailiffs.

The human right to respect for private and family life is engaged and it is important to consider whether it is proportionate to issue a distress warrant. The defendant must be clearly warned about the issue of a distress warrant.

Practical

When a postponed distress warrant is issued the defendant must be warned that the warrant will issue upon one missed payment and will result in the bailiffs visiting the defaulter's home and collecting goods/payment of the outstanding amount. When a vehicle is involved, it is helpful to the bailiffs if the registration number is obtained in court. The reality is usually for the vehicle to be clamped by the bailiffs until payment is forthcoming.

It should also be pointed out that the defaulter will be liable for the bailiff's expenses in addition to the penalty, even if cash is paid in full to the bailiff. A further point of interest to the defaulter is the fact that the sum raised by the sale of the goods is unlikely to be the price he paid and he will be responsible for any outstanding balance of the fine.

Distress warrants tend to be an effective measure of obtaining payment for fixed penalties as the amounts are relatively small and the offence carries a good likelihood of ownership of a vehicle or, at least a lifestyle which allows for driving a vehicle. They are also effective when used to enforce fines payable by companies, where there are likely to be distrainable goods to pay the fine if necessary.

DISTRESS

YES!

Available goods and no good reason why they should not be taken
No cost to the court
Postponement allows the opportunity to pay as ordered.

NO!

Defaulter does not own sufficient goods
Property is subject to hire purchase or joint ownership
Removal will deprive defaulter of livelihood and means to pay.

3.4.2.   Attachment of Earnings Order (AEO)

•   **Legal**

The order may be made at imposition with the consent of the defendant. When an existing defaulter appears before the court in circumstances which cannot be disregarded, and he is fined again and is in employment, the court must impose an attachment of earnings unless it is impracticable or inappropriate. Thereafter, an attachment must be considered as a first option on default.

There is no requirement for consent of the defendant if there is default. The employer is not consulted. The employer may deduct an administration charge.

Both the defendant and the employer must notify the court of any change of employment. It is an offence for the employer to fail to comply with the order. The order may be discharged or transferred to a subsequent employer.

- **Practical**

Full employment details must be obtained - employer's name/address/ telephone number; wages office details if different; payroll number.

The previous requirements to fix a normal deduction rate and protected earnings rate are now overtaken by national fixed figures. The figures are set out in a table of national periodic deductions, and payment is at a percentage rate, but no deductions will be made on wages up to £55 per week/£220 per month. For instance, wages between £165 and £260 per week are deducted at the rate of 12%; between £260 and £370 are deducted at the rate of 17%. This is no longer a matter for the court to determine. Simply fix the fine itself on the income figures and make the attachment of earnings order.

If there is default and non-productive enquiries are made with the company, the defaulter will be brought back before the court and the attachment is likely to be discharged and another option pursued.

AEO

YES!
MUST! - Default cannot be disregarded + not inappropriate/impractical
Avoids temptation to spend the money
Large organisations are familiar with debt deductions
Anonymity can be preserved in a large organisation
Likelihood of payment is high if secure employment.

NO!
Inappropriate or impractical
Earnings are less than £55 per week/ £220 per month
2 attachments of earnings already
Knowledge of conviction may put job at risk
Inconvenience of payment may put job at risk
Firm may be too small to cope efficiently with order
Defaulter is on a short-term or temporary contract.

Current estimate of AEOs made = 9,300 per year (2003). This is expected to increase substantially from April 2004.

3.4.3. Attachment of Benefits Order (ABO)

Legal

The order may be made at imposition with the consent of the defendant. When an existing defaulter appears before the court in circumstances which cannot be disregarded, and he is fined again and is in receipt of benefits, the court must apply for an attachment of benefit unless it is impracticable or inappropriate. Thereafter, an attachment must be considered as a first option on default.

The court makes application to the Department of Work and Pensions (DWP) for the financial penalty to be deducted by weekly amounts from benefits. The qualifying benefits are Income Support, Job-Seekers Allowance (income based and contributory), or Pension Credit. A defaulter who is too ill to work may mistakenly believe that he is in receipt of Incapacity Benefit which is not a qualifying benefit. However, it is worth checking as he may not be in receipt of Incapacity Benefit - it is more likely to be Income Support if he has a poor work history and this is a qualifying benefit. An additional possibility is that he may be in receipt of a top up of Income Support which could bear the deduction.

The current deduction rate is £2.80 per week (2004/5), which is 5% of the basic scale rate of a single claimant over 25.

Only one application may be entertained at one time, albeit it may contain several fines that have been consolidated. New fine impositions therefore cannot be 'tagged on' as ABOs to existing orders. The instalment order itself can be made to follow on, but the ABO can only be applied for subsequently.

Practical

- Check the full name of the actual claimant.

- Obtain date of birth, benefit office and national insurance number in order to expedite the application.

- DWP will check for any existing deductions, unless the defaulter is certain that he already has 3 deductions (less than 3% of those in receipt of relevant benefits have the maximum of 3 debt deductions - March 2004). The maximum deduction is 3 arrears orders and no other deductions may be ordered. Arrears deductions for housing costs, fuel charges, water charges, council tax/community charge arrears take priority, but the court will be informed of when any priority debt will cease.

Some courts fix a return date to court if payments have not been deducted, i.e. the application has been unsuccessful. With careful inquiry, the vast majority of applications are successful and if not, the court can issue a summons to the defaulter if the DWP subsequently inform the court that the deductions cannot be made.

Whilst immediate payment at the default hearing itself is always to be encouraged, there is an administrative problem in ordering further payment during the period prior to attachment. This is because the application will be made in the sum applied for at the time of the court hearing and excess deductions may then follow.

ABO

YES!

MUST! - Default cannot be disregarded + not inappropriate/impractical
No additional expense to the defaulter
No effort required of the defaulter
No choice for the defaulter
Administrative benefit of bulk payments from list of defaulters
High likelihood of payment.

NO!

Financially able _and_ capable of the discipline of paying
substantially more than fixed deduction rate.

In February 2004 there were 18,300 attachment of benefit orders to pay fines. From April 2004 there is an estimated increase by 29,000 of automatic orders which will be made at imposition/first default based upon a percentage of the total 126,000 offenders who are classed as defaulters.

3.4.4. Money Payment Supervision Order (MPSO)

Legal

The order may be made on conviction or subsequently. Whilst consent is not required, it is relevant to the assessment of co-operation. The order may be made in absence, provided that a written notice is issued. The supervisor must be specifically appointed e.g. a court enforcement officer or named probation officer.

The supervisor's duty is to 'advise and befriend the defendant with a view to inducing him/her to pay the sum adjudged to be paid and thereby avoid committal to custody, and to give any information required about conduct and means'. A report should be obtained before committal which will briefly outline the efforts to encourage payment and any response.

The order may be discharged at any stage e.g. failure to respond to correspondence or personal visits.

Whilst all options must be considered to be 'unsuccessful or inappropriate' before imposing custody, there is an additional specific statutory requirement to give reasons why it is 'impractical or undesirable' to place a defaulter who is under 21 years old on a money payment supervision order before imposing custody. Case law also urges the making of an order particularly on single parents with low income before considering custody.

Practical

The order is not a probation order and in busy courts the liaison may be based upon the defaulter taking the initiative and making contact for any advice rather than on home visits. When this is the situation, it should therefore be made clear that the service is essentially the access to advice and assistance by telephone number, if and only if, a payment cannot be made.

The Clerk to the Justices will normally give delegated powers to court money payments supervision officers to vary payment rates and due dates of payment. This may be particularly helpful in situations where the court wishes to avoid unnecessary warrants for missed payments in short-term, problematic situations.

If there is already a Community Rehabilitation Order, it may be helpful to name the supervising probation officer and notify so that the fine payment becomes part of the supervision plan.

MPSO

YES!

Defaulter incapable of managing finances and already has 3 benefit deductions or is working
Single parent or carer and already has 3 benefit deductions or is working (custody is highly unlikely to be proportionate to the interference with private/family life)
Court foresees genuine temporary difficulties - e.g. hospital stays, re-housing.

NO!

Defaulter able to manage finances - previous payments, sustained catalogue payments
Unlikely to respond - previous breach of community orders
States that he will not co-operate.

3.4.5. Attendance Centre Order

Legal

An important sanction particularly for the youth who is made responsible to pay his/her own financial penalty. The court may order a person under 25 to attend an attendance centre for a minimum of 12 hours and a maximum of 24 hours (to 18 years) and 36 hours (to 25 years), in default of paying a financial penalty. The defaulter must be present when the order is made and culpable neglect/wilful refusal must be found. All other options should therefore be considered first.

The centre must be available locally and be reasonably accessible. Part payment will reduce the hours pro-rata.

On failure to attend without reasonable excuse, or on breach of the rules, the defaulter may be brought back before the court in breach proceedings. The options are to (a) allow the order to continue, (b) fine for breach (additionally!) and allow to continue (c) revoke the order and consider other options - possibly custody will be the only remaining option.

The venue and date of first attendance should be notified verbally before leaving the court and by formal order.

ACO

YES!
Substantial restriction on liberty
Not as severe as custody - and cheaper!
Social skills training and discipline may be beneficial.

Facility is not available in locality
Defaulter states that he will not attend
Previous breach of community penalties.

3.4.6. Committal to prison

The following aspects must be satisfied before a defaulter is committed to prison:

- The defaulter must be present and a means enquiry must be held.

- Wilful refusal or culpable neglect must be found. Wilful refusal means a deliberate refusal to pay. Culpable neglect means a reckless disregard.

133

Culpability, or blameworthiness, requires a purposeful unwillingness rather than sheer inability. A useful test is to ask whether the court feels that this defaulter is actually 'capable of being culpable'? If not, the court may be limited to one day detention after other options have been considered.

- The court must consider or try all other methods of enforcing payment and it must appear to the court that they are inappropriate or unsuccessful.

- The court must be of the opinion that no other method of dealing with the defaulter is appropriate.

- Legal representation must be considered and the court records must be disclosed to the defaulter if sought, with proper facility for the preparation of the defence. In the community charge case of Benham v. UK 1996 the applicant was imprisoned for non-payment of community charge. The European Court held that legal aid should have been granted because the proceedings were 'not straightforward'; the test for culpable neglect was hard to understand and the deprivation of liberty was at stake. The proceedings were classified on this basis as 'criminal proceedings' which brings with it the right to legal aid, disclosure and proper facility for the preparation of the defence. In practical terms, it is likely to be a referral to the duty solicitor.

- Imprisonment is a major interference with private and family life and the court must consider whether imprisonment in default is proportionate or not, particularly if children are likely to suffer and the amount outstanding is small.

- Reasons must be given, verbally in court, and in writing, for discarding all non-custodial options in respect of all defaulters.

* The above restrictions do not apply if the defaulter is already serving a custodial sentence.

Imprisonment may be imposed forthwith on the following scale. If part payments are made then the period is reduced proportionately.

Maxima

To £200	7 days
£201 to £500	14 days
£501 to £1,000	28 days
£1001 to £2,500	45 days

Where separate warrants are issued and consecutive terms are allowed in law, the court should consider the totality and nature of the offences and the extent of the default in determining an appropriate period e.g. 8 fines of £100 each could carry 7 days each = 56 days. However this may be considered over punitive if they are all minor road traffic matters and on a single commitment they would carry only 28 days, and if served concurrently would only be 7 days.

As with any custodial penalty, it is very important to determine an appropriate period based upon the particular facts rather than simply imposing the maximum period available. 'What does this carry?' is only the start of the decision, leading to 'What period shall we impose?' Normally there is the psychological cushion that the period may well not be served because a suspended committal is imposed so that payments may well be made. In reality, payments are missed and the defendant does not attend court again before being taken straight to prison. 1,455 defaulters were imprisoned in 2001 and the majority followed a suspended committal.

"The purpose of all enforcement measures is to compel payment and commitment to prison is no exception. If a defaulter actually serves a period of imprisonment, enforcement in his case has failed." (Lord Chancellors Division Best Practice Guide 1992).

3.4.7. Suspended committal

Legal

If the court 'thinks expedient to do so', it may fix a term of imprisonment and postpone the issue of the warrant on payment terms e.g. pay £5 per week or serve 7 days imprisonment in default.

The terms may subsequently be varied and the commitment may be further postponed if circumstances change.

Following default, the defaulter must be notified in writing of the date and time when the issue of the commitment will be considered by the court. The court must be satisfied that the defaulter is aware of the notice and cannot proceed to commit in absence if the notice is returned in the post.

The date set for consideration must be at least 21 days after the notice is issued. The defaulter is invited to attend or make written representations as to why the commitment should not be issued e.g. employment has ceased and income has reduced substantially. In such circumstances the order may well be varied by reducing the instalment rate and re - suspending the commitment.

When the defaulter fails to respond to the notice, the commitment may be issued in the absence of the defaulter and he may be arrested and taken straight to prison unless the full amount is paid. It is true to say that few defaulters do attend court on notice and most defaulters do not attend default court again after a suspended committal has been issued. There must be a recognition that a suspended committal is therefore a serious order to make.

3.4.8.   High Court/County Court

Such orders are effectively pursued by the Justices' Clerk. The court may usefully identify whether there is any possibility of such an order and if so, then retire to consult the legal adviser. The occurrence of such orders is very low. They are complicated to pursue and the reality is that substantial assets are usually available and the defaulter is either in a position therefore to pay up or be subjected to a distress warrant. The mere threat of applying for a garnishee order, charging order or appointing a receiver may well be sufficient to encourage payment.

• Attachment of debts and garnishee proceedings

Defaulter's own debtors are ordered to pay debts direct to the court if the debts have already been proved. This arises in the situation where a defaulter says that he would pay 'if only his cash-flow was sorted out and he was paid all that he was owed'. Basically the court can join in to take the monetary orders straight from his debtors.

• Charging order

Impose a charge on land or on an interest in land of the defaulter, or on his securities if the property is owned absolutely. He owns his house solely and outright but will not pay the £1000 compensation – a charge for the £1000 can be imposed on the house.

• Appointment of a receiver for land or rent and profits

This could arise if the defaulter is a landlord whose income is essentially rent. The court cannot make an attachment of earnings but this is the second best option – to appoint a receiver for the rents and hand them to the court. It is important to check that there are no 3rd party rights to the rent.

In all three situations the court must consider the potential expense of taking the action and the prospects of recovery of the sum due. A distress warrant should always be tried first.

3.4.9. New measures - pilot areas only at March 2004

• Appointment of local Fines Officers who have responsibility to manage fine collection within their powers e.g. to vary the payment rate on application.
• Provision of debt advice.
• Failing to supply financial information to the Fines Officer is an offence.

Upon default:

• Fines Officer must make an attachment of earnings order or apply for attachment of benefit on first default unless it is impracticable or inappropriate,
• If an attachment is not made or it fails, the fine may be increased by a percentage (25% in some pilot areas and the full 50% permitted by the legislation in Cumbria), but if a payment arrangement is complied with, the increase will be rescinded.
• Sanction of unpaid work.
• Registration of the debt along with civil debt judgements.
• Car clamping and eventual sale of the vehicle if payment is not made.

Other provisions appear in the legislation, but have not yet been implemented.

3.5. Specimen means enquiry and structured decision

3.5.1. Facts of the case and introduction

D is a male aged 20 years old. Six months ago he was fined £100 for driving without insurance and ordered to pay costs of £40. He was ordered to pay at the rate of £10 per week. Nothing has been paid.
A warrant has been outstanding for several weeks and he appears before the court in custody. He has declined legal representation.

The defaulter will take the oath or affirm. The legal adviser will identify the defaulter by asking for his name and address - rather than simply checking the address on the court record. Other identification features are the national insurance number and telephone numbers if they can be obtained. The defaulter will then be asked if he accepts the outstanding amount. The legal adviser will then describe the history of the account - how much imposed and when; whether defaulter was in court; payment rate; payments actually made; correspondence outcomes; previous court appearances and outcomes.

Questioning by the bench is likely to be in the form of open questions, and also leading questions which assume an answer. These are helpful in inquisition mode. They push the defaulter to explain if the situation is different to that assumed by the questioner. This is more likely to generate quality information rather than leading a defaulter into a string of closed questions and 'yes' and 'no' responses.

3.5.2. Means enquiry

Chairman - C
Have you completed a means enquiry form?
(Culture of form completion as a starting point)

Defendant - D
No, I'd rather just tell you.
(The right of the defaulter)

C. Nothing at all has been paid on this fine. Bearing in mind that the court may send you to prison today for 7 days because you haven't paid, please explain to us why you have not paid.
(Ability and attitude?)

D. I lost my job after the court case because I was disqualified from driving. I've been on job seekers allowance since then and have a lot of debts which I took on when I was working. I've been through a really bad time and the fine was the last thing on my mind.

C. How much money do you have with you today?
(Not - 'do you have any money?' Assume there is some money.
Can a forthwith order be made?)

D. About £8 – but I need my bus fare to get home and I was going to do some shopping.

C. What action did you take to sort out the fine?
(Culpability?)

D. I kept meaning to pay it. My mum said she would come down and sort it all out but she didn't get round to it.

C. What did you do when you got the reminder letter?
(Assume that he did get the letter rather than asking whether he got it, which gives an easy way out of 'no'.)

D. I had a letter a few weeks ago and it said that I had to pay up or there would be a warrant. I couldn't pay it all at once so thought it would be better to wait until I could.

C. When did you become aware of the warrant for your arrest?
(Culpability? + warrants often record lengthy efforts to make contact.)

D. My neighbour said someone had been round looking for me last week, but they didn't come back until this morning.

C. What is the difference in your income now?
(Possible remission based on change of circumstances - need the previous income as well as the current to assess whether fine was fixed above or below the banding for the revised amount).

D. From about £150 take home pay down to £30.65 Job Seekers Allowance.

C. How much do you have in savings?
(Rather than the closed question of 'do you have any savings?' Assume and be corrected if necessary! Lump sum payment?)

D. Nothing at all. Not now.

C. So your income is £30.65 per week. What other income do you have?
(Extra's?)

D. None - that's it.

C. Are any deductions being taken from your benefit to cover debts?
(The follow-on question whenever the income is Income Support or Job Seekers Allowance. Explore suitability for deduction of benefit – maximum of 3 deductions.)

D. Yes. £8.40 a week for gas, electric and rent arrears. £2.80 for each of them for the arrears and they take another £5 a week for the current gas and electric - that's to stop me getting into arrears again. That's why I only end up with just over £30 a week.

C. So your full benefit is about £44 per week then, when your bills are paid off.
(Net income does not include deductions for debts and this figure is needed for any re-calculation of fine amount).

D. Yes, it will be.

C. How will your income vary in the near future?

D. I'm going to sell raffle tickets at the football ground from next Saturday and I'll get about £10 a week for that.
(Assume that it will vary. Immediate prospects of financial change? Saturday commitment rules out attendance centre order)

C. Tell us now about what you have to pay out each week?
(An open question as a starter may produce a more accurate list than a series of closed questions from a long list which almost suggests that there should be something paid out on every item e.g. car insurance, life insurance?).

D. About £20 on food and £4 a week on a catalogue.

C. What are you buying on the catalogue?

D. A television.

C. When did you take on that payment?
(Evidence of culpability?)

D. Last year when I was working.

C. How much is left to pay?
(*Possible distress if imminent ownership*)

D. About £30.

C. Do you pay your catalogue regularly?
(*May rule out any need for supervision order*).

D. Yes – or they'll take it back.

C. Do you have any other items on credit?
(*More likely to reveal items for distress than asking if anything can be sold!*)

D. No.

C. So, all of your other property belongs to you, does it?

D. No, I'm in a furnished flat. I don't own any of it. I'm moving in with my girlfriend soon and her flat is furnished as well. We don't have anything of our own, except the television.

C. You've mentioned moving in with your girlfriend. It would be helpful for the court to have your address and telephone number there as well - just in case we need to contact you urgently. It will be easier to ring you or write to you rather than having to arrange for the enforcement officer to come looking for you - it might save you the embarrassment of that happening to you again.
(*Critical tracing information is identified and obtained*).

D. Fair enough. It's 4 Long Street, Anytown and the number is 09976421. My mobile might be best, that's 078026701.

C. And the car. This can be checked – who is the registered owner of the car?
(*Traffic offence - may have the registration number - bailiffs and distress potential?*)

D.   It was mine, but I had to pay £20 for it to be towed away.

C. If you are allowed your liberty today, how would you propose to pay this fine?
(*An offer from the defaulter may carry more commitment to pay than one which is imposed – it may also be higher!*)

D.   £5 a week.

3.5.3.   Fine enforcement – A structured approach

1.   Getting the bill right. Is the fine figure appropriate?

Remission of the fine is appropriate because of the change in financial circumstances. A reduction of net income from £150 per week and a band B fine of £100, reduced to £43 per week and a fine with the credit would be say £30 (rounded figure) + £40 costs.

2. Consider all options – inappropriate or unsuccessful? Why?

- Distress warrant – *no goods apart from clothes and a television on hire purchase.*
- Attachment of earnings – *unemployed.*
- Attachment of benefit – *maximum 3 deductions already taken.*
- Money payment supervision order – *capable of managing finances if so desires – catalogue payments sustained.*

3.   Is there evidence of wilful refusal or culpable neglect?

Yes. Defaulter is capable of being culpable. He understood the obligation and had the money to pay. He was aware that proceedings were being taken for default and chose to avoid paying.

4.   Is a community order appropriate?

Attendance centre order is not appropriate as he has a Saturday job and can pay the fine from the income.

5.   Is there no other method of dealing with the defaulter?

No. Custody of 7 days.

6.   The purpose of committal is to compel payment rather than serve a custodial sentence. Should the opportunity be given for payment by instalments in this case?

Yes. Pay £5 per week or serve 7 days detention.

See Adult Court Bench Book at 1.43 Fine Enforcement - A Structured Approach.

3.5.4   Decision with reasons

"We are going to help you today. The fine will be reduced from £100 to £30 because your financial circumstances have changed since the order was imposed. The costs of £40 will also have to be paid. That's a total of £70.

Secondly we have considered all options but feel that they would not be appropriate. We cannot issue a distress warrant on your goods because you do not have anything which could be sold. We cannot deduct directly from your wage because you are not working at the moment. We cannot ask for a deduction directly from your benefit because there are already the maximum of 3 deductions for other debts. We do not think it is necessary for a money payment supervision order to be imposed because you are quite capable of paying your catalogue on a regular basis and we believe that you can manage to pay your fine as well so the order would be undesirable.   We cannot send you to the attendance centre as you have a Saturday job and we will not deprive you of the income.

We find that there is culpable neglect in this case. You were well aware of the obligation to pay and you have had the money to pay. You will therefore pay £5 per week or serve a period of 7 days detention in a Young Offenders Institution. You will not have to serve the 7 days provided that you pay the £5 every week. The first payment will be made today and every Monday by 4pm.

Failure to pay a single instalment on time means that the commitment may be issued and you will be arrested and taken straight to the Young Offenders Institution.   So, how much every Monday? Or what will happen? Do you understand?"

(A notice will be sent advising that the commitment falls to be issued. This allows the opportunity to attend court and apply for re-suspension based upon a change of circumstances, but the reality is that very few defaulters do respond to the notice and attend court, so the commitment warrant will normally be the next action which engages the defaulter).

See Adult Court Bench Book at Pronouncement 49 and Checklist 1-43.

3.6.   Enforcement of council tax

The enforcement of council tax is a regular activity in court. The process is as follows:

(a) Pre-court:

- Local authority serve (i) Demand notice (ii) Reminder notice (iii) Final notice.
- Local authority make complaint for a liability order.
- Issue of a summons by a single Justice or Justices' Clerk.
- Date fixed for applications for liability orders to be made.

(b) Court hearing:

The council must satisfy the court that:

- The council tax has been set by resolution of the authority – a certified copy of the resolution.
- A sum has been demanded in accordance with the regulations i.e. appropriate notices served – computer records compiled by the authority are admissible if legally certified as 'evidence compliant' (legal adviser will check).
- A summons has been served.

(c) Liability order:

A liability order must be issued unless the court is not satisfied on one of the above elements. The order will include costs and gives the local authority the power to take enforcement action e.g. issue distress warrant, attach benefits.

(d) Committal proceedings:

- Local authority must attempt to levy distress before committal
- When measures are ineffective the local authority may request a means enquiry with a view to committal to prison in default
- Summons or warrant issued
- Defaulter must be present
- The Administrative Court has confirmed that 3 years should be the maximum period for payment of council tax arrears i.e. compares to compensation order maximum
- Legal representation must be considered
- Court papers must be disclosed if sought
- Private and confidential facilities must be available for the defence
- Means enquiry must be conducted.

The court may impose a period of up to 3 months imprisonment if satisfied that failure to pay was due to wilful refusal or culpable neglect.

- Relevant period to assess culpability begins with the issue of the liability order.
- Consider all options as for a fine defaulter and suggest use of fine default custody maxima as a guideline.
- Give reasons.

(e) Courts powers.

- May issue warrant of commitment
- May issue suspended warrant of commitment – there will be a further hearing before the actual issue
- Adjourn or dismiss the application
- Remission – seek representations of local authority before taking this step.

There has been much controversy about the payment of local taxes over the years and enforcement must be conducted efficiently so that there is a clear message that everyone has to pay - either the cash, or the consequences.

Effective enforcement of money orders is important. Many people do pay – often with enormous difficulty. Ensuring that everyone 'pays their dues' is one of the greatest acts of fairness and equality performed by magistrates.

CHAPTER 4
Fairness of approach

Using the Judicial Oath as a starting point, this chapter considers a variety of practical points which will assist in dealing with the rich diversity in our society so that the court complies with the Human Rights Act and enables people to feel that they have been dealt with fairly.

4.1.   The judicial oath

This section focuses on the practicalities of personal compliance with the Judicial Oath: -

---

JUDICIAL OATH

I ... do swear that I will well and truly serve our Sovereign Lady Queen Elizabeth the Second in the office of the Justice of the Peace, and I will do right to all manner of people after the laws and usages of this realm, without fear or favour, affection or ill will. So help me God.

An affirmation may be made as an alternative to the oath.

A multifaith, multicultural, multiracial society makes special demands on magistrates as it poses challenges in court which require an immediate and well-informed response as soon as they arise. In the words of The Lord Chief Justice 'there is a great deal more to understanding the feelings and concerns of ethnic minorities than simply being polite and patient.'

The range of people in our society swings across race, religion, culture, sexuality, mental and physical ability, and age. The full range will appear before the courts. Appropriate communication needs to be varied for each individual so that relevant information is given and received in an atmosphere which is comfortable to that individual. This is not just about extending common courtesy.

Anyone who appears before the court wants to feel that they have been dealt with fairly and equally 'no matter where they come from and what they come with.' Whether they come from a country mansion or from the notorious estate in town; whether they are intelligent, articulate and smartly dressed or with learning difficulties, uncontrollable anger and the clothes they woke up in. They may well be dealt with equally but the true test is how the individual perceives the fairness of the court process. The same penalty for the same offence, but one defendant was encouraged to give his side of the story and felt that the outcome was fair - the other remained silent and confused in court and left with feelings of resentment.

The concepts of institutional racism and unwitting discrimination further increase the importance of some knowledge of social diversity, all of which are discussed below.

4.1.1.   Dealing with diversity

What is diversity? 'The state or quality of being different'. The court deals with a vast range and variety of people every day and it is essential to recognise that different personal attributes will call for different treatment in order for justice to be seen to be done. Whilst every individual is different, there are some attributes and common features which fall into specific groups in the community. This chapter focuses on differences in religion and on the particularly vulnerable groups as an aid to generate awareness and behaviour, so that fair treatment is more likely to be perceived.

4.1.2.   Some basic principles about race, religion and culture

These are copied directly from 'Race and the Courts' published by the Judicial Studies Board, 1999:

- Treat everyone who comes to court with dignity and respect - 'do as you would be done by'.
- Everyone has prejudices. Recognise and guard against your own.
- Be well informed - being independent and impartial does not mean being isolated from issues which affect people from minority communities.
- Don't assume that treating everyone in the same way is the same thing as treating everyone fairly. It would not be fair to treat a wheelchair user in the same way as someone who is able to walk, for example expecting him or her to climb stairs to reach a courtroom.
- Be 'colour conscious' not 'colour blind'. Fair treatment involves taking account of difference.
- Don't make assumptions: all white people are not the same. Nor are all black, or Asian, or Chinese or Middle Eastern people.
- Don't project cultural stereotypes; for example that all young black people avoid eye contact. Most young black and Asian people are

second and third generation British born citizens and may be no different from any other teenager when faced with authority figures.

- Don't perceive people from ethnic minority communities as 'the problem' - the problem may lie in the working methods and traditions of some institutions which may put some groups such as women, people from racial minorities at an unfair disadvantage.
- If in doubt - ask. A polite and well-intentioned inquiry about how to pronounce a name or about a particular religious belief or a language requirement will not be offensive when prompted by a genuine desire to get it right.

4.1.3.   'Equal treatment - do's and don'ts'

These are summarised from the JSB publication 'Equality before the Courts' (2001):
(N.B. In the court setting it is now preferable to speak and think of 'fair' treatment, rather than 'equal' treatment. It would not be 'fair' to treat a person with some type of special need in exactly the same way as someone else, as they would effectively be disadvantaged. Similarly if justice were delivered 'equally' then the guidelines would be tramlines instead).

Do
- Recognise that Christians have 'Christian' names - others do not.
- Ascertain how parties wish to be addressed.
- Obtain details of any disabilities or medical problems of the parties and allow more time for special arrangements.
- Plan in advance for disabled people so that their needs are accommodated.
- Ensure that appropriate measures are taken to protect vulnerable witnesses - children, those with mental or physical disabilities and those who are distressed.

Don't
- Underestimate the stress of appearing in court, particularly when the ordeal is compounded by an additional problem such as disability or appearing without professional representation.
- Overlook the use - unconscious or otherwise - of gender-based, racist, religious or homophobic stereotyping as an evidential short-cut.
- Allow advocates to attempt over-rigorous cross-examination of children or other vulnerable witnesses.
- Use words that imply an evaluation of the sexes, however subtle e.g. 'man and wife', 'businessman'.
- Allow anyone to be put in a position where they face hostility or ridicule.

4.2. Ethnicity and religion in England and Wales - Census 2001

As a starting point, the figures below describe how our population is made up.

4.2.1. Ethnicity

	Total population %	Minority ethnic population
White	92.1	
Mixed	1.2	14.6
Asian or Asian British		
Indian	1.8	22.7
Pakistani	1.3	16.1
Bangladeshi	0.5	6.1
Other Asian	0.4	5.3
Black or Black British		
Black Caribbean	1.0	12.2
Black African	0.8	10.5
Black Other	0.2	2.1
Chinese	0.4	5.3
Other	0.4	5.0
All minority ethnic population = 4.6 million	**7.9**	100

Of people living in England, 87.4% gave their county of birth as England, and 3.2% of the population came from other parts of the UK.

4.2.2. Religion

Religion	Percentage
Christian	71.6
No religion	15.5
No religion stated	7.3
Muslim	2.7
Hindu	1.0
Sikh	0.6
Jewish	0.5
Buddhist	0.3
Other religions	0.3

Just over three-quarters of the UK population reported having a religion. The census religion question was a voluntary question, but nevertheless over 92% of people chose to answer it.

(Source: <http://www.statistics.gov.uk/cci/nugget.asp> accessed 2/2/2004)

4.3.   Religions

An awareness of a person's religion is an integral element of being aware of fair treatment issues and it is often a key element of a person's identity and family life. There follows a few key points in respect of the religions which are followed by the greatest numbers in England and Wales. In an effort to provide useful information, it is necessarily generalised. It is fully acknowledged that everyone must be treated as an individual who may hold individual beliefs and individual choices of manifestation. The headings for the 5 predominant religions in England and Wales follow the description used in the census.

4.3.1.   Christian

The Christian religion developed out of Judaism and is centred on the life and work of Jesus of Nazareth. During his life he chose 12 men as disciples, who formed the nucleus of the Church as a communion of believers called together to worship God, who is the creator, through Jesus Christ. Humankind, as his creation is essentially good, but in practice is sinful. At the heart of the Christian faith is the conviction that through Jesus' life, death and resurrection, God has allowed human beings to find salvation. Belief in Jesus as the Son of God brings forgiveness of all sin.

The 'Gospel' of Jesus was proclaimed by word of mouth, but by the end of the 1st century it was committed to writing and became accepted as the authoritative scripture of the New Testament, understood as the fulfilment of the Jewish scriptures or Old Testament.

Separate doctrines and practices apply to the Eastern or Orthodox Churches, the Roman Catholic Church acknowledging the Pope as head, and the Protestant Churches stemming from the split with the Roman Church in the Reformation.

Public worship takes place at least every Sunday, with holy days of Christmas Day (birth of Jesus Christ); Maundy Thursday (the last supper); Good Friday (the crucifixion); and Easter Sunday (the resurrection). Most Churches recognise two sacraments, baptism and the Eucharist/Mass/Communion as essential.

4.3.2. Muslim

Islam is an Arabic word which has translation as 'to enter into peace' or 'submission' to the will of God, and the followers of Islam are called Muslims in their holy book, the Holy Qu'ran.

The 'five pillars of Islam' are:

1. The declaration of faith that there is only one God (Allah) and Muhammed is His Prophet.
2. Prayers are said 5 times per day, either individually or in congregation, before sunrise, noon, afternoon, late evening and night. Before saying prayers a Muslim should wash the parts of the body that are exposed. Adult male Muslims should go to the Mosque for the noon prayers on Friday.
3. Fasting during Ramadan, the 9th month in which the Prophet first began to receive revelations from God. Muslims are required to fast from food and drink for 29 or 30 consecutive days from dawn to sunset, with the exception of the very old, the sick and pregnant or nursing mothers. Extra prayers will be said and many Muslims attempt to read the entire Holy Qur'an divided into equal daily parts. It is a month of self-discipline, appreciation, and generosity to others. The end of the fasting is marked by the festival of Eid-ul-Fitr and is marked by a holiday to celebrate. ('Eid' literally means 'recurring festivity').
4. Giving money or alms to the needy and good causes annually. 'Zakat' is payable at the rate of two and a half percent on cash, bank savings and the value of gold and silver jewellery and is regarded as a right and not charity, which can be given at any time.
5. Making the pilgrimage to Makkah at least once during a Muslim's lifetime if this can be afforded (Hajj). It is a journey to the house of Allah in Makkah, Saudi Arabia. Hajj symbolises the unity of mankind and is the annual international assembly of about 2 million members of the Muslim community and it reinforces the idea of a Muslim belonging to one but one creator, and also the equality of humankind. The second festival prescribed by the Prophet is Eid-ul-Adha and this coincides with the pilgrimage to Makkah (Hajj).

Men may wish to keep their head covered at all times. Muslim women may wish to remain completely veiled and this may cause some difficulty in communication, but it is not a refusal to co-operate but in response to Islamic teaching to wear modest dress which covers the whole body and to avoid unnecessary contact with strangers.

Most marriages are arranged in some form by the families involved. Monogomy is the norm but polygamy for men is allowed in certain circumstances. Divorce is met with disapproval.

4.3.3.   Hindu

Hindu dharma (religious philosophy and way of life) is believed to be the world's oldest dharma - over 8500 years old, and its roots lie in the Indian subcontinent. There is no mortal founder. It does not require an express commitment to one particular core belief or doctrine nor one deity. The Supreme Reality, God Almighty (Brahman) becomes manifest in various forms and is known by various names. Whenever righteousness declines and unrighteousness rises, God incarnates himself on earth to restore righteousness. There have been many Incarnations and ten are glorified, and include Shri Rama (the Prince) and Shri Krishna (the Great Teacher) who descended to make the world a better place.

The five main recognised principles are the Omnipresent God Almighty; prayer; life after death and the eternal soul; the law of karma, 'as you sow you shall reap', and compassion for all living beings.

Most Hindus are vegetarian and refrain from eating beef. The cow is regarded as a 'mother' and the slaughter of cows is strictly prohibited. Many do not smoke tobacco or drink alcohol, or sometimes tea and coffee, which are also considered to be intoxicants. In most Hindu homes there will be a small altar dedicated to God. Daily prayer is offered twice or three times a day and portions of the family's food will be presented for blessing before being eaten. There is little congregational worship in Hindu temples as religion is considered to be a matter for the individual. Festivals include Diwali, the festival of lights in the Autumn, and the Holi in the Spring. There are many others.

Marriage is valued as the key institution and is usually arranged in accordance with rules of caste. Divorce is relatively uncommon and is stigmatised, especially for women, because it represents a violation of ideal norms.

4.3.4.   Sikh

The main features of the Sikh religion include the following:

1.   Founded by Guru Nanak, who was born of Hindu parents.
2.   The belief is that the 'divine spiritual light' first possessed by Guru Nanak was passed in turn to each of the successive Gurus, and

following the death of Guru Gobind Singh in 1708, it now resides in the Holy Scriptures, the Guru Granth Sahib.

3. The lowest is equal to the highest in race, creed, political rights and religious hopes.
4. Rejection of the caste system.
5. Many practising Sikhs wear the 'five Ks' at all times:

- Kesh - 'hair', which is regarded as gift from God. The hair is a symbol of faith and keeping long hair confirms a Sikh's belief in the acceptance of God's will and teaches them humility and obedience.
- Kanga - 'a wooden comb' which is worn in the hair as a symbol of cleanliness.
- Kacherra - slightly longer type of underwear and is symbolic of continence and high moral character.
- Kara - 'link' which is a special bracelet worn on the wrist and signifies that the wearer is bound both morally and spiritually to the teachings of the Gurus. The circle is also a symbol of restraint.
- Kirpan - a small sword which is worn as a symbol of power and freedom of spirit. The Lord Chancellor has provided guidance to court security staff that this should be limited to 6" and should be worn beneath clothing whilst in court.

Some Sikhs abstain from drinking tea and coffee, and practising Sikhs are vegetarians and tea-total. Marriage is regarded as a person's entry into a new spiritual stage and from a religious point of view it is regarded as indissoluble.

4.3.5. Jewish

The central belief of Judaism is the belief in one God, the creator of the world who delivered the Israelites out of their bondage in Egypt, and chose them to be a light to all mankind. He revealed his law (Torah) to them, as the revelation of God's will to Moses, and this sets out the commandments. God's compassion permits the atonement of sin. The Hebrew Bible is the primary source of Judaism.

There is a preference for expressing beliefs and attitudes more through ritual than through abstract doctrine. The family is the basic unit of Jewish ritual, though the synagogue, which is the centre for community worship and study, has come to play an increasingly important role.

The Shabbat (or Sabbath) is observed as a day of worship, rest and peace. It is observed on Saturday which is believed to correspond to the seventh day of the creation on which God rested from creating the earth. Shabbat begins about half an hour before sunset on the Friday evening and ends at nightfall on the Saturday night and the time varies from week to week, starting later in summer and earlier in winter. During Shabbat it is forbidden for Jews to engage in any activities which are considered as work. This is interpreted in different ways and for some will include not driving a car unless there is a danger to life.

There is an annual cycle of religious festivals with High Holy Days, Rosh Hashanah (New Year's Day), Yom Kippur (The Day of Atonement) and Peasach (The Passover). When a male is aged 13 years or more, a special service is held in the Synagogue and represents his coming of age - the Bar Mitzvah. The Orthodox Synagogue usually have a blessing for a girl from the age of 12 - the Bat Mitzvah.

Men may wish to keep their head covered at all times, usually with a skull cap. In Orthodox Judaism neither men nor women are permitted by Jewish law to take an oath on the Hebrew Bible/Old Testament and they will affirm. Most observant Jews will only eat kosher meat e.g. from sheep, cattle, poultry, which has been slaughtered in accordance with Jewish religious custom.

4.3.6.   Buddhist

A tradition of thought and practice originating in India, deriving from the teaching of Buddha, who is regarded as one of a series of enlightened beings, or 'he who knows'. Images of the Buddha portray him as serene, wise and compassionate. This is what Buddhists aspire to. Many practising Buddhists would view Buddhism as a philosophy of life rather than a religion. There is no belief in a creator God. The teaching of Buddha is summarised in the four noble Truths, the last of which affirms the existence of a path leading to deliverance from the universal human experience of suffering, a middle way of life between austerity and comfort. A central tenet is the law of karma, by which good and evil deeds result in appropriate reward or punishment in this life or in a succession of rebirths.

Through a proper understanding of this condition, and by obedience to the right path, human beings can break the chain of karma. The Buddha's path to deliverance is through morality, meditation and wisdom. The goal is nirvana which means the 'blowing out' of the fires of all desires and the absorption of the self into the infinite.

Underlying the diversity of Buddha belief and practice is a controlling purpose. The aim is to create the conditions favourable to spiritual development, leading to liberation or deliverance from bondage to suffering. This is generally seen as involving meditation, personal discipline and spiritual exercises. Buddhists follow a path of teaching that centres on cultivating the mind so that it can be freed from greed, hatred and delusion - the three factors that create our suffering. The common purpose has made it possible for Buddhism to be very flexible in adapting its organisation, ceremony and pattern of belief to different social and cultural situations.

Practising Buddhists are often vegetarian, particularly those westerners who have adopted Buddhism as a way of life. There are five precepts which guide Buddhists' behaviour:
- Not to destroy living beings
- Not to take that which is not given
- To refrain from sexual misconduct
- To avoid incorrect speech
- To avoid alcohol and drugs that lead to carelessness.

4.4. Practical aspects

4.4.1. Naming systems and forms of address in court

It is surely a basic issue that names and forms of address are used appropriately in court if we are to demonstrate some personal sensitivity and ensure that personal dignity is instigated and preserved on both sides of the bench. Most defendants would feel at least patronised, probably insulted and possibly even pre-judged if they were referred to purely by surname. Similarly, by using the first name only there could well be a feeling of over-familiarity by the chairman and the formality and authority of the court may well suffer.

Traditional Muslim male names most commonly consist of a personal name and a religious name - either may come first, and the personal name is only used by family and friends. There may also be an hereditary name. All names should therefore be used unless permission is given to do otherwise, e.g. Mr. Mohammed Rahman, Mr. Mohammed Rahman Khan. Referring to Mohammed Ali as Mr. Ali can be likened to saying 'Mr. God'.

Female Muslims should also be referred to by both names, usually a personal name and a title or second personal name e.g. Mrs Amina Begum, Miss Yasmin Nesa. Referring to Mrs. Begum can be likened to saying 'Mrs. Mrs.'

In Sikh naming systems, Singh (male) and Kaur (female) are religious designations and it is normally inappropriate to treat these as surnames without permission e.g. Mr. Kamarjit Singh and Miss Jaswinder Kaur should therefore be referred to by both names.

As a matter of both politeness and dignity, it is appropriate to ask how someone wishes to be referred to in court - there will be a number of occasions for using names, other than the full formal identification. The usher may well be happy to do this outside court when taking names and then refer to the preferred name when calling the case into court

Check pronunciation and note it phonetically on the register as the defendant or witness says it. Even the simplest names can be misheard and we have probably all had the irritation of being referred to incorrectly. It is not an answer to say that no one has complained. Arguably this could suggest that the level of expectation of respect is fixed at a very low level?

4.4.2. Appropriate terminology

X	Coloured
X	Negroid
→	Black people (Caribbean or African origin), Black British

X	Asian if exact origin is known
→	Asian if exact ethnic origin is not known
→	Region of origin e.g. Punjabi, Bengali, Gujarati

X	African if origin is known
→	African if exact origin is not known
→	Nigerian, Ghanaian

X	Afro-Caribbean
→	African Caribbean
→	Black people

X	Half-caste
→	Mixed-race/origin, or dual-heritage

X	Non-white as it indicates a deviation from the norm
✓	Black, Asian, Chinese etc.

X	Ethnic minority
→	'Minority ethnic community' makes it clear that the majority is also an 'ethnic' community'.

4.4.3. Oath and affirmation

The common law originally held that atheists and agnostics could not give evidence in court or serve as jurors, as they could not swear an oath! The law is now contained in the Oaths Act 1978 which states at s.1 (1) 'The person taking the oath shall hold the New Testament, or in the case of a Jew, the Old Testament, in his uplifted right hand, and say or repeat after the officer administering the oath the words 'I swear by Almighty God that ....'.

At s.1 (3), 'In the case of a person who is neither a Christian nor a Jew, the oath shall be administered in any lawful manner'. For this purpose, it is important to make other holy books readily available, namely the Qur'an for Muslims; the Gita for Hindus and the Sunder Gutka for Sikhs.

'Any person who objects to being sworn shall be permitted to make his solemn affirmation instead of taking an oath', and also if it is not 'reasonably practicable' to administer a religious oath. 'A solemn affirmation shall be of the same force and effect as an oath'.

How many people take it upon themselves to object to being sworn and ask to affirm instead? How does the court know whether a person is taking an oath on the religious book which relates to his religion? How does the court know whether a person has any religious belief at all? (almost 23% of the population in the census did not give a religion).

No cause to worry on a legal basis. The case law is clear that an oath on any holy book may be binding. The proviso is that the oath appears to be binding on the witness's conscience and secondly, that they did actually consider it to be binding, e.g. a Muslim may be bound by an oath taken on the New Testament rather than upon the Qu'ran. The statute itself provides that duly administered oaths which are taken by a person without religious belief are binding.

On a religious basis, the holy books must all be wrapped as appropriate, and be kept clean as a mark of respect to all religions (this includes the presentation of the New Testament). Many witnesses who are religious are unwilling to swear on their holy books for a variety of reasons. For instance, they consider themselves to be unclean, or they are not prepared to swear to 'tell the truth, the whole truth and nothing but the truth' because we can only tell what we honestly believe to be the truth. It is important that any perceptions and assumptions about who should be swearing on which book, and whether they are therefore telling the truth or not must be put to one side as irrelevant. Evidence is evidence and perjury can be charged on the basis of any oath or affirmation as stated above.

(The sooner we demonstrate equality of treatment and move to binding affirmations for everyone the better!)

4.5.   Vulnerable groups

Many such groups exist. A few are selected for discussion as being the groups which we tend to see in the courtroom most frequently.

4.5.1.   People with a disability

It is estimated that there are at lest 8.5 million people who currently meet the definition of disabled person under the Disability Discrimination Act 1995. A 'disability' is any 'physical or mental impairment which has a substantial and long term effect on ... normal day to day activities'. It may relate to mobility, manual dexterity, physical co-ordination, incontinence, speech, hearing or sight, memory and ability to concentrate, learn or understand. Courts must be able to accommodate the special needs of litigants, defendants and witnesses and it is unlawful to discriminate against disabled people in the provision of facilities and services.

Various guidance has evolved which includes the following: -

*   Check whether the carer should accompany at all times - even in the dock or witness box.

*   Ensure that waiting time is kept to an absolute minimum.

*   Talk directly to the person with the disability. This includes those with a learning disability. It is tempting to speak instead to the person accompanying them as they will very often be making the responses on behalf of the person.

*   When talking to a person with a hearing difficulty, make sure that your face is in the light, look at them directly and speak clearly and naturally in a strong volume which you can maintain. Keep your hands away from your mouth. Ask them if you are speaking loud enough rather than shouting at the outset.

*   A person who is deaf and without speech is a competent witness if he can understand the nature of an oath. This may be established either

by signs, through an interpreter or in writing. The evidence must be expressed sufficiently clearly to enable it to be faithfully interpreted.

- When talking to a blind person, introduce who you are and ask each speaker to introduce themselves before beginning their speech so that the person can orientate himself first.

- Ask if a person needs any help, but wait until it is accepted before doing anything.

- A wheelchair is part of the body space of the person using it and nobody in the court should simply move it without permission.

- Consider whether more food or drink is required. Provide opportunities to take medication and arrange for easy request for toilet breaks.

Appropriate terminology:

X   Wheelchair-bound
✓   Wheelchair-user

X   Handicapped, invalid, cripple, spastic, disabled
✓   Person with a disability

X   Mental, mental handicap, mental problems
✓   Person with a learning issue

4.5.2.   Children

Children may be called as defendants and as witnesses in adult court and obviously require every possible support in order to give their evidence as confidently as possible. A parent/guardian should accompany and remain next to the child throughout. First names should be used and the proceedings should be as informal as possible in order to avoid any feelings of intimidation. A child under 14 will give evidence unsworn and should be presumed competent unless the contrary is shown.

Special measures directions are available for child witnesses in cases involving sex and violence. A video recording of an interview may be admitted as evidence in chief and evidence may be given by live link so that the child is in a separate room with an independent witness supporter, but can be seen and heard by the magistrates and legal representatives. Alternatively, screens may be considered so that the witness does not see the accused in court. The court may be cleared if a child is giving evidence in cases against decency or morality.

A press restriction direction should always be considered whenever a child is 'concerned' in adult court proceedings, whether as a defendant, a witness or in respect of whom the proceedings are taken. The order will prevent publicity which reveals particulars which are calculated to lead to the identification of the child e.g. name of school. In considering whether to make an order the court must weigh the public interest in full reporting of the crime, including the identification of the defendant, against the need to protect the victim from further harm. It is particularly important when an adult is charged with sexual offences and child victims are named in the charge and therefore in open court. Similarly it may be appropriate in cases involving non-school attendance where the adult is brought to court but the child is concerned in the proceedings and may be adversely affected by the accompanying publicity which may well include sensitive family issues.

It is more difficult in the cases involving children who are made the subject of Anti Social Behaviour Orders in the adult court There is a balancing act between the child being thrust into the public eye and the benefit of the community being made aware of the order. See 4.9.2. (b).

4.5.3.   Sexual orientation and preference

The level of approval and acceptance by society varies but homophobia (hostility and fear towards homosexuals) is widespread and perceptions of prejudice by the gay and lesbian community extend to their experiences in court.

A research project by the London Lesbian and Gay Teenage Group provides an insight into the lifestyle of some homosexuals which may be helpful for magistrates to be aware of. 416 individuals completed the questionnaire as to whether they felt that the various situations applied 'because they were lesbian or gay':

- 6 in 10 had been verbally abused
- 1 in 5 had been beaten up
- 1 in 10 had been thrown out of their home
- 1 in 5 had attempted suicide
- 1 in 5 had had contact with the police
- 1 in 2 had had problems at school

Some awkwardness may occur particularly with transsexuals who are in the process of change. The treatment usually involves living in the new role for at least a year, usually on hormones and then progressing to undergo a series of operations to bring the body into line with the chosen gender if desired. Whether they are 'pre-op' or 'post-op' they should be referred to by their new gender. Transsexuals normally change their name by statutory declaration.

The process is complex and it is important to the person concerned that their chosen new name is used with ease and acceptance rather than incredulity. 'Jane' Smith may well have some facial hair but that is 'her' name.

In the court room there is the potential for some of the greatest fears to be made manifest - a fear of public embarrassment and a perception that some may feel they 'ask for all they get' - those fears can be largely allayed by a sensitive bench.

Appropriate terminology:

X   Queer, bent
✓   Homosexual, gay, lesbian

X   Your husband? wife?
✓   Your partner?

4.5.4.   'The poor and ignorant'

The words above the Old Bailey summarise a crucial duty upon the court, to 'protect the poor and ignorant.' Words and behaviour can be misinterpreted if the expectations and evaluations of them are based on the code of the 'richer and wiser.'

Examples:

- *A defendant attends court and wears dirty, torn clothing. Is he being deliberately disrespectful and provocative? Is he making some kind of political statement? Is he making the point that he cannot pay a high fine?*
  or
  Is he wearing the only clothes he has?

- *A defendant says that he has nothing to say about the offence. Is it because he has no mitigation at all? Is it because he might make*

matters even worse for himself? Is he purposely refusing to show
appropriate remorse?
or
Does he feel too intimidated, too inadequate or too inarticulate to
speak up?

Being open to various possibilities and interpretations is important to social justice. Financial priorities may be affected by the stress of being on a low income, being without employment, being alone for much of the day and having children who are making the money demands of their peer group. The means form may well openly confess to a few pounds on cigarettes and a lottery ticket each week but in these life circumstances, are they really chosen 'luxuries' to be taken entirely for a fine instalment, or necessities to 'get by'? The more 'intelligent' or criminally sophisticated on the other hand are more likely to recognise the split between the socially acceptable necessities and luxuries, and load their outgoings into the food and clothing column, which probably include the lottery and cigarettes anyway! A balance?

4.5.5. Women

Women can feel particularly vulnerable in a court situation. It is less 'normal' for a woman to appear before the court than a man. The experience is far less likely to have been shared by female friends and family. The 'code of behaviour' may remain something of a mystery until the day of the court appearance. Criminal statistics show that in 2001, only 19% of known offenders were women, with a 22% proportion of theft and handling charges attributed to women.

Similarly the imposition of a custodial sentence on women is a relatively infrequent occurrence compared to men. Women prisoners make up just over 5% of the prison population (2001).

How may a woman be put at ease? It is helpful to determine the appropriate title of address. Given the comparatively low numbers of women attending court as defendants and witnesses, it is suggested that the usher may have the opportunity to check whether it is 'Miss' 'Mrs' 'Ms' or otherwise when registering the names outside the court. When called into court the defendant may be announced as 'Mrs. Jane Smith'. This saves the chairman having to guess (is she wearing a ring?); questioning title in a manner which may indicate to her that marital status is somehow important, or alternatively using all names throughout the case and avoiding any reference to title. In terms of maintaining some dignity and some warmth it seems far preferential to use a title.

4.6. Discrimination

The Oxford dictionary definition of discrimination is to 'make a distinction, especially on the grounds of race or colour'.

Direct discrimination occurs when an individual is treated less favourably on grounds of race, colour, religion, gender, ethic or national origin, or disability, than others would be treated in similar circumstances. Indirect discrimination occurs when treatment may be equal in a formal sense between different groups but it is discriminatory to one particular group, because of its disproportionate effect and the fact that only a small number of the group can comply with it. This can happen unintentionally. Facilities, on the one hand or punishments, on the other hand, may well be available to everyone, but are they equally accessible to and accessed by everyone? It is recognised by the response to the statement of 'anyone can' by the statement 'some can't' e.g. 'anyone can' pick up and read the explanatory leaflets about their rights - but 'some can't' read. Similarly it is important to avoid and destroy perceptions that maybe 'anyone can' but 'only some are' sent to prison for a particular type of offence.

In a recent research, one in eight Asian defendants in both the Crown Court and the Magistrates' Court perceived racial bias in their treatment. The complaints were most often about perceived 'excessive' or 'disproportionate' sentences as compared with what it was thought a white defendant would have received, from which they had inferred racial bias. (Ethnic Minorities in the Criminal Courts. Lord Chancellor's Department Research Programme. March 2003)

'The criminal justice system has the capacity for both indirect and direct discrimination... knowledge about discrimination in other social fields suggests that it is most likely to occur where certain conditions apply e.g. where decisions depend on subjective judgements rather than (or in addition) to objective criteria'.
(Royal Commission on Criminal justice, 'Ethnic Minorities and the Criminal Justice System' Home Office, 1993).

4.6.1. Equality legislation

There is now a statutory duty on the Secretary of State to publish information annually to facilitate the performance of those involved with criminal justice to avoid discriminating against any persons on the ground of race or sex or other improper ground (s.95 Criminal Justice Act 1991). This enables trends regarding particular groups to be identified and enquiries are made to ensure that they are objectively legitimate.

Examples:

Information collected and published under s.95 in 2001/2:

- *Police stop and search - 12% black people; 6% Asian; 1% other 'non-white' origin. Compared with 2000/2001, across England and Wales (excluding Metropolitan Police) there was a rise of 6% for black people and 16% for Asians and a fall of about 2% for white people. A black person is 8 times more likely to be stopped and searched than a white person.*
- *Arrests for notifiable offences - 9% black people; 5% Asian; 1% other 'non-white' origin. Compared with 2000/1 arrests rose by 12% for black people and 7% for Asians and fell by 1% for white people. Black people were 5 times for more likely to be arrested than white or other ethnic groups.*
- *Prison population - 13% black people; 3% Asian; 4% other minority ethnic groups (31.6.2001). These proportions have remained relatively constant in recent years.*
- *Magistrates' conviction rate in 6 pilot areas - white defendants were more likely to be convicted (64%) than black or Asian defendants (56% and 52%).*

2002

- *Between 1993 and 2001 the average population of women rose by 140% as against 46% for men.*
- *In mid-2001, minority ethnic groups made up 26% of the female population compared to 20% of the male prison population.*
- *37% of women prisoners had previously attempted suicide.*
- *A survey of released female prisoners found only 25% were in employment when interviewed 5-9 months after discharge.*
- *Almost half of all women who were released from prison in 1997 were re-convicted within 2 years.*

Discrimination may be generated by prejudice.

4.7.   Prejudice and stereotyping

What is prejudice? The Oxford dictionary definition is 'preconceived opinion, bias (against of <u>or</u> in favour), e.g. that handsome men are good lovers. Stereotype? An 'unduly fixed mental impression'.

Prejudice is natural. It is part of our daily life and development to build up opinions based on what we see and what we hear - often fleetingly and sometimes without full information or even completely wrong information. Inevitably there is a danger of that prejudice then moving into an unduly fixed mental impression - a stereotype. This may well go on to influence our thoughts, words and actions in the future. Once we have a mental picture of someone or something, it is natural to develop assumptions and probabilities around it. This is where we need to recognise the dangers of prejudice and stereotyping and be very clear that whenever decisions are to be made about other people, there will never be an element of prejudice or stereotyping entering into the decision.

Perhaps the expression 'a little bit of information can be a dangerous thing' best summarises the potential problem. It is a fact that on the 13th June 2001, 51% of the black people in prison were sentenced for robbery or drugs offences; 17% of white people were sentenced to burglary compared to 9% of black people. This can convert to a generalised stereotype that black people tend to be the robbers and drug dealers and white people by comparison tend to be the burglars. This awareness may well be of interest and value for various reasons, but in the courtroom everyone is innocent until proven guilty and everyone is entitled to unconditional bail and any acknowledged prejudice must be put to one side.

This may be more difficult for a magistrate who has recently been robbed or burgled. They may well recognise that for the time being they simply cannot put to one side their opinion of anger towards anyone who is charged with such offences. The mental picture of their own ravaged house or the frightening face of the robber is just too strong and it is fixing on to each case. It may be appropriate not to sit on such a case until emotions have calmed and a blank screen can be created for each case. The feelings of being a victim are real enough though and will go on to become valuable in an objective sense.

On a more day to day level there is the potential for all who pay their car insurance to form a preconceived opinion against those who do not pay. Many of us are paying for the facilities for those who do not pay - that is a fact. This naturally creates feelings of irritation and can generate calculations of unpaid premiums and visions of bad driving and accidents - typical stereotyping. It is essential to put aside preconceptions and stereotypes, and look at the insurance case in a judicial way. What is the actual evidence? It is one single offence on a single day (no relationship whatsoever to annual premium); there is no allegation of bad driving at all and there is no evidence of any injury being caused to anyone - those are the prosecution facts of the case for this particular defendant.

Similarly the prohibited 'what if' thoughts and discussions are far more likely to generate from situations where there is a potential for negative prejudice and stereotyping - probabilities built on a mental picture. In the insurance case, the comment may well be made 'what if there had been an accident?!'. By comparison, a similar thought or remark on a criminal damage case 'what if someone had been stood near the window when it was broken?!' would be recognised immediately as being inappropriate in the light of the actual evidence.

The calculation of annual premium may equally be raised - a daily multiplier as a potential aggravating feature on the nature of the offence. By comparison, a similar remark about 'assuming that he takes cannabis every day then, let's multiply and see how much he would have taken in a year - goodness that must be worth committing to Crown Court!' This would be recognised immediately as being inappropriate in the light of the actual evidence.

With evidence of bad driving - disqualify to protect others. With evidence of driving without insurance twice - points disqualification to punish - the fine has not worked. But a first time stand alone offence - check for prejudice?

Prejudices, stereotypes, labelling, assumptions and generalisations must be recognised - they are natural, but must be left firmly at the court door.

Defendants will also have their prejudices, which may well be negative pre-conceived ideas or stereotypes of the magistrates and the court system. This may be based on a wide range of experiences e.g. programmes on television, seeing all criminal justice agencies as being 'in it together', court experiences as relayed by friends. There may well be myths to dispel and new mental pictures to be created in order to earn and maintain trust in the criminal justice system.

4.8.   Challenging stereotyping and discriminatory comments

To 'let remarks go' is to passively collude with discrimination. Very often remarks are made which either demonstrate a generalised view or terms are used which belittle another person without any intention to demean at all. On the other hand, the comment may well be the tip of the iceberg of underlying beliefs and attitudes which could affect decision making and fair treatment today and in the future.

Challenge needs to be made. This may be done through feedback, enquiry or simply by repeating back the comment.

4.8.1. Giving feedback

This should be specific, objective and focus on what has been done or said. Whilst giving feedback will depend to some extent on the particular people involved and the relationship, there are some 'basic rules' and a few suggestions to consider.

(a) Describe what the person has said or done because this is a fact. Don't start off or finish off with judgement.

NOT 'You're thoughtless' ...'That remark was homophobic'. **X**

Start off with something on the lines of 'There's something I'd like to say ... Do you mind if I just make a comment about ....?

Then give the facts of the words or actions e.g. 'You used the word 'queer' when describing the last witness ...'

(b) Explain the effect this has on you because this is a fact.

'I think 'queer' is an unfortunate word to use, especially in the court setting. I think it makes it seem as if gay people are not normal, not equal and somehow valued differently. It's just my own view.'

(c) State what changes you'd like to make.

'I'd be a lot more comfortable if you used the word 'gay'.

(d) Explain the advantage of the change and use it?

' I think you'll find that it's more acceptable generally and in the court setting it doesn't set apart from others in the same way. He did describe the defendant as his boyfriend so yes, I agree with you, I think he is gay.'

4.8.2. Using enquiry

This may be the more appropriate method if generalisations are being made. It involves asking the speaker questions to clarify exactly what has led him to the particular view expressed. The questions would need to be asked respectfully rather than as an interrogation.

Example:

'Stealing cars is a way of life on that estate - they're all at it'.

What makes you say that?
How can you be sure?
What evidence is there?

4.8.3.   Repeating back

Simply repeating the comment back in a tone of mild surprise to check that it has been heard correctly can be quite sufficient, with a pause to allow for an immediate withdrawal. The message that a comment is not acceptable is conveyed more through tone and body language than by making any comment whatsoever. This strategy can be very effective and far easier than engaging in discussion. From the point of view of the maker of the statement, he may genuinely wish that he had not made the remark and this option allows the opportunity to make a short apology and move on quickly.

4.9.   The Human Rights Act 1998

4.9.1.   Introduction

The Act encapsulates the rights and freedoms of the European Convention on Human Rights and Freedoms agreed in 1950, and brings them into our domestic law, along with the case law which has built up under the Convention. Domestic courts must take into account the judgements, decisions, declarations and opinions of the European Court of Human Rights based in Strasbourg. Whilst this is a potentially complex topic area, the reality is that only three Convention Articles tend to be quoted in the Magistrates' Court and the issues are relatively straightforward. Whilst points are sometimes taken in the spirit of 'human rights', the detail is often found in other legislation or case law. The relevant Articles are discussed below, along with the associated legal provisions which also relate to the points discussed.

*   Article 6 - the right to a fair trial and specific provisions in relation to criminal matters
*   Article 5 - the right to liberty
*   Article 8 - the right to respect for private and family life.

4.9.2.   Article 6 - The right to a fair trial

Everyone is entitled to a fair and public hearing within a reasonable time by an independent and impartial tribunal established by law. The judgement shall be pronounced publicly unless exceptions apply.

(a) Hearing by an 'independent and impartial tribunal.

So far as independence is concerned, in the United Kingdom we have a separation of power between the legislature, the executive and the judiciary. So far as impartiality is concerned, this is covered by statute law and by case law which goes back to 1924, stating;

'It is not merely of some importance but is of fundamental importance that justice should not only be done but should manifestly and undoubtedly be seen to be done."

The situations below indicate when a magistrate may not be regarded as being 'impartial' and they should not therefore adjudicate in a particular case:

- Members of a local authority must not sit on any cases brought by or against the authority, or by way of an appeal from a decision of the authority or an officer of the authority.

- Magistrates who have dealt with a bail application and considered previous convictions must not sit on a trial of the same defendant in the same proceedings. Similarly magistrates sitting on a trial who are aware of previous convictions through dealing with a legal aid application in the same proceedings should not sit.

- If previous convictions become known during the course of a trial – a trial before a fresh bench will be usually be required. Disclosure of other allegations or future trials is not of itself a basis for disqualification.

- If a magistrate is a party to a cause, or has a relevant interest in the subject matter. Therefore a magistrate who has a direct pecuniary interest, however small, or a proprietary interest in the outcome of the case is sitting as a 'judge in his own cause' and is disqualified.

- A magistrate should not sit on a case if there is 'apparent bias'. The test to be applied is, having ascertained all the circumstances which have a bearing on the suggestion that the magistrate was biased, would those circumstances lead a fair-minded and informed observer to conclude that there was a real possibility that the tribunal was biased. Bias means that the magistrate might unfairly regard with favour or disfavour the case of a party to the issue under consideration. If there are legitimate reasons to fear impartiality, a magistrate must withdraw. An objection cannot be based on religion, ethnic origin, gender, age, class or sexual orientation. Similarly, an objection could not ordinarily be made on the basis of social or employment background or that of his family; previous political associations, or membership of social, sporting or charitable bodies. In borderline cases, disclosure should be made to enable parties to make submissions whether the magistrate should withdraw.

- The Lord Chancellor has issued guidance to local advisory committees as to various situations which may require care in the selection process e.g. applicants who are related to local serving police officers.

Whenever a magistrate knows that there could be an objection to his sitting on the case, he should let the chairman know so that the matter can be brought to the attention of the parties with the offer of withdrawing from the case. Arguably the withdrawal should take place by remaining in view of the parties by moving well away from the bench or sitting in the well of the court. The difficulty of simply going into the retiring room is that the bench may subsequently wish to retire and discuss the case.

(b) Judgement to be 'pronounced publicly' and reporting

There is a general obligation on the court to give reasons for judgements in the spirit of a fair trial so that both the defendant and the public know the basis of the decision. There is also a specific statutory requirement to give reasons in certain situations in any event e.g. upon refusal of bail, imposition of custody, when refusing to order compensation, when finding special reasons for not endorsing a licence.

The test for adequacy of reasons is whether a person with notice of all the facts and representations made to the court would be able to understand the basis of the decision including the conclusions reached by the court on disputed facts or contentious submissions.

The compilation of reasons is discussed at 2.5 (verdict) and 2.7 (sentence).

The Press may attend the adult court and may report freely on what they hear unless legal exceptions apply or the court makes restrictions. The principal exception is in both youth and family courts where reporting is generally prohibited as a starting point. In the adult court, the starting point is full publicity unless one of the exceptions below applies and an order is made to restrict publicity:

(i)   Children and young people - adult court. This is the most often used statutory restriction on Press coverage:

'The court may direct that no report shall reveal the name, address or school, or include any particulars calculated to lead to the identification of a child or young person concerned in the proceedings. This may be either as being the person by or against or in respect of whom the proceedings are being taken, or as a being a witness therein' (s.39 Children and Young Persons Act 1933). Publication in contravention of such a direction carries a level 5 fine.

There must be reasons to outweigh the legitimate interests of the public in receiving fair reports of the proceedings and knowing the identity of those in the community who have been guilty of criminal conduct. Publicity must never be regarded as being part of the punishment.

Examples of restrictions on identification:

• *Child victims of sex offences.*

• *The child of parents who are convicted for failing to send the child to school.*

• *An application for an Anti Social Behaviour Order (ASBO) against a young person in the adult court. (As an ASBO is a civil application it cannot be heard in the youth court, as compared to a bolt-on order to a criminal penalty which is heard in the youth court).*

So far as ASBOs are concerned, it is interesting that since January 2004, the usual bar on publicity in youth court proceedings does not apply automatically to a bolt-on ASBO in youth court in criminal proceedings.

Various matters must be considered before making a publicity restriction order. In considering an ASBO application, the court might consider such matters as:

• Does the local community need to know who the order is made against and what the actual conditions are, so that they can report any breaches to the police?

- Is the order of little real benefit to the victims of the behaviour unless it is well publicised?
- Are the risks of publicity for the defendant proportionate to the need to protect others?
- Should there be a Press restriction whilst a disputed youth ASBO case is heard because it may ultimately be dismissed?
- Should the restriction be reconsidered if the case is found proved so that details can be published?

(ii)   Allegations of rape and other sexual offences, where, generally no material should be published or broadcast to identify the victim.

(iii)   Prohibition of names or matters as appear to the court to be necessary. This is rare.

(iv)   Postponement of publication for a period as the court thinks necessary to avoid a substantial risk of prejudice to the administration of justice.

(v)   Restrictions on committal for trial proceedings where there is an application to dismiss the case. Publicity is limited to identifying the people concerned, the offence being inquired into and the decision, unless restrictions are lifted.

(vi)   Fraud cases in relation to applications to the Crown Court for dismissal of the charge and preparatory hearings.

Submissions should always be sought from the parties and the Press if the court intends to exclude the Press or restrict reporting in any way. The general criteria will always be whether it is in the interests of justice to restrict the information reaching the public or not. The precise terms of the restriction must be announced - normally it is names and anything which could lead to the identity being discovered - be clear in open court and in written form - because 'something' is likely to be reported. (See Adult Court Bench Book 1-7)

4.9.3.   Article 6 - specific provisions relating to criminal offences.

Some provisions of Article 6 apply only to criminal proceedings in order to give greater protection than in civil proceedings. 'Criminal' proceedings for these purposes extends to cases where the party could face severe penalties e.g. custody, even though they would not normally be classed as criminal proceedings e.g. non-payment of fines/community charge, so that the rights below apply to those proceedings.

- *Everyone charged with a criminal offence is presumed innocent until proved guilty according to law.*

And the rights:

- *To be informed promptly and in a language which he understands, the nature and cause of the accusation against him.*
- *To defend himself in person or through legal assistance of his own choosing, or have free legal assistance if of insufficient means and the interests of justice so require.*
- *To time (and confidential) facilities to prepare defence.*
- *To examine or have examined witnesses against him and to obtain the attendance and examination of witnesses on his behalf under the same conditions as witnesses against him.*
- *To have the free assistance of an interpreter if he cannot understand or speak the language used in court. (The court is under an obligation to provide an interpreter to the defendant when this is necessary, without any cost to the defendant regardless of his means).*

(a) Equality of arms

The principle of 'equality of arms' underpins Article 6 as one feature of the concept of a fair trial. Essentially this means ensuring that one party is not placed at a procedural disadvantage as against the other party and there is equality in all aspects e.g. receiving advance disclosure about the case. This also extends to very simple principles.

Example:

> *A professional prosecutor is unlikely to have any diffidence at all in letting the court know if he cannot hear what the defendant or a witness is saying. A defendant should equally be able to hear what the prosecutor is saying about the case so that he may participate effectively. However he is likely to be far more reticent or may well feel that 'this is how it is done' if the prosecutor directs a quiet, fast outline for the magistrates' ears alone.*

> *Equality of arms requires the bench to ensure that both parties can equally hear exactly what is said. Move the defendant; move the prosecutor; ask him to 'shout up and slow down'; look and see whether the defendant is responding; make it clear that it is 'o.k.' to say "I can't hear' especially from behind the glass screen in the dock.*

(b) Trial in absence

Clearly it is important to take every step to ensure that the defendant is allowed to participate effectively in the case and presence at the trial is the ideal, but this is not an absolute right. A denial would otherwise be an easy way to avoid the case proceeding - simply never attend court!   An amendment to the Trials in Absence Direction was handed down by the Lord Chief Justice in January 2004 and reads as follows:

'A defendant has a right, in general, to be present and to be represented at his trial. However, a defendant may choose not to exercise those rights by voluntarily absenting himself and failing to instruct his lawyers adequately so that they can represent him. In the case of proceedings before the Magistrates' Court, there is an express statutory power to hear trials in the defendant's absence (s.11 Magistrates' Courts Act 1980). In such circumstances, the court has discretion whether the trial should take place in his/her absence.

The court must exercise its discretion to proceed in the absence of the defendant with the utmost care and caution. The overriding concern must be to ensure that such a trial is as fair as circumstances permit and leads to a just outcome.

Due regard should be had to the judgement of Lord Bingham in R v. Jones 2003 in which Lord Bingham identified circumstances to be taken into account before proceeding, which include:

* The conduct of the defendant
* The disadvantage to the defendant
* Public interest
* The effect of the delay
* Whether the attendance of the defendant could be secured at a later hearing
* Seriousness of the offence and likely outcome if the defendant is found guilty

In the case of summary proceedings the fact there can be an appeal that is a complete rehearing is also relevant, as is the power to re-open the case ....'

As a simple test, it is suggested that if the grounds exist for a warrant without bail to be issued, i.e. there is no acceptable reason for absence, then the grounds exist for the case to go ahead in absence.

4.9.4.   The right to liberty - Article 5

(1) Everyone has the right to liberty and security of person. No one shall be deprived of his liberty save in the following cases and in accordance with a procedure prescribed by law;
(a) the lawful detention of a person after conviction by a competent court
(b) lawful arrest or detention of a person for non-compliance with the lawful order of a court or in order to secure the fulfilment of any obligation prescribed by law
(c) the lawful arrest or detention of a person effected for the purpose of bringing him before the competent legal authority on reasonable suspicion of having committed an offence or when it is reasonably considered necessary to prevent his committing an offence or is fleeing after having done so.

Other provisions deal with educational supervision, illness and unauthorised entry into the country.

(2) Everyone who is arrested shall be informed promptly in a language which he understands, of the reasons for his arrest and of any charge against him.

(3) Everyone ... shall be brought before a judge or other officer authorised by law to exercise judicial power and shall be entitled to trial within a reasonable time or to release pending trial unless there are relevant and sufficient grounds to justify detention. Release may be conditioned by guarantees to appear for trial.

The police operate under strict statutory Codes of Practice which cover the whole interaction with a defendant from the point of arrest and the courts must comply with statutory custody time limit provisions, so our national law is compliant with the Convention. Additionally the Bail Act provisions begin with a right to unconditional bail unless there are 'relevant and sufficient grounds'.

4.9.5.   The right to respect for private and family life - Article 8

(1) Everyone has the right to respect for his private and family life, his home and his correspondence.
(2) There shall be no interference by a public authority with the exercise of this right except such as is in accordance the law and is necessary in a democratic society and in the interests of national security, public safety or the economic well-being of the country, for the prevention

175

of disorder or crime, for the protection of health and morals, or for the _protection of the rights and freedoms of others._

The key words are underlined, and basically we have the right to do as we please in our private lives but we may be restricted in this so far to whatever extent is necessary to prevent disorder and crime or to protect the rights/freedoms of others.

This right 'engages' with virtually every bail condition and with every sentence of the court. There will almost inevitably be some interference with the defendant's private life, from having to remain indoors under a curfew to the ultimate restriction on liberty with a custodial sentence. From being excluded from a particular area under an ASBO through to having to spend money on a fine instead of private life.

There are 3 requirements to consider whenever imposing a restriction on a qualified right:

(1) Is it lawful? Usually no problem at all as bail restrictions and sentences all derive from clear, accessible legal criteria and limitations.
(2) Does it pursue one of the legitimate aims? Usually no problem at all as bail restrictions and sentencing will normally be imposed in order to prevent disorder/crime, or protect the rights and freedoms of others - the very reasons for being able to restrict the right.
(3) Is it no more than is necessary in a democratic society? This is the 'one to watch'. The nature of the restriction must be proportionate to the problem and not a 'sledgehammer to crack a nut'. For example it may well be lawful and legitimate to impose a 6 month curfew order on a defendant found guilty of drunk and disorderly, but it would be wholly disproportionate to the charge.

Example:

R v. Gwent Magistrates' Court ex parte Katrina Stokes 2001

Single mother with 3 children under 16, owing £455 fine/compensation and with an income of £174 per week, committed to prison for 12 days.

On appeal, Lord Justice Brooke said 'In cases of this kind decided today, when a court concerned with fines enforcement is contemplating making an order which would separate completely a mother from her young children and send her to prison for a period of time with unknown consequences of the effect of that order on her young children it must take into account the need for proportionality. It must ask itself, given the

176

seriousness of the intervention it is minded to make in terms of taking a mother away from her young children and imprisoning her: Is the proposed interference with the children's right to respect for their family life proportionate to the need which makes it legitimate? The committal was quashed and the magistrates were invited to consider instead a money payment supervision order.

See Adult Court Bench Book 1.1. Human Rights - A structured approach.

Fair treatment and human rights

Two concluding comments:
1. 'Just as justice needs to be 'seen to be done' so fairness must be 'seen to be demonstrated' in order to generate trust. (Stephen Lawrence Inquiry Report, para 46).
2. The Human Rights Act gives rights and freedoms to the defendant and equally to the victims who require protection from further harm.

CHAPTER 5
Personal development and working as a member of a team

This chapter focuses upon personal responsibility and development in order to be an effective team member both in the courtroom and in the retiring room. Effective teamwork rests very much upon the chairman and a fuller picture of court preparation and management of the proceedings is covered in chapter 6 which is recommended reading for wingers as well as chairmen.

5.1.　The basic reference tools

So far as keeping up to date generally, the Magistrates' Association publishes 'The Magistrate' journal on a monthly basis and it covers latest information. There are also locally published bulletins and handouts through the court and probation service. The media usually gives a view on new legislation and current issues (see chapter 7). Additionally there are several useful web-sites listed in the bibliography.

The principle reference book for court is the Adult Court Bench Book which is produced for every magistrate by the Judicial Studies Board and contains:

- Checklists with a structured approach to all key decisions e.g. bail, sentencing
- National Mode of Trial Guidelines
- Magistrates' Court Sentencing Guidelines and
- Pronouncements

It is well worth becoming familiar with the lay out of the Bench Book so that reference can be made quickly in court to all relevant aspects. Normally the chairmen will allocate only one reference task to each winger.

Examples:

- *Domestic burglary*

Reference:
✓ *Sentencing Guidelines: p.18 entry point is committal to Crown Court*

- ✓ Mode of Trial Guidelines: 2-5 information as to factors which would suggest committal to Crown Court
- ✓ Pronouncement: 3-37 committal for sentence, and 3-25 remand in custody.

- Driving with excess alcohol

Reference:
- ✓ Checklist: Sentencing: p. 1-35
- ✓ Sentencing Guidelines: p.70 entry point penalty determined by level of alcohol (pink section for traffic cases)
- ✓ Pronouncements: 3-50 fine, and 3-54 disqualification, and 3-57 attendance on drink driver rehabilitation course
- ✓ Reasons: p.103 of the Sentencing Guidelines (blue section for helpful information. Reasons forms are usually available as separate sheets for completion in court).

Another crucial reference tool is the court register and it is helpful to be fully aware of how to identify all the information it provides, e.g. the nature of any plea entered previously, number of previous listings.

The chairman will usually wish to have a note of the following:

- Names of legal adviser, usher, prosecutor(s), and duty probation officer.
- Likely adjournment dates e.g. any slots within the next 7 days for community sentence reports; 3 weeks for full pre-sentence reports; the next pre-trial review date.
- Disqualification reduction dates for defendants who are convicted of drink/driving offences and opt to attend the rehabilitation course.

Also see 6.1. - pre-court briefing.

5.2.   Effective participation and communication in court

5.2.1.   Listening and body language

Listening - the most important skill in court. Listening is not about being able to hear. It is much more. Can you repeat back what someone has just said? You heard it surely, but did you listen? Particularly in long proceedings, or in 'standard proceedings', listening requires real determination and conscious effort. In court, every word can make a difference to the outcome and everyone who speaks is well aware of this and they are desperately looking to see that the bench are listening. The only way for a speaker to assess that this is happening is to look for the outward signs. They need to be there - attentive eye contact, nodding (not nodding off!), leaning forward, making notes and looking up again, jotting down a question, and demonstrating that you are referring to it later. Looking away from someone who is speaking, or looking down for lengthy periods is tantamount to saying 'not listening - I've already made my decision'.

Just as facial expression and purposefully leaning forward can demonstrate concentration and interest, the very opposite can equally be conveyed. Slumping, hand over face, frowning, doodling and glazed eyes can give the impression of boredom, lack of interest, disbelief in what is being said and 'switching off'.

Head shaking whilst discussing matters on the bench should be avoided at all costs. It is a massive and open statement which says 'whatever is said, I don't agree with it' - not good for a team decision which is being watched very carefully by the very person who is going to be affected by it. Similarly, it is easy to smile at some people in court e.g. solicitors who we happen to socialise with outside of court, as opposed to those who we do not know. Consider what this may say to the defendant, when the prosecutor gets a friendly smile and greeting at the start of the court whilst his solicitor from out of town is treated with expressionless formality. Smiles and expressions which can be construed as friendship are excluding behaviours towards other people - acts which can say 'we're on the same side'. Being polite is fine, but being friendly can shout out bias. From the bench - smile at everyone, or no one!

5.2.2. As a note-taker

What is the legal responsibility of a magistrate to take a note? None. The legal adviser does have some specific statutory responsibility to take notes, e.g. of any full argument for bail and also 'the substance' of oral evidence in family proceedings. However, the Practice Direction 2002 states that:

'At any time, justices are entitled to receive advice to assist them in discharging their responsibilities. If they are in any doubt as to the evidence which has been given, they should seek the aid of their legal adviser, <u>referring to his/her notes</u> as appropriate'.

This carries the inference and expectation that the legal adviser will take some notes in order to perform their responsibilities. However, there are practical advantage for the magistrates to take their own notes.

•   Useful to refer and check back in the decision-making process.
•   Assists in drawing up reasons for a decision.
•   Assists if the magistrates are asked to state a case for appeal.

- Assists an individual to concentrate on the case.
- Creates a visual impression of careful interest being taken - remember to keep looking up and making eye contact to demonstrate that the writing relates to the case, rather than a shopping list!

Avoid trying to take a verbatim note except where key issues are being covered, e.g. statements as to what was said, descriptions. Be ready to alert the chairman to ask witnesses or advocates to slow down.

In the trial scenario there is a school of thought that notes should not be taken during the opening and closing speeches, but only of the actual sworn evidence. This is to emphasise that the magistrates are not considering mere representations as evidence.

Fortunately it is becoming more common for advocates to disclose the basis of the 'not guilty' plea at the pre-trial review and/or at the outset of the case. This alerts the bench to the relevant key issues e.g. mistaken identity, self-defence, and these matters can be noted more fully and underlined for easy reference.

When taking notes it is helpful to split the notes into the structured headings in readiness for the decision making process under the headings. The structures coincidentally flow in the same way as the information will be presented. For example, on a guilty plea, the prosecution will focus upon the offence, and the defence will focus predominantly upon the offender. Quotations of remarks made are likely to be significant features of evidence and are worth noting, both on sentence and more particularly, on trial. Questions can be noted as they occur.

Example :

An offence of common assault.

- *Aggravating features*
Laid in wait outside victim's home at 2am - planned
'I've got something for you' – 2 blows to the face – clenched fist
Black eye
Defendant on bail - trial next month for driving over prescribed limit
Record – assault last year – compensation £250 ordered (question - is it paid?)

- Mitigating features

Provocation – victim flirting with defendant's girlfriend

Both parties in drink – both asked to leave club

- Offender mitigation

Immediate admission to police – arrested at home at 4am

Guilty plea today – 1st appearance 3 days after incident

21 years old – single – full-time work as trainee supermarket manager

Has signed on for 'drink control' course (<u>question - has he attended yet?</u>)

- Objectives

Punishment - money last time - no effect

Rehabilitation - seems motivated to address drink problem

Prevention - relationship - likely to recur? - bind over?

- Options

Entry point - common assault – community.

Black eye - compensation £125.

£180 per week net income. Flat provided. No debts.

Community Rehabilitation Order? – ETS? ASRO?

Add bind over?

In an application for a remand in custody, it would be helpful to at least make a note of the exception(s) and reason(s) put forward to justify those exceptions. Again, noting any questions to be raised through the chairman.

Example:

A bail application - offence of aggravated taking motor vehicle without owner's consent.

- Prosecution
- ✓ Fail surrender to bail

2 fail bail convictions in last 12 months (no need to record details as the previous convictions will be taken into the retiring room for reference).

- ✓ Nature and gravity of offence/probable sentence, and strength evidence

Caught on CCTV as he drove out of the car park and crashed into oncoming vehicle.

- Defence

12 separate convictions in last 3 years - only 2 failures to attend - only fined so clearly mitigation accepted - otherwise good record of attendance.
Full co-operation with police - has pleaded guilty immediately.
Lives with sister. Job to start on Monday.

- Questions

Have probation provided bail information that the address is available and sister is happy for him to return? (Different to address given on charge!)
Any evidence about the job - previous work history - stability?

So far as means information is concerned, a standard means form should ideally be completed by all defendants prior to coming into court (April 2004). However, there are various reasons why this might not have happened and it is a key task for one of the wingers to complete the information so that there is a consistency of detail either given or sought in court.

Failure to make notes is not a sign of incompetence. Some magistrates have excellent memories and the appraiser will see that they are contributing fully in the decision-making process and have clearly missed nothing. Most of us simply do not have that facility!

5.2.3. Questions and prompting in court

Every member of the bench must feel that they have a full picture of the circumstances necessary to make an informed and effective decision. This is a personal judicial responsibility. The example notes above indicate how questions and 'gaps' may be identified as the advocates, defendant and witnesses address the court. When the chairman asks whether there are any questions it is helpful to be ready with succinct wording and if necessary, a clear reason why the information is needed if this is queried.

Both the prosecution and defence have their own agenda. The prosecution will emphasise the offence seriousness. The defence will emphasise the offender mitigation. Somewhere in the midst of this, the bench have to look at the balancing exercise from the eyes of the victim and the community. The Press are potentially poised to report the facts which are emphasised the most - this is the report on which the bench is likely to be judged by the public. Always imagine the headline of 'What the victim thinks of the decision!' Were sufficient questions raised in open court to understand the victim's standpoint, so that this can be included as appropriate in the reasons and assist in really explaining why the decision was reached.

Example:

Prosecutor ' The police have had numerous complaints about disorderly behaviour in this area …..'

This indicates that there is a problem in the area and people will be very interested in the outcome of the case and may well be hoping for a strong deterrent penalty. The questions in open court must probe carefully the actual involvement of the defendant on the day and on the offence before the court. He cannot be sentenced for ongoing problems which may have no connection with him whatsoever. The community needs to know the 'full story' about this defendant and the actual evidence against him.

Questions by the bench:

So far as previous incidents in the area are concerned, is there any evidence that this defendant was involved?
You say that the disturbance began at 9 p.m. - what time did the police become aware of D's presence?
Please summarise now for us exactly what D actually did and said? (Summary is for the bench and for the public e.g. if there is a protracted and serious incident but D is on the periphery).

Similarly the bench have the right to take the initiative in pursuing a number of ancillary penalties and questions from the bench will often be necessary to identify whether they are appropriate or not. No one else will do it. The prosecutor is keen to obtain a conviction and a sentence which reflects the seriousness of the case - the actual cocktail is not within the prosecutor's domain. The defence solicitor is keen to ensure the minimum interference with his client's liberty. It would be an unusual defence mitigation to introduce the notion of additional penalties, over and above the recommended community order.

To suggest that a client should properly pay compensation for the terror caused to the victim, even though there has been no formal claim from the prosecutor? To open up the fact that a preventative measure should certainly be attached as it is quite clear from the remarks made that there could well be repetition. To gratuitously advise that an anti-social behaviour order would be amply justified, but perhaps a bind over would be adequate - in a substantial sum of course…? Unlikely! So who is going to identify whether ancillary penalties are appropriate? This is an avenue of questioning and clarification which falls to the bench.

The general approach about questions from the bench is that the court may ask anything in bail proceedings, fine default proceedings and after conviction with two provisos. It must be relevant to the outcome, and it must not amount to implication of another offence, e.g. Did you steal because you are a drug user? Do you have any more cases in the pipeline? In trial proceedings, any questions must simply be as clarification of points already taken, and the bench must not enter the arena - even if there is a glaring question which would surely convict or acquit the defendant!

Prompting may be necessary in various situations. These range from picking up omissions in pronouncements by writing a note or nudging (gently!) to say 'and costs'. It may be a prompt about procedure e.g. reminder to allow re-examination of a witness. It may arise from the role of being the eyes and ears of the bench. A good chairman will be engaged almost exclusively with the person addressing the court. It is helpful for a winger to point out that the probation officer has now returned to give a stand down report, that someone is drinking beer at the back of the court, that the legal adviser is having a coughing fit etc.

5.2.4. Discussion through a structured approach

Awareness and acknowledgement of the various checklists towards a structured approach is key to effective team discussion. The contribution can begin on the bench by turning to the relevant checklist in the Adult Court Bench Book e.g. bail, sentencing. Whilst the checklists can of course be referred to, the usual sentencing decisions simply rest upon the 4 'O's - the offence, the offender, the objectives and then the options. In the retiring room it is important to encourage others to use a structured approach. This means avoiding the temptation to join in any immediate judgements e.g. 'I think community punishment would be a good idea', or 'Perhaps we could let him out on bail but with stringent conditions.'

See also 2.2.8 bail structure and 2.7 sentencing structure.

5.3.   Effective participation and communication in the retiring room

5.3.1. Listening and body language

Again, listening and being seen to listen are key skills. A wide range of behaviours are obviously available in a discussion, beyond looking interested and engaged. Reflecting back and checking what the speaker has just said, questioning, and acknowledging every contribution either by nodding or commenting.

From an internal point of view, there is a need for a disciplined approach. A recognition that thought is faster than speech and it is easy to race ahead with our own assumptions, rather than continuing to listen at the speed of the spoken word - someone else's! Assumptions need to be checked out by questions. What exactly does the speaker mean? The worst assumption we can make is that we always 'know best' ourselves - the biggest brick wall of all.

Lean forward, uncross arms and legs, be open to what is being said, nod the information into the brain and not into mid-air, keep attentive eye contact with the speaker, stay with him to the end and save up any questions - the best practical tool to aid listening.

See also 6.9.2. and 6.9.3 for listening.

5.3.2.   Questioning

Asking questions of one sort or another accounts for at least 25% of most conversations. Formulating questions helps to make us listen and is the best demonstration that we are listening (or not). In the retiring room discussion it is essential to understand exactly what someone else is proposing, and more significantly why they are making that proposal. Getting alongside someone else's thoughts usually needs a few open questions and then some closed questions to clarify the finer detail.

Questions can be used for various purposes

Examples:

To check understanding e.g. 'So you think that a daytime curfew would stop him from shoplifting?'

To challenge e.g. 'But surely there are plenty of late night shops in that area?'

To seek views e.g. 'What about addressing the underlying drug problem instead?'

Questions can focus more directly on the problem. Simply saying 'I don't understand', whether in a probing or exasperated tone can bring forth a mere repetition of what has already been said - perhaps in a louder voice. Asking a question flatters the speaker because it demonstrates both listening and also interest in the viewpoint and allows another opportunity to re-phrase and try to sell an idea.

Questions demand answers, whereas statements can be politely ignored.

See 6.3.3 for discussion of the various types of questions and how they can be used.

5.3.3.   Assertiveness

Assertive behaviour is simply about believing that your views are equally as important as anyone else's. Not less important - this results in submissive behaviour. Not more important - this results in aggressive behaviour. We use all three behaviours, but generally it is the assertive behaviour which brings long-lasting positive outcomes and relationships flourish.

Where do the differences lie?

Assertive behaviour is about standing up for our own rights in a way that does not violate another person's rights. It is an honest, open and direct expression of a point of view which respects and 'takes on board' other viewpoints.

Submissive behaviour is about failing to stand up for our own rights in such a way that others can easily disregard them. This may be because thoughts, feelings or beliefs are expressed in an apologetic, cautious or self-effacing way or alternatively no view or feeling is expressed at all.

Aggressive behaviour is about standing up for our own rights in a way that we violate the rights of another person. Thoughts, feelings and beliefs are expressed in inappropriate ways - often in a patronising, bullying or hostile manner - even though they may very well be the 'right' thoughts. Being more experienced in a particular area can be a key for aggressive behaviour because we may well feel that our opinion is therefore more valuable and important. Assertive behaviour is about using our experience to draw people alongside by explaining the salient features - 'years of experience' are never required for any decision - it is the small, relevant snippets from those years which can usefully be shared.

Assertive statements are usually to the point and we take responsibility by using expressions such as 'I think', 'I believe'. We make clear what is opinion and what is fact, and ask questions to fully understand other viewpoints.

Submissive statements tend to ramble in an effort to try and justify, and 'I' statements are qualified with expressions such as 'well, it's only my opinion' or 'I don't have much experience of this'. Qualifying words are used such as 'maybe' and filler words such as 'sort of' or 'you know'. Phrases are used which indicate an ease in backing down such as 'it doesn't really matter', or 'well you two are agreed, so I'll leave it there'.

Aggressive statements tend to transfer personal opinion into facts, 'That will never work' rather than 'I don't think it will work'. The views of others are not canvassed or responded to, or they are met with expressions such as 'You cannot be serious'. In a retiring room this cannot be tolerated and the two other members of the bench have to re-establish an assertive discussion. Behaviour breeds behaviour and assertive behaviour is infectious because it makes good sense and will lead to a better outcome.

5.3.4.   Contributing to discussions with the legal adviser as appropriate.

Most chairmen prefer to act as the spokesperson to the legal adviser and it is usually easier to act as impartial adviser to the bench as a whole through one person. It also means that the chairman can take the matter through discussion of the facts with colleagues and then identify the areas on which 'the bench' require legal advice. Obviously there are times when the chairman will indicate that he is quite happy for wingers to ask additional questions or seek clarification directly.

Discussions with the legal adviser should be solely about the law, practice, procedure, penalties and structure and in the main should begin with 'we would like to know' from the chairman, rather than 'I would like to know' from a winger. Identifying the issues for the legal adviser is a team effort.

The legal adviser also has the responsibility to assist, where appropriate in the formulation of the reasons and the recording of the reasons. Provided that the chairman has led a structured decision-making process, the reasons will flow from the chairman's lead. Contribution to the decision-making therefore runs in tandem with contributing to the formulation of the reasons.

5.4.   Giving and receiving feedback and post-court review

Whilst some courts have always held post-court reviews, this will expand to all courts as a requirement under MNTI 2. It is a short, informal opportunity for feedback. One of the main criticisms of the appraisal process is that one magistrate simply receives feedback from one appraiser on one single sitting every three years. Many situations arise in the intervening period which should usefully be identified and addressed. The post-court review is about team discussion so that everyone benefits from a short informal feedback session. The big question basically is 'how do we think we did?' It is a 'we' assessment, rather than a 'you' assessment. The only place for 'you' comments is within the context of how the bench and legal adviser have worked together as individuals within the team, or if a magistrate invites comment on a particular aspect of their own performance.

There is no national, formal prescribed paperwork, but it is expected that any identified training needs will be conveyed to the Justices' Clerk or Training Manager. A note will help to ensure that this happens!

The focus of the review will ideally be identified in the pre-court briefing. It may be largely 'business based' upon new practices and new targets, and/or 'support based' to a new chairman/magistrate or an experienced chairman who is dealing with an unfamiliar procedure. The competence framework will always be relevant. Time is at a premium and there will be little support to generate a review which has a long list of topics. We are talking about a couple of focus points which are relevant to the court list and/or the individuals on the bench for the day which will take no more than 5-10 minutes either during a pause in the proceedings or at the end of the list. The potential for opening up communication and for general improvement is great. The MNTI 2 Handbook describes the spirit of the review as an 'open, frank and free exchange between the members of the bench and the legal adviser. Any feedback given should be balanced, objective, clear and specific'.

Constructive feedback is helpful. We rarely give meaningful compliments to each other - a vague 'well done' is uplifting for the day, but a few more words of detail will help to reinforce good practice because it is clear what exactly was 'well done'. By the same token, we rarely give meaningful negative feedback. It can be uncomfortable to criticise within a conversation and at the end of a court list, there is the assurance that the court has finally ended and the same team may not come together for a long time, so it is easier to walk away - until next time. The post-court review is a window to compliment each other and to identify problems and perhaps even find some solutions or refer them on as appropriate.

Feedback is the entitlement of all members of the bench and the legal advisers. No feedback = no learning. This is different to feedback on an appraisal which carries the notion of the appraiser taking a lead and reaching a conclusion about performance. Post-bench appraisal is not about anyone being more responsible than anyone else. It is about comment on a level playing field. Sharing personal feelings rather than questioning or judging. Recognising that this is the time to ask each other for suggestions rather than telling someone else what to do. There is no individual action plan except for actions which are taken on voluntarily - often the most effective. There are a few golden rules of feedback.

- Be specific and give reasons.

What exactly is being reinforced as good behaviour? The tighter the issues at the pre-court briefing, the easier to be specific later e.g. exactly how many enforcement options were attached to default cases and if not, why not. Give some evidence for every comment. Say how you feel because that is the main reason for taking the trouble to give feedback - there is a personal effect.

If a chairman is new to a particular situation, the necessary support should be identified at the pre-court briefing. Both the chairman and the wingers can expect feedback. Praise specifically - say why - and most important of all, do it.

Examples:

X *You were brilliant today. In fact we made an excellent team. Well done. Let's go.*

➡ *To the winger, 'Thank you for making the notes for discarding each of the fines options - very clear and easy to read - as you know it was my first default committal'.*

➡ *To the chairman, 'Although you said that you were nervous, it didn't show at all - very clear and authoritative, and I thought it was a good idea to ask the defaulter to repeat back the terms of the order and when he had to pay'.*

- Focus on the behaviour and not the person.
- Avoid starting the comment with 'you are'.
- Describe rather than judge.
- Avoid starting the comment with 'it was'.
- Own the opinion you are about to give.
➡ Start with 'I' think/saw/feel' because … (and I may well be wrong!)

Examples:

X *It was far too long a pronouncement and he just turned off.*
➡ *I saw the defendant turn away as you were speaking. I really don't think he was listening.*

X *You just ran the court with Bob. I could have been invisible.*
→ *I noticed that you always turn to Bob first on the bench and then faced me with the decision of the two of you. That would be the majority, so I felt excluded from any real involvement.*

- Allow for solutions before giving them.
- Encourage 'asking', rather than simply 'telling'.
- Lead the person to think he spotted the problem for himself and solved it for himself.
- Make 'asking for help and advice' ok,

We all make mistakes and we often recognise them immediately. It is more dignified to be given the opportunity to put things right ourselves without being told to, or reflect for ourselves on how we might approach a situation differently. To be given a ladder to climb out is welcome, and avoids the temptation to go into defensive mode. Questions often generate the admission and acknowledgement that help is needed, without losing face. Asking a colleague how they might tackle a situation, is very different to the colleague simply proffering advice or giving an unsolicited mini training session.

Examples:

I've said what I think. What do you think?
Do you always do it like that? How?
Would you do it differently another time?
Have you come across this situation before?
No. Well, I can share a similar experience I had if you think it would help?

- Reach a positive closure

As stated, this is not an appraisal and no one has responsibility to create an action plan or make any form of judgement on another person. Post-court reviews are about striving for general improvement in the way we behave - magistrates and legal adviser. Personalities cannot be changed. Behaviour can be changed but it is about someone choosing to do so and therefore seeing a good reason to do so. Not every piece of feedback will be eagerly taken on board and result in immediate transformation.

Once feedback is given, it has to have some sort of closure, so that everyone concerned is aware of what is going to happen as a result of the review. Even if the answer is 'nothing', then at least there can be an assurance of confidentiality and the incident is closed, e.g. if a sexist remark is challenged in the retiring room and the speaker acknowledges and withdraws the comment. This is distinct from the situation where there is a higher level of concern and the review can be used to check out the facts with everyone present and allow the opportunity for a response. One of the magistrates may well chose to refer the matter on - they would have done so, with or without a review, but at least the situation is clear. Where compliments are given, it may simply be a matter of recognising and applauding the actions so that they are valued and repeated.

Sometimes the bench may feel frustrated by the actions or omissions of another agency which have impacted on effective performance. Where there is a worrying trend, rather than an isolated matter, the cases may be identified specifically for the legal adviser to take forward the concern through the Clerk to the Justices, e.g. cases where CPS actions had not been completed during adjournment period.

Where concerns are recognised, it is just as important to receive feedback in a constructive manner as well as give it, in the spirit of general improvement. It may assist to 'get there first' and at the beginning of the court ask for feedback at the end on an area of uncertainty e.g. a first trial, an effort to increase volume when making pronouncements, giving more detail about the credit given for a guilty plea. Similarly at the end, it is more comfortable for colleagues to give feedback based upon an introduction by the person who recognises a problem e.g. losing patience with a difficult defendant.

- Receive feedback

When receiving feedback, clarify exactly what is being said and avoid moving quickly into a defensive stance. As stated above, the hope is that the need for change is recognised and resolved by the recipient. If not, the positive response to a negative comment is to ask for positive suggestions from colleagues. 'I'd welcome some suggestions on how to deal with that in future'. There is no signed contract required if the suggestion is not acceptable! End on a positive - at least agree to think about it. We usually do, whether we want to or not!

The clearest outcomes are when the team recognises a need for specific information and training. This can be conveyed to the Clerk to the Justices or Training Manager. For example, a first application for an Anti Social Behaviour Order reveals a need to understand the different types of evidence, the burden of proof, the standard of proof and some guidelines on publicity regarding child defendants.

See also 6.11 post-court review.

5.5.   Training, mentoring and appraisal

5.5.1.   Magistrates Courts Committee (MCC) →Judicial Studies Board (JSB)

The local Magistrates Courts Committee currently has responsibility for magistrates' training. The Committees will cease to exist on court unification in April 2005. The Judicial Studies Board (JSB) will adopt a strengthened role in relation to magistrates' training. The JSB already provides substantial guidance and training materials, including the Adult Court Bench Book which has been produced in partnership with the Justices Clerks Society, The Magistrates Association and the Senior District Judge. The JSB has been responsible for the design of the new training, appraisal and mentor scheme, MNTI 2 and is responsible for the monitoring and training under it. At a local level, the Bench Training and Development Committee deal with the management of the appraisal and mentor scheme (see below), with the Magistrates Courts Committee responsible for the training.

5.5.2.   Magistrates National Training Initiative (MNTI 2)

Magistrates' training has been based upon a competence structure and appraisal model since MNTI 1 was introduced in 1999. MNTI 2 replaces the previous competence framework, training and appraisal scheme (MNTI 1) with effect from April 2004 for new magistrates, and from April 2005 (at the latest) for existing magistrates. In 2001 the Auld Review recommended that MNTI 1 should be refined to provide: 'a less complex, weighted set of competences for magistrates, supported by clear national standards'.

At appraisal, there is a greater emphasis upon observed behaviour, rather than upon knowledge. There are now 3 competences relevant to adult court, and a 4th competence for the adult court chairman, each with specific elements, as follows:

Competence 1 - Managing yourself
1.1 Before the hearing: preparing yourself for your role in the judicial process
1.2 In the court room: conducting yourself effectively in the judicial process
1.3 Engaging in ongoing learning and development

Competence 2 - Working as a member of a team
2.1 Making an effective contribution to judicial decision making
2.2 Contributing to the work of the team

Competence 3 - Making judicial decisions
3.1 Using appropriate processes and structures to facilitate effective decision making (example below)
3.2 Making impartial decisions

Competence 4 - Managing judicial decision making
1.1 Working in partnership with the legal adviser to ensure the effectiveness of the court
1.2 Managing court proceedings using appropriate communication skills
1.3 Seeking and enhancing the contribution of colleagues in order to ensure effective decision making
1.4 Engaging in ongoing learning and development

Each element carries definition of performance criteria, knowledge and assessment guidance. The previous MNTI 1 did not carry agreed standards. An example appears below:

Competence 3 - Making judicial decisions
Element 3.1 Using appropriate processes and structures to facilitate effective decision making

Performance criteria	Assessment guidance	Knowledge	Assessment guidance
b. Sifting the relevant information from all that is available and clarifying it when necessary	Contributing relevant information to the discussion and identifying issues where clarification is needed. Using questions to or through the chairman or legal adviser to clarify information or raise issues that are directly relevant to the decision being made	The doctrine of precedent and the role of the higher courts' decisions. The different order of proceedings for civil and criminal proceedings and the standard and burden of proof applicable to each.	The difference between adversarial and inquisitorial proceedings. When the court should adopt an inquisitorial approach in gathering information. Presumptions (e.g. of innocence). Rights (e.g. to a fair trial). The fact that rules prescribe a different order of proceedings for civil and criminal cases. An understanding of the phrases, 'beyond reasonable doubt' and 'balance of probabilities'.

See Appendices 1 and 2 for summary of comeptences and references for MNTI 2, and Appendices 3 and 4 for MNTI 1. Permission was not given by the Judicial Studies Board to reproduce the full MNTI competence framework as an appendix - hence the summary. See Magistrates National Training Initiative published by the Judicial Studies Board for full detail.

5.5.3   Magistrates New Training Initiative (MNTI 2) - new magistrates from April 2004

The training scheme and the various stages are summarised below with the relevant minimum periods in brackets:

*   Introductory training (3 hours) - introductions to the organisation, the court-house and personnel; the judicial oath and arrangements for swearing in.
*   'Core' training (12 hours) - Key themes e.g. diversity issues: key knowledge e.g. sentencing: key skills e.g. team working. Optional workbook.
    And 3+ structured court observations recommended to include bail, trial and sentencing.

*   Begin sitting in court.

*   Mentored sittings (6 sittings in 12 - 18 months) - with a mentor who will advise, support, guide and interpret throughout the period, and also review following each of the mentored sittings.
*   'Consolidation' training (12 hours in 9 - 12 months) - review, re-visit and reinforce key knowledge and skills.
*   Visits (3 within 12 months) - adult remand prison, young offender institution and a probation office.
*   Appraisal (12 - 18 months) - review of individual performance by self-assessment, feedback from post-sitting reviews and appraisal.
*   'Continuation' training prior to appraisal (every 3 years following first appraisal).
*   Specialist panels - appraisal within the past 3 years before going on to train in any new role and an appraisal in the new role will take place following the training.
*   Chairmanship - 'should have been appraised on at least one further occasion following his first threshold appraisal'. In practice this will normally mean that the magistrate will have been sitting for 4 years if the 3 yearly appraisal pattern is followed. However it may be appropriate to conduct the two appraisals within a shorter time frame to ensure that there are sufficient chairmen coming through the system - this would be a matter for the local BTDC.

5.5.4.   MNTI 2 and existing magistrates as at April 2004

Dealing firstly with the similarities with MNTI 1. Again, there is a competence framework and assessment will continue to be based on observed evidence in court by appraisals which will continue to be conducted every 3 years. The role of the mentor and the progression of trainee chairmen remains primarily the same. The Bench Training and Development Committee will continue to manage the appraisal and mentoring process, and identify training needs.

The key differences are as follows:

*   The competences carry standards of performance and detail of the required knowledge base (see example above).
*   All magistrates will undertake 'continuation' training, of a minimum of 6 hours, every 3 years. The training should be within 6-9 months of the magistrates' next appraisal. It will include all core areas of decision-making, e.g. bail, sentence, and also, winger competences. This is distinct from 'update' training which will continue to be provided in response to changes in law and procedure.
*   Chairmen will attend 'chairmanship continuation' training, of a minimum of 6 hours, every 3 years. It will include core areas of decision-making, e.g. bail, sentence, and also, chairmanship competences.
*   Post-sitting reviews at the end of each court sitting to enable continual, informal review of performance.
*   Quality control of the appraisal process by some cross-bench appraisal (20%), or other approved process.
*   The first appraisal of new magistrates will take place within 12 -18 months, rather than within 2 years.
*   Mentored sittings are reduced from 8 -11 over 2 years, down to 6 sittings within 12 -18 months, and 3 of them may be conducted by a mentor who is not specifically assigned to the magistrate if necessary.
*   Trainee chairmen will take the chair on 6 appraised occasions following attendance on the basic chairmanship course, with the additional stipulations that between 2 and 6 different appraisers should be used, and 2 of the appraisals will be from the well. The BTDC will receive all 6 reports for consideration.

5.6. Self assessment and learning styles

5.6.1. Self assessment

The MNTI 2 scheme puts greater emphasis on individual magistrates taking responsibility for their own learning and development and undertaking regular self-assessment following a normal court sitting. In practical terms, the new magistrate will have the benefit in particular of the 6 mentored sittings, and all magistrates will have the benefit of post-court reviews, and appraisals at least every 3 years. Remember that all occasions are opportunities to ask for information or training. The most effective outcome of self assessment is when the magistrate asks the mentor/legal adviser/appraiser to provide information or take forward a suggested topic for training - these are always the most popular topics - magistrate-generated.

The competence framework is not intended simply as a reference prior to appraisal - it represents an ongoing set of standards to reach and maintain. Every court brings the potential to identify gaps in knowledge or areas of interest where more information will be useful. The Training Manager will usually be able to locate information or assistance in some shape or form.

5.6.2. Learning styles

The same learning aids are not necessarily the most effective for everyone and it is worth identifying what type of learner we are so that we can tap into the best sources for ourselves. There are four recognised learning styles - activists, reflectors, theorists and pragmatists.

✓ Activists

The philosophy of the activist is 'I'll try anything once'. They thrive on new challenges, and enjoy the 'here and now'. They tend to act first and think later.

✓ Reflectors

Their response to new information is 'I'd like time to think about this'. They will gather information first and consider all implications before reaching a conclusion. They are good listeners and observers of others and may need encouragement to get involved.

✓   Theorists

Their philosophy is 'If it's logical its good'. They think problems through in a logical way and feel uncomfortable with subjective judgements, lateral thinking and anything flippant.

✓   Pragmatists

Their philosophy is 'if it works it's good'. They search out new ideas, enjoy experiments and like to solve problems. They tend to be impatient with ruminating and open-ended discussions.

This is significant in two ways. About 35% of us fall into one single group, but of the remainder, only 2% possess attributes across the range. The advantage of the full range is that we would have facility to work methodically through the learning cycle of having an experience, reflecting upon it, drawing theoretical conclusions from it and then pragmatically deciding what changes to take forward. For 98% of us, this is an ideal which does not come naturally and we need to discipline ourselves to act - reflect - draw conclusions and then change accordingly if we are to learn. The post court review and supervised sittings for chairmen are based on this model.

By recognising what type of learner we are, we can pursue 'what comes naturally' in terms of choice of learning methods. The activist may well find it difficult to read and concentrate for lengthy periods, and may learn more from attending discussions and taking an active part in role plays and scenarios. The pragmatist will welcome workbooks, exercises and computer web sites, with real situations rather than unstructured activities. The reflector will be able to engage for long periods with a lecture or video and may feel uncomfortable with spontaneous role play. The theorist is perhaps best suited to reading a variety of materials to stimulate their own views.

Development should ideally touch on all of our senses - each reinforcing the other:

I hear and I forget
I see and I remember
I do and I understand

Training and development for a magistrate is about being equipped at all times to put justice into practice. The law changes on a weekly basis. New options become available. Court practices are constantly revised to create quicker and fairer outcomes.

There is only one advocate for the victim and the community and that person is not legally qualified - it is the magistrate. Current knowledge of key issues is essential to make the most of individuality and life experience in the retiring room. The legal adviser will advise so that the decision is legal, but a well-trained bench will make sure that the decision is also the best.

CHAPTER 6
Chairmanship and
Managing judicial decision making

Most of the chairmanship competences are dealt with in this chapter. They are covered as they arise in the court process, from the point of pre-court briefing through to the courtroom, to the retiring room, to making the pronouncement and then concluding with the post-court briefing. See Appendices 2 and 4 for full list of chairmanship competences and where they appear in the book.

The lynchpin of an efficient court relies upon creating an effective relationship with the legal adviser. It has to be a 'double act' so that between the two, every piece of information is made available to the bench, the defendant, the witnesses, the usher, the probation officer and the advocates. That is no small task, and it is impossible for the chairman and legal adviser to operate in isolation from each other and present a well-managed court. Co-operation and communication are vital to the smooth running of the court. See 1.6.8 for role of legal adviser.

6.1.   Pre-court briefing

6.1.1.   Content of the court list

This is something beyond the enquiry "Is it a heavy list? What time can we expect to finish?" It is the opportunity to be prepared for the types of case which the bench will face and the kind of information you will need to hand.

Examples:

(i)   *What type of list is it?*
        Largely arrest warrants and bail applications and then a trial.
(ii)   *Could you remind me if there are any new practices around bail -*
        it's a long time since I sat in a remand court.
        Yes, we had a Direction in January that the court should normally
        sentence any failure to surrender convictions immediately unless
        there is a good reason to adjourn to sentence with the original
        offence. The starting point is a community penalty.
(iii)   *Are there any multi-handed cases? How many people will be lined*
        up in court?

A 6-handed case which includes 2 youths who will be with parents - all separately represented.

Identifying the case on the court register in advance together with the names of the solicitors and noting which defendants are the youths.

(iv)	*Are there any cases with a lengthy history which need to be expedited?*

Yes, we have an application to adjourn a 2nd trial date.

Turn to case management enquiries in the Adult Bench Book as an aide memoire to make progress with directions if the case is adjourned.

(v)	*This is my first time in chairing a trial - I'd like to try and manage it, but will you jump in if I miss anything and give me some feedback at the end of the court?*

The pre-court briefing is also the opportunity for the legal adviser to inform the bench about new practices and options, and also, to identify any current issues which the court is attempting to address. This will provide a useful basis and focus for the post-court review.

Information may include, for instance:

✓	A new probation service programme and the relevant criteria
✓	New listing practices to expedite cases
✓	Using more community sentence stand-downs (specific sentence reports) rather than pre-sentence reports if appropriate
✓	Using enforcement measures on fine defaulters rather than excessive orders simply to carry on paying (latest figures?)

Pre-court - What are we doing today? Post-court - How did we do?

### 6.1.2.	Agreeing speaking roles with the legal adviser

This may vary between various partnerships, depending upon individual strengths and preferences. There is no legal requirement about who says what and when. This creates the danger of both the chairman and legal adviser speaking at once, or a defendant being faced with an intermittent barrage from both without any clear picture emerging about who is actually in charge of the court and making the decisions.

The 5 main areas for agreement are:

1. Who will identify and charge?

   If this is the legal adviser, it is helpful to ask the defendant to give his name and address 'to the magistrates' so that eye contact is directed to the bench from the beginning, and the defendant is asked to speak and interact immediately. (It is useful to ask for the address to be supplied, rather than simply checking the address details given at the time of charge!)

2. Who will put any breaches of conditional discharge to the defendant? Lest they be forgotten!

3. Who will explain the course of the proceedings to an unrepresented defendant?

   Whilst this may properly be delegated to the legal adviser, there is much to be said for the chairman dealing with this at least on guilty pleas. Some 'hand over' words from the legal adviser such as 'May the defendant be seated?' will make it clear that the legal adviser has completed all matters relating to charge. If the chairman explains what is to happen, it also demonstrates who is actually in charge of the court and lifts eye contact and interaction to the chairman and the bench, rather than to the legal adviser. It also avoids overlooking the fact that the defendant remains standing until an advocate interjects to ask for permission for him to be seated - let the chairman give that permission either before or after giving the explanation.

4. Who will draw out the mitigation?

5. Who will conduct the means enquiry?

Obviously this would not preclude the legal adviser or chairman asking supplementary questions to obtain a full picture. The one who is actively listening is more likely to identify the gaps than the one is asking.

6.1.3. Delegation and who is going to do what?

Delegation is a management skill and is more than simply 'asking someone else' to do a job. The chairman retains accountability. Any decision to delegate will therefore depend upon the ability and experience of the winger. The winger will naturally wish to do the job well and will appreciate the opportunity to either say 'no' or question exactly what is required. What exactly do you want them to do? As in any other setting, what does a 'good job' look like to you? Explain clearly to the winger.

Examples:
- *Turning to the Sentencing Guidelines – depending upon your personal preference, you may ask for this to be done whilst the defendant is being identified. Stress that it should not be done*

during any interchange between the bench and the defendant or defence solicitor and certainly never during a trial! Full attention must be observed from the well of the court.
- *Turning to the Pronouncements - this is particularly helpful when several different orders are being made, e.g. fine and disqualification.*
- *Assessment of net income figure and 'doing the maths' of tying this to the relevant band - especially when variations are involved e.g. speeding.*
- *Completing a draft checklist of fine default options in readiness for reasons to be drawn up for discarding each option if necessary – make sure that the winger is familiar with any local form and the requirements before delegating the task.*
- *Completing the areas of the reasons form as they are agreed.*

6.1.4. Practicalities on the day

Different types of list and different groups of 3 will usually call for some identification of how you will work together. Having identified that the list is essentially made up non-attendances on a TV licence list, it may be helpful to identify the norm penalty and then set the parameters for when this will apply before going into court. This will save checking with each winger on every case.

Wingers will welcome the invitation to prompt, and the chairman may wish to identify just how he would prefer to be alerted. Be ready for when it does happen though! 'I am grateful to my colleague for reminding me that we also agreed that you will pay £60 costs' is a more dignified and open acknowledgement than nudges and nods in mid-pronouncement. Keep the 'running commentary' (describing what is happening) going from start to finish - that is open process and open justice.

And finally, before going into court, note the names of the prosecutor, legal adviser, usher, court probation officer and the routine adjournment dates e.g. 3 weeks time for the reports cases.

6.2. Managing the proceedings in court

6.2.1. Opening the court proceedings

Although courts may have slightly different local practices, the most common starting point is that the bench will enter court at the court starting time, whether or not there is any work to proceed with. This demonstrates that the court is ready to proceed and enables the chairman to establish some authority, greet those present and openly make such enquiries as:

- Is there anything we can proceed with e.g. paperwork, assisting other courts?
- Who is bailed to attend at 10 a.m.?
- Have they attended? If not, this can be taken up with them when they do attend.
- Which solicitors are we waiting for? Do we know where they are? In practical terms it is impossible for solicitors to be in 2 courts at once, but as a matter of courtesy and list juggling it is critical information for the court to be given.

In liaison with the legal adviser it may then be preferable to either fix a time for return so that everyone is aware that there is a real expectation of making a start and at least re-assessing the difficulties, or alternatively, awaiting notification from the usher.

6.2.2. Authority and the 'running commentary'

This is simply about making sure that everyone in court, from the defendant to the usher to the members of the public, know exactly what is happening and who is running the court. Open justice is visible <u>and</u> audible. Management from the chair is far preferable to unexplained whisperings and shufflings which can seriously distract the proceedings and leave people confused about what is going on.

With the exception of a very small minority, most defendants wish to treat the court with appropriate respect. The difficulty is that they frequently do not know what is expected of them. Once in court, they are immediately in the spotlight and there is no time to 'get the feel of the situation' and take the 'cue from others'. 'Do I stand?' 'Do I sit?' Questions which they are bound to ask themselves. It is very helpful to say from the outset 'Please sit down, and then stand up when we ask you to speak to the bench'.

Examples:

- *Defendant pleads 'Not Guilty'. Remains standing. All is quiet except for the legal adviser making a prolonged whispered telephone call to someone. Who? The witnesses? Are they coming today? The police?*

So much better if the chairman says 'We are going to fix a date for the trial and the legal adviser is going to obtain some dates so that we can fix a date that is convenient to you and all the witnesses. This may take a few moments - do sit down'.

- *A case is proceeding. Probation officer arrives in court to conduct a stand down enquiry on the previous case. He does not know where the defendant is and what the enquiry is about. He asks the usher to identify the defendant, then has a conversation with the legal adviser to ascertain the reason, then interrupts the prosecutor to obtain the file and then tells the relevant defence solicitor how long he will take. Meanwhile another advocate is attempting to mitigate effectively in the current case. The bench is distracted by the inevitable noise and movement.*

So much better if the chairman finds a place to pause and says ' Mr. Advocate could I just interject briefly so that we can give you our full attention. Mr. Probation we have stood down the case of Mr. Defendant (point to him) to consider a community punishment order. Mr. CPS do you have the file for the probation officer? Thank you.
Now, Mr. Advocate you were saying ....'

6.2.3. Gathering information in court - effective questioning techniques

Whether the defendant is represented or not, and whether the case consists of dealing with an application, a trial or sentence, all 3 magistrates must be in full possession of the information they need, rather than simply the information which is volunteered from the floor of the court.

It is important to recognise that all 3 magistrates are on the information trail, albeit the questions will normally be asked by the chairman. The reality is that the chairman will often be absorbed with the defendant and advocates, and it is the wingers who will have the greater facility to observe, and process the information and be the 'eyes and ears' of the bench. The most important question in most cases is the genuine question to each winger, 'do you have any questions?' - is there anything else we need to know to make a fully informed decision?

Many wingers are anxious that their questions may be inappropriate or inadmissible and unfortunately it is very easy to destroy confidence in this important area. The basic approach is that virtually any questions may be asked on a bail application and after conviction, provided that they can be justified as being relevant to the decision. However, only 'clarifying' questions can be asked during a trial - nothing new can be brought into the arena. If the chairman feels concerned about the relevance or legality of a question, he might simply state in open court that he wishes to check whether a question can be raised with the legal adviser, who will be happy to advise - or re-phrase! It is well worth a few moments with a disappointed winger after court to explain the problem, possibly with the legal adviser present, so that there is some clarity and reassurance for the future.

Questions are wonderful tools to obtain information and also to show that the court is interested and listening attentively. Specific examples follow at section 6.3 in the context of dealing with an unrepresented guilty plea, but first, some general principles on types of questions and what they might achieve.

Question type	Purpose	Example	Suggested use
Open	Cannot be answered by a 'yes' or 'no'	What happened? Why did you do that? What do you pay out each week?	Start up of any interaction with an unrepresented defendant and in the retiring room
Closed	Aim is to get a 'yes' or 'no'	Are you sure that you will start work on Monday? Will you pay as ordered this time? Do you understand that you could go to prison if you don't?	'Need to know' critical features of decision-making. Flags up in simple terms stark realities. Asking and checking is always more effective to get messages across, than simply 'telling'.
Reflective	Mirrors back to encourage more.	So you say that you were not thinking straight at the time … and why was that …?	A listening/caring approach is likely to draw out helpful information.
Probing	Follow-up for more	Did you take out the bank loan after the fine was imposed? Why do you think a conditional discharge is appropriate?	Funnelling down from broad statements into critical information. Retiring room to clarify views.

Hypothetical	'What-ifs' to assess possibilities	What problems might you have if you were excluded from going into X street?	Where there is a range of possible outcomes which depend upon a range of scenarios.
Leading	Based on expected or anticipated answer	So you knew full well that the victim was in the house at the time? So you have had the money to pay the fine? So how much state benefit do you get?	Only in cross-examination to challenge the listener with the questioner's legitimate version of events. Never if genuinely gathering information - never lead with assumptions or stereotyping!
Multiples	Several questions rolled into one	Will you tell us about the incident and exactly what time it happened and what you saw?	Never. Pause after the first question for a response instead and avoid multiple interrogations

Example:

An argument of exceptional hardship to avoid a points disqualification.

- *What is your employment? (Open)*
- *You say that you need a licence to do your job, tell us more about what your job involves?(Reflective)*
- *How many times each week do you have to deliver cars? (Closed)*
- *Is this actually part of your job description?(Probing)*
- *Would it be possible for someone else to do the deliveries? (Hypothetical)*

Keep the questions short. Explain, if necessary why you need to know. The defendant may well misinterpret what or why you are asking and may be unnecessarily wary of giving the answer. Be ready to re-phrase if there is no helpful response.

Example:

A means enquiry.

- *Who lives with you?*
No response. Defendant may not wish to give names or relationships in open court.

Re-phrase:
- *We need to have a picture of your financial situation so that we can fix a fair fine. Do you have any dependants to support out of your income?*

6.3.   Dealing with the unrepresented defendant on a guilty plea

Assume that the legal adviser has identified the defendant and dealt with the formalities of identification, advance disclosure, charge/plea. The defendant does not wish to take advantage of legal representation or advice and the legal adviser then asks the chairman whether the defendant may be seated, i.e. he has completed his part. What next?

Most defendants desperately want 'to <u>do</u> the right thing at the right time' in court. The court can ensure that at least that concern is allayed and leave the defendant free to consider the crucial aspect of what he needs to <u>say</u> to the court.

If the agreement is for the chairman to take control, a suggested process is described below, which should ensure that both sides of the case are presented in as much detail as if a defence solicitor had been instructed.

6.3.1.   Explanation of procedure

A brief commentary is essential so that the defendant is able to fully understand who is who, and what is happening at each stage of the proceedings, and contribute effectively to a fair hearing.

Example:

'Mr. X, you may be seated now. The prosecutor for the Crown (show who you mean) will give the court an outline of the prosecution version of what happened. Listen carefully. Then you will have the same opportunity to tell us your version of what happened.

An important factor is to use the same words for each input e.g. 'version of what happened'. It does not create an even-handed appearance if the prosecution input is described as 'the prosecution facts' and the defendant's response is encouraged by the words 'and then we will hear your story'!

A comment such as 'same opportunity' as above, helps to underline parity, and also the expectation of similar air-time.

It may be appropriate to offer notepaper and a pen, but this should be considered with some care, particularly on a guilty plea. The legal adviser will have checked that any advance disclosure has been served. It may even be in the hands of the defendant at the time, and this should provide a satisfactory summary of what is to be said. It may be necessary to check that the defendant has actually had time to read the disclosure and has been able to do so. Any inference that note-taking is expected may create a feeling of disadvantage if it is not taken up for any reason. In unfamiliar circumstances note-taking is a challenge for most people.

The chairman and/or wingers should ensure that the bench takes notes so that particular points can be pursued as appropriate.

On a 'not guilty' plea, the trial procedure is set out in 6.3.6. and the bench should consider openly delegating responsibility to the legal adviser to assist with framing questions.

6.3.2. Gathering information and encouraging mitigation by open questioning

Ideally this should begin with some open questions which may be successful in obtaining information. It may assist to begin by setting the scene and demonstrating that the court is listening, fully engaged and is genuinely alongside the defendant in their mitigation.

Examples:

Now, Mr. X, we would like to hear your version of what happened. What did happen?

So Mrs. Y, it's last Monday morning at 10 a.m. and you are in XXX store. Please talk us slowly through exactly what happened.

What was happening in the pub just before the police arrived?

And what were you doing?

And then?

Why did you do that?

The 'big avoid' - *Would you like to tell us what happened?*
This is a closed question and the answer may well be 'no'.
Compounded by a second closed question, 'Are you sure?'!

6.3.3.   Encouragement to the defendant who is not engaging

Some further explanation may be necessary to deal with concerns such as 'dropping myself in it even more' and advice such as 'least said - best mended'.

Example:

'Mr. X, it's important for us to fully understand exactly what happened so that we can fix the most appropriate penalty for you. To do that, we need to hear both sides of this incident'.

'Mr. Y, we must disqualify you for at least 6 months because you have 12 penalty points now, <u>unless</u> you can convince us that you will suffer exceptional hardship, that is, that you will face problems which would be worse than normal for a disqualified driver. Before we sentence you, we need to know if you would have any serious difficulties without a licence'.

6.3.4.   Questioning on the key issues from the prosecution facts which are likely to affect your decision

It is important to jot down notes of the factors which are likely to aggravate, so that the defendant is given the opportunity to respond to them before they appear in the reasons as facts.

Example:

Chairman: 'Mr. X, the police officer says that he told you to go home 3 times and you simply ignored him - what can you tell us about that?'

Defendant: 'I was just so drunk I can't remember him asking me to do anything. If I'd been sober, I'd have gone straightaway. I just wish I had.'

The response may well satisfy the bench that this was not a deliberate lack of co-operation as it may at first appear, and that there is some remorse about the situation.

6.3.5. Means enquiry - questioning

Details of finances are required almost invariably, if only because there is usually an application for a contribution to costs. Additionally, it helps to provide a picture of the defendant's lifestyle and circumstances without appearing to be unnecessarily intrusive. The court needs to know whether/how the costs are to be paid and this depends upon the individual circumstances. So, always remember to obtain means information before retiring. A standard means form came into operation in April 2004. Many people are unable to complete such forms and the enquiry will be verbal and in court. It is an offence to fail to give details of income and outgoings on request and it is also an offence to give false information.

Example means enquiry:

- *Have you filled in a means enquiry form?*
Remember, the answer may be 'no' because of inability rather than defiance.
- *Explain why the bench needs to know e.g. because we are intending to impose a fine and/or costs.*
- *What is your income?*
- *How many people is that to support?*
Often there is no need to ask if 'norm benefit' figures are available on the bench.
- *How much do you pay for rent/mortgage/council tax (essential roof costs - if any)?*
- *What else do you pay out?*
An immediate detailed list of potential outgoings may well evoke a figure for every suggestion if that appears to be the expectation!
- *What is the situation with the previous fines? (outstanding total/payment rate/enforcement?)*
If the defendant is already in default the court must now impose an attachment of earnings or apply for an attachment of benefit at the imposition of a new fine, unless it is inappropriate or impractical (see 3.2.3).

Consider avoiding embarrassing and unnecessary questions:

- *Are you married? Does the children's father live with you?*

What do the personal relationships of the household matter? The only issue is how many people live on the income described and in a public court, any further detail is unnecessary.

- *How much is spent on beer/cigarettes/lottery/DVD player/Sky TV?*

Some people's luxuries are the necessities of others - we are a diverse society. Why should the court order a housebound smoker and beer drinker whose only entertainment is Sky TV to pay more per week than the person who chooses instead to spend his 'household norm' on good red wine within the food bill, leisure club subscription and live theatre. The fine surely comes first after 'normal family expenditure' in any event. We all have some ongoing awareness of how much is needed for essential day to day life and that amount should be protected - even though choices as to how a limited budget is spent will vary. The minutiae of how every pound happens to be prioritised is surely irrelevant and subjective judgement. The open question of 'what else do you pay out?' will glean the unusual expenses and debts, which may affect ability to pay.

6.3.6. Dealing with an unrepresented defendant on a 'not guilty' plea

Specimen script and procedure checklist for chairmen (see also 2.4):

1. EXPLAIN PROCEDURE TO DEFENDANT "The prosecutor (name?) will tell us about the case and will then call witnesses to give evidence. After each witness has given evidence, you will have the right to ask questions of the witness. After that, you have the right to give evidence and to call your witnesses. Finally, you can address the court before we retire to consider our decision.
Have you brought any witnesses. Names? The witnesses will have to wait outside the court until called, which is likely to be about .... (prosecutor's estimate). In the meantime the usher will show them where to wait.
Do you require a pen and paper to make notes?" (Seating with a table).

2. PROSECUTION OPENING SPEECH

3. LEGAL ADVISER WILL EXPLAIN THE IMPLICATIONS OF ANY STATEMENTS BEING READ OUT TO THE COURT

4. EXPLAIN PROCEDURE TO PROSECUTION WITNESSES
"The prosecutor (name) will ask questions first and then the defendant (name) may ask you questions. Please keep your voice up and please speak slowly because notes are being taken – keep an eye on the legal adviser's pen as you speak. Would you prefer to sit down as you give your evidence?"

5. EXAMINATION BY PROSECUTOR

6. EXPLAIN RIGHT TO CROSS-EXAMINATION TO DEFENDANT
"You will have the chance to state your own side of the case later. At this stage, you may ask the witness questions about anything he has said, especially if you disagree, or about anything he may have left out. We would like the legal adviser to help you to frame the questions if necessary."

7. RE-EXAMINATION BY PROSECUTOR

8. QUESTIONS BY THE BENCH – check with both wingers and ask through the chair

9. THANK WITNESSES FOR ATTENDING

10. CONSIDER WHETHER THERE IS A CASE TO ANSWER
- Is there any missing evidence required to prove an essential element? e.g. intention to permanently deprive the owner of the property on a theft allegation.
- Is the evidence so discredited as a result of the cross-examination or so manifestly unreliable that no reasonable tribunal could safely convict e.g. witnesses describe widely different circumstances and give different versions during their own evidence.

11. EXPLAIN RIGHTS TO DEFENDANT
"You can now make your defence to the charge. You do not have to say anything unless you wish to do so. However I must warn you that the court may draw its own conclusions and feel that you may have something to hide if you choose not to give evidence.

If you want to say anything in your defence, you must give evidence on oath, and afterwards answer questions put to you by the prosecutor. Again, if you do not answer any questions without good reason, then the court may draw its own conclusions.

Do you wish to give evidence or not?"

12. DEFENDANT'S EVIDENCE
- Legal adviser requested by the bench to assist in presenting relevant evidence in a logical sequence.
- Cross-examination by the prosecutor.
- Questions by the bench.

13. DEFENCE WITNESSES
- Explanation as for prosecution witnesses.
- Cross-examination by the prosecutor.
- Re-examination by the defendant.
- Questions by the bench.
- Thank the witnesses for attending.

14. DEFENDANT'S ADDRESS
"Now is your chance to summarise your case and draw to our attention any particular points which have been made in the evidence given."
- Prosecutor may reply on legal points and with leave may call rebuttal evidence if unforeseen evidence is put to the court.

15. RETIRE
- " We will retire now to consider the evidence. Would the legal adviser wish to advise us on any points of law before we retire?"
- " We expect to take at least half an hour and you may wish to go for a coffee, and let the usher know where you are so that we can call you back into court".
- " When we have reached our decision we will call for the legal adviser to assist us in drawing up our reasons. If we require him to join us for any other reason we will return to court first.

6.4 Case management - the inquisitorial approach - dealing with applications to adjourn

6.4.1. Questioning adjournment applications

The important point is that adjournments are granted by the court, and in granting an adjournment, justice can be delayed unnecessarily. This will have some effect on both the victim and the defendant - and potentially the wider community. Justice delayed is often justice denied.

Most questions from the chairman are likely to be of the closed variety in order to establish exactly what is happening to the case and ensure that there will be some specific progress in readiness for the next listing. The officers of the court will of course provide information to support, oppose or describe the application, but have they covered the full picture?

Adjournment applications are inquisitorial in nature which means that any question can be asked to obtain relevant information.

- *What is the reason for the application to adjourn?*
- *How many previous listings have there been?*

Beware of creating an impression that a 'first listing' will be a 'nod through' - adjournments should never be easy and should get progressively more difficult.

- *Has the defendant attended on each occasion?*
  A good bail record suggests that there is no attempt to evade justice. A bad bail record indicates a lack of co-operation and the potential for further bail risk and delay.
- *What was the anticipated action today?*
  This is where there is great reliance that the previous bench were VERY clear. A reason such as 'for enquiries', will hardly assist a robust line at the next hearing! What particular enquiries - what, with whom and by when?
- *What exactly is the problem?*
- *What steps have been taken to prepare for or resolve the problem described?*
  This question is regularly omitted. Few problems suddenly arise on the very day of the hearing and they were both foreseeable and avoidable.
- *Why can't it be resolved today by standing the case down?*
  A negative line of enquiry may be more helpful than simply asking whether it can be resolved - an easy answer to that question would simply be 'no, I'm sorry'.
- *If not – what is the realistic, minimal period for progress?*
  Realism is critical at this stage. 'The next available date in the diary' is likely to appear punitive rather than robust. Furthermore, it simply generates a reasonable excuse for non-compliance on the next occasion.

The views of the other party should always be sought. They are views, rather than a binding consent or agreement!

Every adjournment should carry a reasoned and clear description of what will happen on the next occasion.

Example:

We cannot go ahead today because ....
At the next hearing we expect ...
We are also making the following directions ... see 6.4.8
(Pronouncement p. 3.19)

6.4.2. Adjournment of a trial - background information

In terms of case management, the adjournment of a trial is one of the greatest problems, because of the wasted court time, the inconvenience to witnesses, and balancing the rights of the defendant and the victim. The national statistics on trial completion at 1st hearing does not present a satisfactory picture - about 1 in 3 trials actually go ahead.

Terminology first. There are 4 scenarios.

1   An *effective* trial proceeds to verdict. The best outcome.
2.   An *ineffective* trial is when expected progress is not made due to action by one of more of the prosecution, the defence or the court and a further listing for trial is required. The worst outcome.
3.   A *cracked* trial may occur when the defendant makes a late plea change or pleads guilty to an alternative or is bound over i.e. there is a 'result'. The shame is that this did not happen earlier, but at least there is a result.
4.   A *cracked* trial may alternatively occur if the prosecution either offers no evidence or ends the case because a witness is absent or has withdrawn or the defendant is found unfit to plead, i.e. no 'result'. There are a multitude of reasons why this will always happen in some cases.

The national 'ineffective' trial rate for July to September 2003 was 29.6% and the 'cracked' trial rate was 37.6% (22.6% of which had a 'result'). This leaves a mere 32.8% as being effective - around 1 trial in 3 is actually going ahead!

The focus is most heavily on 'ineffective' trials. The reason is simply that with effective case management they should be effective instead. Information must be shared; sensible directions must be made and complied with and sufficient time must be given to ensure that preparation is efficient. Occasionally there are bound to be problems. The Public Service Agreement target is to reduce ineffective trials in the Magistrates' Court to 23% by March 2006.

So how to tackle the problem? It is helpful for chairmen in particular to be familiar with the local paperwork completed at pre-trial review and also any local certificate of trial readiness so that there is an awareness of the issues covered and the information provided. This may well form the basis for decision on whether a trial actually proceeds or alternatively any subsequent directions.

A pre-trial review form will normally include:

- Details of which statements are agreed so that those witnesses need not attend.
- Number of witnesses who are to be called for prosecution and defence (required to determine timing).
- Names of witnesses to attend are sometimes given (no obligation).
- Consideration of whether any special measures should be arranged e.g. video-link arrangements for children's evidence in sexual/violent cases.
- Whether alternative charges were fully explored, or binding over.
- Basis of the 'not guilty' plea may be given, e.g. identification (no obligation).
- Nature of any legal argument and agreement to serve skeleton argument before the trial.
- Directions made at the pre-trial review (see 6.4.8).

A certificate of trial readiness (where used) basically states that the party (defence and prosecution) completing the certificate is ready to proceed and this would normally be directed by the court to be filed at least 14 days before the trial booking. It confirms that all directions made at pre-trial review have been complied with; that witnesses are warned and confirmed; whether any issues/evidence have arisen since the pre-trial review; whether there are any outstanding issues relating to disclosure; whether alternative charges have been canvassed. It is also an opportunity to check that the defendant has been advised about the provisions for credit for a guilty plea!

Applications are usually based on a limited range of scenarios and some suggested questions and outcomes are suggested below.

See also 7.2. Criminal Case Management Programme.

6.4.3.   Adjournment of a trial - the absent witness

- *Was this witness listed to appear at the pre-trial review hearing?*
- *When/how was he told of the hearing date?*
- *Can he be contacted by telephone or a visit?*
- *Has he supplied a witness statement/been interviewed by the defence?*
- *What material evidence does the witness contribute to the case?*
- *What is the nature and significance of his evidence?*
- *Ask for representations on whether the case should proceed in his absence.*
- *Ask for representations on whether the case should be part-heard.*
- *Is there a basis for a witness summons?*

The greater the effort to secure his attendance, the more likely that he is genuinely considered to play a vital part. If there is evidence that he has blatantly failed to co-operate and will not attend voluntarily, then a witness summons should be considered.

On the other hand, there may be very little evidence of genuine effort to bring the witness to court. Was he listed by name as a witness at the pre-trial review? What contact has been made with the witness by the party calling him? A letter, a visit, a telephone call? Once? When? Has he made a witness statement at all? Negative answers without explanation to such questions may persuade the bench to go ahead without the witness.

An adjournment part heard with a final opportunity to call the witness on the next occasion might be a 'middle-road' option if so persuaded, but much will depend on the period of adjournment before the bench can continue the case - memories fade.

6.4.4.   Adjournment of a trial - the absent defendant

- *What reasons, if any, are given for the non-attendance?*
- *What is the case history, including the bail history?*
- *Did the defendant attend the pre-trial review hearing?*
- *When did he give instructions for the trial to his solicitor?*
  This will be particularly relevant if the previous bench have identified a bail risk and made a bail condition to keep an appointment with solicitor prior to the next hearing. A failure to comply with this condition effectively creates a good reason to acknowledge that there is a general lack of co-operation and proceed in absence.

Generally the approach should be to proceed with the trial in the defendant's absence if a warrant is justified, i.e. there is no apparent reasonable excuse for failing to attend court. The issue of a warrant and yet, the adjournment of the trial simply do not fit together in logic. When witnesses are present and the case is ready to proceed - hear it, and then if necessary issue the warrant after conviction if the defendant is required to attend for sentence.
See 4.9.3.for further discussion on trials in absence.

What if the defendant has had an accident on the way to court? The case may be re-opened if such a reason emerged and the interests of justice so required. Similarly, the right to appeal against conviction/sentence will lie to the Crown Court. All is not lost.

6.4.5. Adjournment - case to tie or link with other matters

- *Is there any reason why a plea cannot be entered to this matter today?*
  Once a plea is entered, actions can follow. A report can include the new matter; an interim driving disqualification can be imposed; credit for an early guilty plea is beneficial to the defendant; pre-trial planning can begin on a not guilty plea, and a plea may affect the overall view of the case by the Crown Prosecution Service.
- *What is the history of the case so far - including bail history?*
  A good bail record is more encouraging for attendance on yet another day.
- *Are the offences of a similar nature and gravity?*
  If offences are likely to aggravate each other, there may be some value in dealing with them together. Together they may well move from community entry points in isolation, into custody or a more intense community programme. If there is a short time-frame, a short delay may clarify a single final outcome e.g. three weeks for a definite finale by pre-sentence report. By comparison, there is little practical sentencing reason to adjourn minor traffic matters warranting a fine/endorsement to tie with offences carrying community or custody entry points. The adjourned hearing may be a timely opportunity to check the fine payments!
- *What stage has been reached in the other matters?*
  It is more appropriate to tie to a case if it is a convicted matter and a report is already commissioned, than to a 'not guilty' case which is set down for pre-trial review and the prospect of a trial is many weeks away with possible acquittal.
- *Can the other matter be brought forward and resolved today?*

If necessary a penalty of a fine or community order imposed on the first offence can be remitted or discharged if the defendant is sentenced to custody on a later date in respect of the subsequent matter.

Consider doing what you can when you can! Consider the benefit of the defendant being physically present today - a bird in the hand etc....

6.4.6. Adjournment - for pre-sentence reports

This request is often made by the defence at a very early stage in the proceedings as a 'helpful suggestion' on the lines of 'there is a lengthy record in this case and I concede that a pre-sentence report would be helpful to the court'.

Pause and consider whether that is the route which the court wishes to take. On the one extreme, the case may be worthy of immediate committal to Crown Court, and on the other it could be dealt with by a recent report, stand down report or indeed, a report may be totally 'unnecessary'.

To wingers: The entry point is custody - are we seriously considering custody or committal to Crown Court based on the prosecution outline?

If the answer is committal:
To the advocates: We are considering committal to Crown Court in this case, do you wish to make any representations on that course of action?

Adjournments for reports without considering Crown Court can prevent subsequent committal unless it is clearly included as an option. The reality is that even with the option of Crown Court left open, there is a strong defence argument for a sentence within Magistrates' Court powers if a bench have nodded it through for reports in the Magistrates' Court, rather than committing immediately.

If the answer is custody:
To the probation officer/defence advocate: I see from the previous convictions that the defendant was sent to prison 3 months ago, could that report be made available today please?
To the defence advocate: Do you wish to address us on any changes in Mr. X's life since his release? Is there anything to persuade us that the content of the report would be substantially different now? If not, we will go ahead with the previous report. (Or even deem a report to be 'unnecessary' for further custody).

If the answer is neither committal nor custody as a starting point:
To the defence advocate: At this stage we would like to have the benefit of hearing the mitigation first.
The likelihood is that the case will be disposed of as a community penalty which can be resolved on a stand down report from court on the day. The only exceptions to community orders being made on a stand down report are if there are issues of domestic violence, sexual offences, mental illness or the prospect of a drug treatment and testing order or an intensive supervision order.

A result on the day!

6.4.7.   Adjournment - breach of community order

This application is likely to arise when a defendant is brought into a crime court on warrant, having failed to attend a community order breach court. The additional problem is that the court is taking the risk of a failure to attend court on the next occasion, in the face of an allegation of failure to attend court and also failure to comply with a court order. Not an optimistic scenario for bail!

- *Can a plea, at least, be entered?*
  If admitted, the court may be minded to consider revocation of the order, and a pre-sentence report can then be requested during the adjournment, along with details of the original offence. Progress can then be made during the adjournment with the expectation of completion on the next occasion. Ideally, the prosecution file should be available with the court probation team, and a recent report may be sufficient to proceed. Is a pre-sentence report really 'necessary'?
  If denied, the court can conduct an immediate pre-trial review to identify the basis of the denial. If it is simply that there is a 'reasonable excuse' for failure to attend, then a short stand down for the defence to read through the file, may result in proceeding on the day simply with sworn evidence from the defendant as to the nature of the excuse. It is unlikely that any other witnesses will be required.
- *Is it likely that the defendant will attend court voluntarily after an adjournment?*
- *What is the bail risk, and can this be dealt with by conditions e.g. a condition to attend for a specific PSR appointment?*
- *Are the probation service content for the defendant to continue/start the order during the adjournment?*
  If so, can the first appointment be fixed before leaving the court? This may be a critical factor at the next hearing - did he comply with the last chance or not? Make the adjournment worthwhile.

6.4.8.   Adjournment - identification of relevant directions

The questions on adjournment should be pursuing 3 outcomes:

- Progress - some at the very least.
- Clarification of the difficulties experienced or anticipated.
- Identification of what exactly needs to be done, by when, by whom, before the next hearing which will often trigger relevant directions from the bench which are very much part and parcel of the decision.

The following examples may be considered:

- Full instructions must be given to the defence solicitor before the next hearing date by imposing a bail condition if there is evidence of delay in the past.
- The prosecution and/or defence must be in possession of a full file with up-to-date details of when their witnesses can come to court so that the trial can be fixed at the next hearing.
- Primary disclosure must be served on the defence by ….
- Prosecution to request XX evidence from the police within the next 4 days and supply it to the defence within 4 days of receiving it.
- The prosecution is to serve on the defence copies of statements/video tape/ copy exhibits by ….
- A summary of the legal argument to be relied on at trial is to be served on the prosecution/defence/court by ….
- The parties are required to notify the court at once of any change of circumstance likely to affect the time listed for the trial
- A certificate of trial readiness must be completed and filed by … (see final paragraph).

It is suggested that directions on the lines of 'the case must proceed next time' are both counter-productive and pointless. Surely every single case is adjourned for a sufficient period and with sufficiently clear expectations that every single case 'must proceed next time'.

By adding the direction to some cases and not to others, there is an inference that, without the direction there is always a fighting chance of getting a final adjournment - a final persuasive card to play by the applicant who will respectfully seek that authoritative and galvanising last chance!

Also, it actually counts for very little as every application must be dealt with on the information on the day if justice is to be achieved. A refusal to adjourn a case because the previous bench had stated that no further adjournments would be allowed was overturned on appeal. The court said that the comments of the previous bench were relevant to the decision but all factors had to be considered and the previous statement was not binding on a subsequent bench who had a duty to exercise their own judicial discretion (R v Aberdare Justices ex.p DPP 1990).

By comparison, failure to comply with specific directions can be passed on to the Local Criminal Justice Board in respect of the police and CPS, and to the Legal Services Commission in respect of defence failures to comply without reasonable excuse. In serious cases the court may also consider making a wasted costs order against the offending party. The other sanction of course is that cases are ordered to proceed in any event and for want of evidence they are dismissed or discharged.

6.5.   Contempt of court

Different chairmen expect different standards of behaviour and this may also depend upon the particular defendant. Some will take the view that any defendant who is chewing gum and standing with his hands in his pockets should be reprimanded immediately. Always consider that maybe he has no belt on and is holding up his trousers (especially if in custody). That maybe his mouth is just moving with nerves; that it is uncomfortable bravado in front of his friends, or maybe, he is in fact being deliberately difficult and wants to show his disrespect to the court. Maybe?

If he is represented, then his solicitor will no doubt welcome the opportunity to 'have a quiet word'. If unrepresented, what should the chairman do? Recognise the danger of making a false assumption and that the situation can escalate. A defendant could immediately feel at a disadvantage and will fulfil the apparent expectation and take the role of the difficult defendant. He would then find it impossible to rise to the occasion on an adult to adult basis with the chairman. Protracted episodes of finding paper for the disposal of chewing gum and hands moving from pockets into an arm-folded stance are unlikely to generate an atmosphere for meaningful communication. At the end of the day, he has at least attended court. He needs to be calm enough to formulate exactly what he needs to say so that the court is properly informed about the case - not easy, even without a negative start to the occasion. It is worth overlooking a little and preserving energy instead to build up a lot of patience. To set a calm example by words and behaviour and hope that it will be mirrored very quickly.

Members of the public who shout out in the midst of proceedings may not initially understand the sanctity of the courtroom. It is unlikely that the bench will know exactly what their relationship is with the current case, and it may equally be a 'friend' of the defendant who thinks that he is demonstrating his support, or, alternatively, an incensed victim. The suggestion is to give that first chance by stopping the case, concentrating on the behaviour and how it is affecting the court and saying something on the lines of 'We're finding it difficult to concentrate on Mr. X's case because of the noise/interruptions. You are welcome to stay and listen provided that there are no more interruptions - otherwise we will have to ask you to leave'.

It is common for relatives and friends in particular to shout abuse to the bench as defendants are being led to the cells. The chairman is seen as the person who has just broken up a relationship for the foreseeable future with no fond farewells, just 'please go with the officer'. Perhaps some measure of 'we didn't hear that remark' will avoid more abuse from a person who is clearly very upset. The danger otherwise is to shunt the incident into protracted proceedings and for what constructive purpose? The actual case concerned has after all concluded with an outcome, and the person shouting abuse will normally be satisfied to have had the last word and then leave. Some level of tolerance in such circumstances may be appropriate and dignity can swiftly be resumed for the next case.

As soon as disruption results in an interchange of more than one remark from the chairman and one remark from the person causing the disruption, it is going to develop into an emotive argument. This must be avoided. Retire to preserve both the dignity of the court, and those involved. Occasionally a defendant or witness may feel that he has been unfairly treated - sometimes he may have a point, and he will not engage until 'it is sorted'. It will usually be far easier for the legal adviser to establish and respond to it in the informality of the court being stood down, perhaps by explaining why another case was called on first or, if necessary, advising about the complaints procedure.

If the situation does not resolve the chairman must always be mindful of the court's powers to deal with contempt of court. It is an action of last resort and consists of the following situations:

- If a person wilfully insults the magistrates, any witness, officer or advocate either during the court or in going to or returning from the court, or
- If a person wilfully interrupts the proceedings of the court, or otherwise misbehaves in court.

The court sanctions are to order the offender to be taken into custody and detained until the court rises, and with penalties of imprisonment up to 1 month or a fine up to £2,500. The court may discharge the committal at any time.

The build up to taking contempt proceedings will normally begin with a polite request. This will be followed by a warning that the court will consider contempt proceedings being taken and a short retirement from the bench to allow the situation to calm down, allow time for reflection, and ensure that appropriate officers are on hand if removal becomes necessary after recommencing the proceedings.

If the defendant is removed, he must be warned of the actual contempt powers and be offered legal representation. At any stage he may be returned back to the court to apologise and this will normally mark the end of the incident.

If formal contempt proceedings are necessary, this will be dealt with at the end of the court list by admission or denial. The defendant may object to being dealt with by the same bench on an admission, and a denial should always be dealt with by a different bench as soon as possible with the consideration of bail in the meantime. The opportunity to apologise should be on offer at all times. Custodial sentences should only be imposed where there is no practical alternative. (See checklist 1-47)

6.6   Maintaining dignity

6.6.1.   Ensuring that witnesses are not bullied

There is a fine line between robust cross-examination, which is allowed to test out the veracity of the witness, and bullying which is using verbal power to coerce others by fear. The line must not be crossed. Answers given in a hostile environment may be motivated simply by wanting the questions to stop and to get out of the room. The chairman may consider various interventions: -

- Summarise what the witness has answered e.g. 'Mr. Y has now said 3 times that he cannot remember the colour of the car - may we move on now?'
- Ask where the line of questioning is leading if it is becoming protracted and unclear. At the least it should focus the mind of the questioner.
- Suggest that the witness may need a short break and the bench will retire after a particularly lengthy or emotional line of questioning.
- Cut off allegations of lying/covering up/making up with the statement from the chairman that they are matters for the court to determine after hearing all of the evidence.

6.6.2.   Dealing with discourteous advocates

How should the chairman deal with advocates who begin a whispered conversation whilst waiting for their case to be called? This can be very distracting for those involved in the present case, and of course the bench. A comment that the bench is finding it difficult to concentrate because of the noise, might usefully carry the suggestion that they conduct their conversation outside of the court, with the assurance that the usher will call them into court as soon as their case is called. It may even expedite another case if they can use the time fruitfully.

We all have bad days. Sometimes advocates do find themselves running very late. It is important to recognise that the client in court wishes to feel that he is being well represented and that his choice of advocate is respected by the court. The discourtesy of arriving late can be dealt with more fully and more sensitively after the client has left the court. There may be a very good reason which the court can understand, but the client may not. If there is no acceptable reason for late arrival and the matter is to be reported, then the client should not be observing this interchange and outcome.

Ignoring late arrivals or negative behaviour is to the detriment of defendants and witnesses and encourages similar repetitions. When a confidential explanation is sought afterwards, and it is reasonable, the incident is then closed on a positive note for the solicitor and the chairman and will avoid future tension.

6.7.   Communication on the bench and body language

As a starting point, virtually all communication on the bench will relate to the parties before the court. In our ordinary lives we would normally consider it rude to talk about someone, in full view, and without them being able to hear what is said. Matters can be made even worse when a few whispered words and phrases are overheard which may well be totally disregarded at final decision.

Consider the defendant and his solicitor watching the 'live decision-making' in front of them. Catching the words 'small fine' from one winger, and then watching the chairman turn to the second winger with a suggestion and he simply nods in agreement. A few seconds of whispering behind closed hands. The decision is announced as an adjournment for reports to consider custody. Someone apparently thought a fine (or something different at least!) was appropriate. Any disagreement, which is demonstrated often by simple body language can easily project as a 'sentencing lottery' when differences are dealt with so quickly and without a 'proper discussion'.

Obviously many decisions are taken on the bench following short discussion and the courts would grind to a standstill if the bench were to retire on every decision.

What does the defendant want to hear and see when his fate is being considered in front of his eyes. Firstly, what does he need to hear and see? A continuation of the running commentary and explanation which began when he came into court, which tells him, what exactly is happening now? The chairman may wish to say something on the lines of 'We are now going to discuss the application/decision - you may sit down'.

Secondly, to see that all 3 magistrates are involved and either they agree immediately without comment, or that they are in a position to hear any comments made and 'talk about it properly - together'. This might be achieved most effectively by drawing back the chairs and moving closer together. The defendant is unlikely to feel confident that there is a 'right answer' if he sees shaking heads - body language in open court should be guarded against, and reserved for the retiring room. A 3-way discussion is likely to take the same length of time as the alternative of a chairmen jockeying comments to either side of the chair. Visually, it is a world of difference in the perception from the well of the court of full bench equal involvement. Additionally, it is usually welcomed by the wingers.

When it is clear that there is a major difference in opinion, it will normally be appropriate to announce that the bench are retiring to consider the matter. This will enable a full exchange in the privacy of the retiring room for the benefit of the wingers, as well as preserving court dignity.

The task of the chairman is often, simply, to summarise the application or suggested penalty and then seek the agreement of each winger. Two nodding heads are fine! Happily this will often be the case, particularly with agreed applications and penalties which fall directly within the Sentencing Guideline. This approach can be agreed at the beginning of a court, particularly if it involves a long list of similar matters and the norm penalty has been agreed in advance. It requires some discipline to turn to each winger in turn as a first reference - we all have our natural turning directions but it avoids any notion of preference.

When contributions arise - huddle and hear. When an alternative is put forward and there is disagreement with it - retire for body language to join in!

Never let a member of the public believe that the wingers are simply administrative aides!

6.8.   Retiring from the bench

When it is necessary to retire to make a decision, the chairman needs to check whether either of the wingers have any questions, and also allow the opportunity for them to point out any omissions e.g. means information, before retiring. Then he must check that there are no other issues with the legal adviser e.g. fine default yet to be put to the defendant, a reminder about potential options etc. Explanation should be given in open court about exactly is happening.

'Does our legal adviser have any advice on the law or any other matters to draw to our attention before we retire?'

'We are retiring now to consider our decision. We will be asking our legal adviser to join us when we have made our decision in order to formally record our reasons. We will telephone when we are ready.'

'If anyone wishes to go for coffee, the court will adjourn now for 30 minutes to allow time for the witness to arrive'. (After checking whether other courts can be assisted in the meantime!).

6.9.   Managing the decision-making process

6.9.1.   Getting the discussion started and summarising key points

Perhaps the most difficult aspect of decision-making in the Magistrates' Court is the fact that the discussion and decision involves 3 people. Obviously this has the advantage of being able to take a majority decision if necessary. The disadvantage is that we tend to have meaningful conversations in 2s - whether sitting or standing. It is easy and comfortable to talk as 2 people. 3 is the potential 'odd one out' scenario. It is so easy for any 3rd person to feel excluded in any gathering. That person might be the new magistrate, the only man with two women, the only one who did not watch a particular television programme the night before, the only one who does not follow football. Even before court, there is a team to build in readiness for decision making later in the day and encouraging full participation of all 3 members even in the general conversation gives a motivating message of value and inclusion.

Once in the retiring room, the first stage is to ensure that everyone is referring to the relevant reference material and ready to work through the appropriate structured approach, following a short introductory summary by the chairman.

Example:

Sentencing on a common assault case
- *See 2.7*
- *Adult Court Bench Book: Sentencing - A structured approach, p.1-35*
- *Sentencing Guidelines: Common assault, p.20*
- *Reasons form for sentencing*
- *Notes*

' *The Guideline entry point for common assault is a community penalty. So let's look at the offence itself first. Mrs. X, would you like to start off with your views on any aggravating features ....*'

The chairman needs to make it clear that he is not going to entertain any discussion about whether colleagues are 'for or against the report recommendation' or take any views at all on options until the case has been discussed. The last words in court will have come from the defence about options and it is essential to re-wind back to the prosecution outline first and work through the structure - Offence, Offender, Objectives and Options.

Example:

Trial of a common assault case
- *See 2.5*
- *Adult Court Bench Book: Guilty or not guilty - A structured approach, p.1-31*
- *Reasons form for verdict*
- *Notes*
(NOT the Guidelines at this stage!)

'*So just to summarise what we have been told in court on the law. The prosecution must prove beyond reasonable doubt that the defendant put the victim in fear of immediate unlawful violence at the least. Any injury proved is an aggravating feature but isn't essential to proving the offence. Is that your understanding?*'

I suggest that the agreed facts are that there was an argument between the two of them and at some stage the defendant did strike the victim in the face with a single blow and cause a black eye. Do we agree that?

The disputed fact is that the defendant says that he struck the blow in self-defence because he really believed that the victim was going to strike him first. The victim says that nothing was said or done to suggest there would be any violence at all. That is the issue and we need to look carefully at the evidence to assess whose evidence we prefer. Do we agree that is what we need to focus on?

Mrs. Y, what is your view of the prosecution evidence from the victim? ....'

This approach will avoid a general discussion which re-iterates again and again what is either agreed or irrelevant. This is particularly easy to fall into if the method of discussion is to go through every line of every witness. After hearing both sides, much of what is said is actually agreed and the 'padding' can be ignored.

By reminding colleagues of the 'beyond reasonable doubt', it can reduce lengthy 'what if/maybe/not sure' meandering. The chairman who quickly focuses <u>and</u> checks out the disputed points for careful analysis will save time and reach a high quality, well-reasoned decision. A clear verdict structure. What is to be proved? What is agreed? What is disputed? Preferred evidence and why?

Example:

Bail decision
*   See 2.2.8.
*   Adult Court Bench Book - Bail decision-a structured approach, p.1-17
*   Pronouncements (reasons included)
    Conditional bail + notes, p.3-23
    Remand in custody, p.3-25
*   Notes

'The prosecution application is to remand in custody based on the exception of failure to surrender because of the two previous failures, and the defence have listed a number of conditions for us to consider.
Do we agree with the one exception to unconditional bail for that reason?
Do any other exceptions or reasons apply?
Now, let us consider whether any conditions would satisfy us?

A bail discussion has the highest potential perhaps to begin with the echoes of the defence submission, 'Well I'd be happy with those conditions'. A competent chairman will discourage 'rubber-stamping' and ensure that the only discussion about conditions will follow on from which exceptions (grounds/risks) the bench have identified.

Fighting for a release on bail may well generate the suggestion of unnecessary and inappropriate conditions on the basis of quantity rather than quality. On the other hand, a 7 day remand in custody is carrying the same restriction as a 14 day prison sentence, usually without conviction, and relevant conditions must be carefully considered first. Imagination and local knowledge are invaluable and should be encouraged to create effective conditions such as exclusion areas by identifying whether any of the magistrates know the area can help to create a practical definition for comment by the advocates.

6.9.2.   Listening actively to colleagues

Listening is easy if we do not have a contribution to make. We can listen with almost full attention to a gripping radio/television programme, and be able to digest much of it immediately and then repeat much of the content. In joint decision-making, that is never the case because there are several processes fighting against each other - listening, thinking hard, forming our own views, wanting to speak. Wanting to stop or interrupt what is being said by someone else because it doesn't accord with our own view, turning off from what is being said because it doesn't accord with our own view. Our greatest problem is that we simply form a view too quickly and this can create a brick wall to our really listening any further. Our mind has left the room, but we sit politely on!

Active listening needs a disciplined approach so that we really benefit from the ideas and views of others and reach genuine, 'added quality' decisions.

6.9.3.   'Make myself listen properly' strategies

- Maintain eye contact with the speaker.
- Lean forward.
- Look interested.
- Nod the information into my head instead of into the mid-air.
- Look like I want to be involved in this discussion.
- Uncross my arms.
- Avoid interrupting (write down an aide-memoire word or two for later).
- Wait - something good might be coming next ...
- Recognise that thought is faster than speech and draw back to what is being said.
- Formulate a question instead of dismissing 'out of hand'.
- Repeat back anything I'm not sure about - first and foremost did I really listen?
- Deal with distractions such as background noise.
- Take a short break rather than 'drifting off'.

- Do not assume and judge the speaker's motives rather than listening to what they say.
- Never be in the situation of someone saying 'well I said that' and thinking 'did you?'
- Acknowledge every contribution from others by doing something with it:
  Agree - 'yes I agree', 'good idea' (instead of just thinking it)
  Ask for more information or reasoning - 'why do you think that?'
  Check it back - 'so you say that ...'
  Put it in the arena for comment by others – 'what do you think of Mrs.X's suggestion?'
- Stop thinking that I always know best.

6.9.4. Contributing to discussions with the legal adviser as appropriate

Most chairmen prefer to act as the spokesperson to the legal adviser and it is usually easier to act as impartial adviser to the bench as a whole through one person. It also means that the chairman can take the matter through discussion of the facts with colleagues and then identify the areas on which 'the bench' require legal advice.

Obviously there are times when the chairman will indicate that he is quite happy for wingers to ask additional questions or seek clarification directly.

Discussions with the legal adviser should be solely about the law, practice, procedure, penalties and structure and in the main should begin with 'we would like to know' from the chairman, rather than 'I would like to know' from a winger. Identifying the issues for the legal adviser is a team effort.

The legal adviser also has the responsibility to assist, where appropriate in the formulation of the reasons and the recording of the reasons. Provided that the chairman has led a structured decision-making process, the reasons will flow from the chairman's lead. Contribution to the decision-making therefore runs in tandem with contributing to the formulation of the reasons.

6.9.5. Ensuring full participation in the decision-making

The role of the chairman changes from directing proceedings in the court room and acting as spokesperson, to facilitating proceedings in the retiring room and acting as one of 3 people reaching a decision together. As a team member the winger wants to know what the task is and how/when he will play his part. The list below builds upon the points already made:

- Make sure that everyone is referring to the Sentencing Guidelines.
- Put the reasons form in a prominent position.
- Summarise the situation.
- Provide the agenda so that irrelevancies don't arise in the first place.
- Be ready to ask why a point is relevant to keep the discussion on track.
- Using the relevant structure, start with the first open question e.g. Sentencing - any aggravating features of the offence? Bail - which exceptions apply (if any)? Verdict - what are the agreed facts?
- Seek starter views from a different winger each time.
- Use closed, probing, hypothetical questions to clarify views.
- Be clear about your own independent view - the chairman is not there to compromise.
- Demonstrate that you really are listening.
- Respond in some way to every contribution.
- Reflect back your understanding of each stage of the decision for the benefit of everyone.
- Be ready to challenge any prejudicial comments and ensure that they do not affect decision-making e.g. repeat back and allow opportunity to withdraw comment: Ask 'why should this case be dealt with differently to the norm?'
- Check the reasons and pronouncement with both wingers, even if it a 2:1 decision.

6.9.6.   Managing disagreement and potential conflict

Disagreement is going to happen and it must be managed so that everyone feels that they have had their best say and everyone has listened effectively. So long as this happens, disagreement can have constructive consequences and is 'ok'. It can increase motivation, innovative thinking and generate a thorough examination of the alternatives.

Conflict arises from various classic conditions and in the retiring room it is usual to find that there are different preferred outcomes. This conflict can be avoided by making sure that outcomes are left right to the end of a structured approach so that the relevant information is identified and agreed first on a stage by stage basis.

In a sentencing case, the early establishment of the level of seriousness will narrow down the outcome to one band or another e.g. community band. The next stage is to identify the sentencing objective or objectives to be achieved. This is often omitted and the discussion of options suffers from a lack of common purpose. If it is agreed that there is realistic hope for rehabilitation or a need for straight punishment, then the outcomes and potential for conflict are necessarily reduced at the next stage. Similarly, it may equally arise that all agree that some prevention is also required, and preventative 'add on' penalties will then fall to be discussed, but a reduced and specific menu is at least agreed. Co-operation and mutual respect is more likely to be generated on the back of some level of agreement and progress together.

Similarly, in bail and verdict cases, there are matters which are likely to be agreed first. Enjoy them. Then be sure to narrow the issue as much as possible before even mentioning final outcome. Initial views may be changing or developing in the meantime and the potential conflict may have ebbed away. If we move forward carefully, we seldom have to go backwards. Going back over old ground, and re-visiting omissions creates unhelpful feelings of irritation and frustration, the more so because it can be avoided.

The tools for managing conflict are:

- Make sure that the visual aids are being used - structured approach, guidelines and reasons form.

- Make statements about what is agreed.

'We agree that the offence seriousness falls within the community band.'
'We agree that the record shows that some preventative measure is needed here.'
'We agree that he is likely to commit offences on bail.'

- Question everything else.

Never tell two people to stop arguing - they probably will not, and if they do, the quietness will be uncomfortable. Make them pause instead by asking a question. A straight 'why' can sound accusing - soften it with a positive if possible.

- *So we have a difference of view to share. Mrs. X, you suggest a curfew order and that is in the community band as we agreed, why do you think it is the most effective choice?*

- Repeat back the argument of each winger to focus and check understanding.

'So you say ... because ...
Is there anything else you would add to support your view?
'And you say ... because ...

234

Is there any anything else to support your view?

- Check out that those in conflict are actually listening and understanding each other's view point rather than concentrating on pursuing their own view.

'Can you see where Mrs. X is coming from?'
' Why do you disagree with it?'

- Identify where the specific facts of the case are distorting into broad emotion or bias.

'I can understand that cases of domestic violence are abhorrent to you. I'm also aware of the high likelihood of previous history, but we have no evidence of any history in this case, do we?'

- Suggest alternatives as an equal member of the team, rather than as a chairman who is trying to compromise.

'I don't believe that the criteria are made out for us to add an Anti Social Behaviour Order in this case. But I do think the facts of the case call for some measure of protection for the future. A short specific bind over would be proportionate and it may help to prevent a repetition. If that is breached, then the criteria would certainly be made out for next time.

'I can see the value to this defendant of a rehabilitation order to work on the drink problem as you say Mr. W. I can also understand the suggestion by you Mrs. Y of curfew to keep him out of the pub. Why don't we reduce the curfew period to 3 nights a week and make it a requirement of a rehabilitation order. Do both?'

- Suggest that the legal adviser is called in to advise on any uncertainties on legal or practice issues which are raised by the wingers, e.g.

'I'm not sure if we can do a curfew and rehabilitation order for the same offence'.
'We don't normally do ancillary bind overs in this court - I don't think we should start something new'.
If we're thinking of doing a bolt-on ASBO, I think we might need to draw up some conditions for the defence to comment on first - it's probably too complicated to bother with.'

6.10. Formulating and delivering the pronouncement

6.10.1. Content

Model pronouncements are produced in section 3 of the Adult Court Bench Book. The aim is to cover all essential elements in plain language, and it is accepted that chairmen may well modify the language and adapt to their own style.

As a basic requirement, virtually every pronouncement will need to cover:

- 'We' (rather than 'I')
- Reasons - Why? ..
- Detail of the order - What? When?
- Explanation - You must ….
- Warning(s) - Or else …

Whenever 'extras', are to be delivered it is important for the bench to agree what is to be said. Wingers should not be put in a position of demonstrating by their body language that they do not wish to be associated with unexpected tirades or threats. The chairman's authority is clearly dissipated in the face of the court by such actions. Check that there is to be a united front first!

6.10.2. Effective delivery

So far as effective delivery is concerned, the key points are:

- Engagement - with the defendant and the court.
- Simple language - no jargon, no acronyms.
- Volume - loud enough for everyone in court to hear easily.
- Pace - slow enough to catch all that is said and remaining steady throughout.
- Pauses - allowing time to digest the last bit before moving on to the next bit.
- Tone - monotone is monotonous and doesn't flag up the warning elements.
- Checking understanding - by eye contact and summaries.

6.10.3. Engaging with the defendant and the power of body language

Engaging - what is it? The words and body language which shout out a clear statement 'you are important' and 'this is between you and me'.

Engagement is critical to ensure that the decision is conveyed and understood. So often, it is said that 'defendants don't listen' and 'pronouncements are far too long and defendants get bored'. The pronouncement is unlikely to be longer than the last conversation they had with a friend, or the last person they listened to on the television, plus the pronouncement has the added interest value that it is all about them. So why do we perceive boredom and disinterest in the courtroom? Much will depend on the body language. At least 55% of our communication is on what we see, with tone of voice coming in second place and the actual words coming in last. Isn't the reality that very often the effort goes almost entirely into getting the words right? Understandable, but ...

A defendant desperately needs to know what will happen if he misses a fine instalment or fails to keep a bail condition. Yet how many defendants are genuinely shocked to be arrested and face custody? No doubt they were told about the warning but were they really encouraged to hear it? The friend and the television presenter would be doing all they could to make sure he was listening and taking interest - engaging. The court chairman and legal adviser should be doing just the same thing. Do we always do that?

Examples:
Body language

Upright posture = 'I am confident - I know what I am doing - we will get this right'.
Open gestures to reinforce messages.
No fiddling with a pen or paperclip = I am totally interested in the proceedings.
Acting as an adult to an adult, rather than as parent to a child or a teacher to a pupil.
Eye contact = I am watching to see whether you understand me or not.

Eye contact is the most obvious body language. It is extremely helpful to assess whether a defendant or witness is engaged with the chairmen or not and whether there are indications of understanding or otherwise. It is unnecessary to hold eye contact for prolonged periods, but something beyond glancing up at intervals to make sure the defendant is still there!

This is a two way process and the defendant's body language may also appear to be giving louder messages than the words they say. We need to beware of misinterpreting those non-verbal signs. Assumptions may be made that direct eye contact by the defendant or witness may indicate honesty and veracity, but care should be taken in interpreting the response to eye contact in this way. Chairmen in particular should be aware that in African-Caribbean culture it may be considered impudent to look at a person in authority directly in the eyes. In some Asian cultures it is considered appropriate to look away from a person in authority to indicate deference and respect.

The most straightforward way that we can engage more effectively is by using the listener's name At the beginning and then again at various points in a conversation. In a long pronouncement, it helps to personalise, provide emphasis to key points, and it can also draw the defendant back into listening mode.

Again, particularly in long pronouncements there is much to be said for following the trainers' strategy

- Tell them what you're going to tell them - it's going to be a fine, disqualification and costs.
- Tell them - give the details of each aspect.
- Tell them what you've told them - so the total due is … and the disqualification is …

6.10.4. Using simple language

We would all no doubt say that we do not use jargon. The reality is that court jargon gradually becomes part of our day to day language and it is actually quite difficult for us to spot the jargon and translate it as necessary. There are a number of regularly used expressions which may need interpretation.

> *Examples:*
>
> *'We feel that you may 'fail to surrender' because … = 'We feel that you 'may not attend court' for the next hearing because ….*
> *'Advance disclosure' = what the prosecutor will be telling the court about your case*
> *Acronyms e.g. PTR, PSR, SSR, ASBO, ETS programme etc. = what the letters actually mean.*

6.10.5. Volume

Volume is likely to be the single most observable aspect of authority. Authority is about confidence and projecting it loud and clear. It is common for volume to be low - too quiet for a defendant to be bothered to strain and listen. He may assume that his solicitor will probably tell him what is was all about, or hope that it will be confirmed by letter. Both are unfortunate assumptions. Volume is particularly relevant to defendants who are appearing in custody behind glass screens. They have the added disincentive to listen carefully because their priority is simply to 'get out' or they are fatalistic about a return to custody in some shape or form.

By reading a pronouncement, it is easy to project downwards instead of upwards. Remember to literally 'throw your voice' like a tennis ball to the back of the room - all the way from start to finish. The volume should be loud enough so that everyone in court can hear easily without having to strain. Low volume is irritating to try and hear, immediately detracts from authority, reduces the likelihood of interaction and, most importantly, reduces the chances of complying with the order - … what order?

6.10.6. Pace

The most common criticism of pronouncements is that they are rushed. This may be due to reading rather than communicating; nerves; or a lack of confidence in the content. The words of a pronouncement are important and the defendant deserves a professional and dignified approach. This message is going to affect his future in some way. It matters, and time and space are needed for it to be digested.

Nerves can make a lengthy pronouncement into a breathless race - breathe slowly and deliver slowly. A lack of confidence can give the impression of 'simply wanting to get it over with.' The old-fashioned advice of taking a deep breath and giving yourself plenty of fuel is good advice. Rather like the graceful swan, the court will only see the graceful delivery and will not see the rapidly paddling legs!

A feeling that delivery is 'slow' is usually a positive indication that it is 'about right' for listening to.

6.10.7. Pauses

Equally as important as speed, is the need to break up a pronouncement into 'digestible chunks'. Keep a steady pace and give the defendant some space in the pauses to give and receive the information. A few seconds for the defendant to digest that the penalty is a community penalty and not custody is essential before he is ready to take on board the explanation of what will be required. Unfortunately in a busy court it is easy to overlook the value of silence – the pauses between each piece of information. Use them and make them work.

6.10.8. Tone

Finally, a change of tone can help to get the message across. Monotones are the kiss of death to the most carefully constructed reasons. Patronising tones are likely to reduce the defendant into the role of a naughty child being 'told off', with the limited response of grumpily agreeing to 'whatever!'

The tone of the explanation may well be warm and friendly to engage attention, but can create a misleading impression if it continues in the same way into the warning element. The defendant deserves to be made aware that there are serious implications and the tone should convey this on an adult to adult basis.

It is worth recognising that our tone of voice carries more weight in communication than the actual words. Just try saying one word, 'yes', in a tone that conveys that you really mean either:
- happy and delighted yes
- unhappy but yes, ok then
- angry yes, if I have to then'
- disbelieving yes
- let's be clear, this yes really means no!

The chairman must sound as if he believes each part of this information is important. It really is. The most flattering response is for a defendant to ask a question at the end. He was listening and he trusts the chairman to have the answer (Possibly to be deflected to the legal adviser though!).

6.10.9 Checking understanding

Not once, but perhaps twice or even three times during a complicated pronouncement which involves several features. The most obvious way of checking is to ask, 'Do you understand?' In reality it is unlikely that a defendant will reply honestly in the negative, given the environment and the occasion. A more realistic way of checking is to look at the body language and determine whether the defendant is looking receptive, 'switched off', or quizzical and expand or change tone as appropriate. Occasionally it may be helpful to ask a defendant to repeat back his understanding of the decision e.g. bail conditions. This should not be phrased as a test question, but on the lines of 'that is quite a lot to remember, but its very important to you, so can I just check with you that I've been clear about exactly what you need to do'.

Sometimes there are implications for others. Does the probation officer understand which options should be covered in the pre-sentence report? Does the victim understand that the compensation will be paid in instalments rather than by a lump sum? Does the dock officer understand that the one day detention is deemed to have been served? Does the press officer understand that reporting restrictions apply?

Relying upon a written notice of decision is insufficient on its own. Many defendants cannot read – even more, do not.

6.11.   Post-court review - purpose and content

MNTI 2 brings with it the introduction of a post-court review by the bench and legal adviser, to briefly review the work at the end of the session. The MNTI 2 Handbook describes the review as follows:

'The aim is to identify and acknowledge good practice, identify what could be improved on and how to do things better, and to emphasise learning from that court sitting'.

The review is 'part of an ongoing process and intended to help us to focus on aspects of the relevant competence framework. Discussions should be kept as brief as possible and be led by the chairman and involve the legal adviser.   The spirit should be one of open, frank and free exchange between the members of the bench and the legal adviser. Any feedback given should be balanced, objective, clear and specific...'

'If an appraisal is taking place, the review gives everyone the opportunity to make comments openly and for the appraiser and appraisee to take these into account in their private session following the review. You may wish to refer to the relevant competence framework for more detail'. The competences are listed as a suggested checklist for this purpose.
(Appendix 10A MNTI Handbook)

Some thought will be needed about how to get the best out of the review to avoid any resentment about staying on after a busy court. Bringing forward the normal finish time by 5 minutes may assist - its amazing how minds focus to finish a court at 1 p.m., so why not 12.55 p.m.? 5 minutes should be sufficient or alternatively there may well be a short natural break during the late morning.

A clear practical benefit is created if the post-court review relates directly to the pre-court briefing. Simply as an opportunity to pause, comment and to measure.

See also 5.4 giving and receiving feedback.

Example:

This relates to the pre-court briefing examples described at the beginning of the chapter but perhaps only one aspect would have been flagged up for review at the end, rather than all of them!

- *The new failure to surrender sentence practice - used, but all recognised that the local defence solicitors were surprised by the change. Action: legal adviser to make sure that it is mentioned at the next meeting with solicitors.*
- *The new probation programme - used, and winger asks whether it is possible to find out if the order is complied with. Action: legal adviser asks probation team to note feedback to the named magistrates after 6 months.*
- *The chairman's first trial - chairman recognises that he had not been prepared for the defendant choosing not to give evidence, and thanks the legal adviser for giving the appropriate warning. Asks for a written note to have in readiness if it should happen again. Wingers compliment the chairman on the clarity of the structured approach in the retiring room.*
- *Efforts to attach enforcement options to fine defaulters - legal adviser congratulates the bench that all of the defaulters left court with an enforcement option. Winger seeks clarification about why benefits could not be attached in a particular case and legal adviser explains that maximum number of deductions were already attached. A supervision order was imposed instead.*
- *Feedback to legal adviser - chairman thanks legal adviser for standing and turning to face the bench to read through the case history - so much easier to hear what is said than sitting and facing the court instead.*

A good morning's work and ... now ... time for lunch.

CHAPTER 7
Current issues

This chapter provides information about current initiatives and issues, and aims to develop understanding to deal effectively with the many cases which fall within the various topic headings.

7.1. Narrowing the Justice Gap (NJG) - 'bringing more cases to justice'

This is a government initiative launched in April 2003, with a target of bringing 1.2 million offences to justice by 2005/6 (a 17% improvement). The NJG Public Service Agreement is managed by the National and Local Criminal Justice Boards as a prime example of inter-agency work across the Criminal Justice Service, with a target of just less than a 6% increase in cases brought to justice each year from 2003 to 2006.

So what is the 'Justice Gap'? This is the difference between the number of crimes which are recorded and the number which are finalised by conviction/caution/taken into consideration. In 2000/1, only 19.8% of recorded offences resulted in the offender being 'brought to justice'. This is clearly unacceptable, with around 80% of crime currently going unpunished. Criminal careers are flourishing.

There are various points in the process where cases fall out of the system:

Crime recorded → police investigation and detection → arrest → charge → bail/remand → case building →court.

The relative ease of detection of different crimes varies e.g. violence against the person at 35.5% detection, compared to only 8.9% for burglary. The practical problems include insufficient evidence to arrest, failing to identify the suspect, lack of witnesses who are prepared to come forward. Following charge, numbers continue to fall because of witness related problems and discontinuance due to insufficient evidence in the view of the Crown Prosecution Service when they scrutinise the police evidence. Once the case hits the court system, there is the problem of failure to attend court, with over 78,000 warrants issued in 2000 and also ineffective trials, with an average of only 1 trial in 3 actually proceeding as a trial on the day.

Various actions have been taken to address the problem. The principle target group are the 'persistent offenders' who are defined as those who have been convicted of 6 or more recordable offences in the last year along with others who are identified as persistent offenders on the basis of local intelligence. It is suggested that this 10% group of offenders commit about a half of all serious crime. Given, the evidence that catching and punishing offenders is the most effective way of shortening their criminal career, this group are prioritised for 'premium services' with senior police/CPS input into expedited preparation of files and execution of warrants. The court will list such cases as quickly as possible.

A similar initiative was launched in 1999 in respect of 'persistent young offenders', to reduce the period from arrest to sentence from 142 days (the average period at the time) down to 71 days through closer, strategic inter-agency working. This has been successful.

Similarly some crimes are prioritised, e.g. a tailored approach to rape cases to lead to more successful prosecutions; high 'street crime' areas provide enhanced victim support to witnesses from the identification parade through to court appearance at trial.

Each Local Criminal Justice Board will have different priorities, and each agency will have some specialist priorities. Most courts are endeavouring to increase court attendance on bail and increase the number of effective trials. Examples of court actions in the NJG plan are given below:

Examples:

- Bail - keeping defendants in the court system.

✓ *Prioritise dispatch to police of warrants for persistent offenders within x hours.*

✓ *Deal with evidence of failure to surrender to court, by bail conditions or remand in custody as proportionate.*

✓ *In conjunction with the Crown Prosecution Service, ensure that the failure to surrender charge is considered in respect of all defendants who are arrested on warrant.*
There are two alternative charges - failing to attend without reasonable excuse and failing to surrender as soon as practicable thereafter e.g. as soon as the medical certificate expired. Both offences carry the same custodial penalty.

✓ *Robust court sentencing to demonstrate that failure to surrender to court is a serious matter.*
This has recently been emphasised by a recent direction to the courts which encourages immediate charge/sentence following arrest, and consecutive prison sentences where appropriate.

✓ *In conjunction with the Probation Service and Police, impose if appropriate bail conditions to attend specific appointment for pre-sentence report preparation.*
This is a stage in the court process where numbers fall out of the system, particularly if under threat of potential custody!

• Trials - ensuring that they proceed.

✓ *Prioritise early listing of trials which involve persistent offenders.*

✓ *Deal with evidence of potential interference with witnesses, by bail conditions or remand in custody as proportionate.*

✓ *Manage effective pre-trial reviews with directions and robust enquiries on application to adjourn a trial.*

✓ *Proceed in the absence of the defendant if there is a reasonable excuse for non-attendance is not presented to the court.*

And the good news, a provisional estimate for England Wales for offences brought to justice in the 12 months ending September 2003, showed a 6% improvement on the 12 months ending March 2002 (<http://www.cjsonline.gov.uk> [Accessed 14.2.04]).

7.2. Criminal Case Management Programme

The national roll out of this programme is expected to be complete by 2006, with pilots currently exploring all elements. The programme supports the drive to narrow the justice gap and brings together 3 major elements of Criminal Justice Service reform:

• Charging
• Effective Trial Management Programme
• Victim and Witness Care (now known as 'No Witness, No Justice' Project).

7.2.1. Charging

This is about dedicated CPS prosecutors working with the police on cases from the start of the investigation to finish. The CPS will advise the police on lines of enquiry, on the evidence that should be gathered and the charge upon which to proceed (if any), in all but minor cases. The intention is that this will reduce the number of cases which are subsequently discontinued for lack of sufficient evidence, increase the number of guilty pleas and reduce the number of ineffective trials when the prosecution are not ready to proceed.

Duty prosecutors will be co-located in police stations to review cases with the police and also provide 24 hour advice by 'CPS Direct' which is a telephone advice facility.

A shadow charging scheme is already in place across all 42 areas and migration to a statutory scheme aims to be complete in priority areas by Autumn 2004. Once the statutory scheme is in place, the police will be required to seek a charging decision from the CPS on all relevant cases and conditions may be imposed on the bail back to the police station (currently police bail back to the police station must be unconditional).

7.2.2. Effective Trial Management Programme

About 2 out of 3 trials currently do not proceed on the day of trial. They fall into 2 types - 'ineffective' and 'cracked' trials. An 'ineffective' trial is one which has to be adjourned to another day for trial (29.5% of trials in the Magistrates' Courts in 2003). The main reasons for this are because the defendant fails to attend, a witness fails to attend, or the prosecution or defence are not ready to proceed. The other type of trial which does not go ahead is the 'cracked' trial. In this type of case, there is a conclusion to the proceedings, and it is not adjourned any further. This is usually because there is a change to a guilty plea at the last moment or the prosecution offer no evidence. Between April and June 2002, there were 27,500 trials which did not proceed in the Magistrates' Courts.

This programme is to ensure that cases are prepared and managed effectively between charge and disposal, and it clarifies the roles and responsibilities of everyone involved. A new case progression function will be undertaken by all Criminal Justice Services agencies and services e.g. by the appointment of specific case progression officers. The programme focuses upon directions and assessments of readiness between the agencies and with the defence.

Examples:

- *Direction to prosecution and defence to provide witness availability dates to the court progression officer at least 3 days before the pre-trial hearing.*

The hearing date can then be identified and checked in advance of the hearing, rather than finding that availability dates have not been obtained or they have become out of date. It also saves the time of everyone checking personal and court diary time in open court.

- *Direction to file a certificate of readiness 14 days before the trial.*

This will be 'chased' by officers with case progression responsibilities and brought back before the court for consideration of vacating the trial to another date if there are insurmountable problems. This avoids witnesses attending for trial, only to be told that the case is to be adjourned, or alternatively, being cancelled on the day before the hearing.

7.2.3.   Victim and Witness Care - 'No Witness, No Justice' Project

There is currently no local system-wide management of victim and witness care on a day-by-day basis, or a seamless focus on the victim from start to finish of the case. In 2003, prosecution witness issues accounted for 26% of ineffective trials in the Magistrates' Courts.

The Project will introduce dedicated Witness Care Units (WCU) across England and Wales and brings together the police and CPS to jointly meet the individual needs of victims and witnesses. At the point of statement, the police will complete an initial needs assessment for each victim and witness - from childcare arrangements when attending court through to dealing with intimidation. There may be tailored support e.g. referral to a relevant support group. From the point of charge, the needs will be managed by the Witness Care Unit, with a single point of contact to provide information at key stages of the case and deal with practical issues such as transport to court.

All pilot areas are demonstrating a higher level of attendance of witnesses at court e.g. 20% increase in witness attendance in Gwent.

7.3.   Anti-Social Behaviour

7.3.1.   Anti-social behaviour

'Anti-social behaviour has been the issue raised by people ...The same things come up time and again' (Prime Minister Tony Blair, October 2003, Queen Elizabeth II Centre, London).

Recent Home Office research reveals that on a day in September 2003 there were 66,107 nation wide reports of anti-social behaviour. Anti-social behaviour includes damage, graffiti, throwing missiles, disorderly behaviour, aggressive begging, vehicle crime, prostitution and dumping rubbish.

The courts have various options available to deal with anti social behaviour, ranging from a binding over order as an order on application, or as an ancillary criminal penalty, at the 'lower end' of behaviour up to the Anti-Social Behaviour Order (ASBO).

7.3.2.   The Anti-Social Behaviour Order (ASBO)

The Anti Social Behaviour Order (ASBO) began in 1999 as an order which could be made by the court following application by 'relevant authorities' and requiring consultation first with the police and local authority. In December 2002 it was extended for use as an ancillary order on criminal conviction (although the actual term of ASBO is not used in the legislation). This 'bolt-on' order to criminal convictions may be made on the application of the prosecutor or on the court's own initiative, and it may involve evidence which was inadmissible in the criminal proceedings.

The requirements for an ASBO are that:

1.   The defendant behaved in an anti-social manner. This is 'a manner that caused or was likely to cause harassment, alarm, or distress to one or more persons not of the same household' as the defendant, and
2.   An order is necessary for the protection of persons from further anti-social behaviour by the defendant.

'Harassment' usually infers some measure of repetition - the likelihood that someone is saying 'We've had enough of this - will you just stop it?' Alarm or distress is about the likelihood of someone feeling a fear of danger, or anxiety and anguish - one incident can be sufficient. Why is an order 'necessary'? There is no requirement to try all other options first, but essentially nothing else is either working or has any real chance of working, e.g. repeated arrests for non-imprisonable offences can only result in arrest/fine/release/return to the scene/return to the behaviour on a regular basis.

The order comprises a list of 'must not' prohibitions with a minimum order period of 2 years. Breach of the order carries 5 years imprisonment at Crown Court on breach of any of the requirements.

The order carries a few peculiarities. It is a civil order which means that hearsay evidence can be used - very useful because members of the community may understandably be unwilling to come forward to give evidence personally because of fear of reprisals. Professional witnesses e.g. housing officers, police, social landlords may be used, giving evidence of what they have been told and why the witness will not attend court. They may also provide helpful information to describe the state of affairs in the locality such as the extent of void properties in a neighbourhood, the difficulties of re-letting and the state of the properties. Evidence may well include video footage and photographs. As the order carries the potential of custody on breach of any of its requirements, the standard of proof is at the higher criminal standard of 'beyond reasonable doubt'. However, the issue as to whether the order is considered to be 'necessary' is a matter of judgement and is not subject to a standard of proof test.

7.3.3.   ASBOs and children/young people

Because the youth court only deals with criminal cases, this means that the applications, which are civil proceedings, must be dealt with in the adult court in respect of children and young people. Magistrates who do not sit on the youth panel need to be alert to the issues arising from dealing with children and young people:

- Parent/guardian should be present and involved in the proceedings.
- Defendant addressed using his first name, and far more informality than with adults e.g. parent and child to remain seated, and possibly the advocates as well provided that there is clear vision and hearing.
- To consider whether reporting restrictions should properly be imposed or not, otherwise the adult court is an open court for reporting, even if the defendant is only aged 10. Representations should be heard so that the court can balance the interests of the community in being made aware of the order and its requirements so that it may be effectively enforced, as against the need to protect the young person. Open publicity is likely to include photographs.

- The court must now consider making a parenting order on the making of an ASBO if the defendant is aged 10 -15 years old if it is considered desirable to prevent repetition of the behaviour. The consideration of a parenting order is discretionary for the 16 and 17 year olds. See 2.13.6.

The youth court will only deal with the orders which are made ancillary to criminal proceedings, i.e. as 'bolt-on' orders with another sentence, and also the breaches of any ASBO, whether made in the adult or youth court. Interestingly the usual automatic restriction on publicity in youth court does not now apply when an ancillary bolt-on order is made - although the restriction would apply to the criminal part of the proceedings.

7.3.4. ASBOs made in absence of the defendant and interim orders

An order on application may be made in the absence of the defendant 'without notice' ('ex parte') if it is considered to be 'necessary' to proceed in this way e.g. witnesses are likely to be intimidated. On the evidence provided, the court must then consider that it is 'just' to make the order - that the application is properly made and there is an urgent need to protect the community. An interim (temporary) order is made to a fixed date and this must be served upon the defendant within 7 days along with a hearing date for the defendant to attend court, otherwise it will lapse. Both the applicant and the defendant may apply to vary or discharge the interim order. Variation may include extending the duration of the interim order. If the defendant chooses not to attend the full hearing, then the final order can be made in absence.

7.3.5. ASBO requirements

What prohibitions should be included in an ASBO? Specific and relevant requirements, rather like bail conditions. Their purpose - to protect victims, witnesses and the wider community.

Example:
Evidence of regular drunken and disorderly behaviour involving noise and spraying graffiti outside a parade of shops/flats.

- *Must not cause harassment, alarm or distress to other people in England and Wales.*

This covers the over-arching evidence required for the order to be made. It may well be appropriate for this type of behaviour to be prohibited throughout the country and will encapsulate any spread of misbehaviour into other areas. It does not restrict any rights.

- *Must not enter the area marked on the plan attached and marked as A and not to cross over B, C, D streets.*

In terms of proportionality such areas should be limited carefully to the problem zones and be very carefully marked and explained. Exclusion for a minimum of 2 years cannot be effectively enforced if there are likely to be reasonable excuses put forward on breach. For instance, crossing main roads which are on the periphery of the problem in any event, or visiting a sick grandmother (representations on the wording of requirements are critical so that any exceptions can be included from the beginning).

- *Must not cause damage to property belonging to another person in X area.*
- *Must not drink alcohol in a public place in X area.*

These conditions are not about the offences of 'criminal' damage which requires proof of intention or recklessness, or being drunk. They simply define behaviour which will not be tolerated any longer from this defendant in this area - simply causing damage and simply drinking alcohol in public may be sufficiently harassing because of the background evidence. It may be appropriate to make the prohibited behaviour areas wider than the exclusion zone as the likelihood is that the behaviour will simply spill out of the exclusion zone and into the next parade of shops.

- *Must not carry aerosol paint sprays or alcohol in a public place in X area.*

A substantial amount of anti social behaviour involves some items, equipment or 'tools of the trade'. This may include sticks, stones, alcohol, fireworks, drug dealer cards - whatever has been involved. The more likely that the 'equipment' has a potential legitimate use, the more restricted the prohibited 'carrying' area is likely to be. Carrying alcohol to his home, or drinking in a public house or in a street café outside of the area is not the problem, as compared to carrying fireworks, for instance, which he has already used purely to frighten people. If he is actually drunk or sprays graffiti elsewhere then it is a criminal offence and also a breach of the wide requirement at number 1 above.

- *Not to associate in public with F and G.*

Bearing in mind that there is already an exclusion in the problem area and causing ASB elsewhere is a breach of the order, the 'non-association' requirement would need strong evidence that when these people are together, there is likely to be trouble anywhere. Some history of joint misbehaviour would be necessary as this engages the freedom under the Human Rights Act to associate with whom we please. It must therefore be proportionate to prevent the level of disorder or crime or protect the rights and freedoms of others as evidenced.

- *Not to approach or communicate in any way with W.*

It may be necessary and appropriate to protect witnesses who are known to the defendant if there is some evidence that there may be negative repercussions.

If the order were made on conviction of an offence, then it is unlikely that there will be sufficient background evidence to justify such a long list of requirements. Perhaps just one condition to keep a specified distance away from the problem area might be appropriate, as compared to an application by a relevant authority which is more likely to be based upon a history of incidents and justify a wider range of prohibitions.

7.3.6. Breach of the ASBO

In September 2003, there were 1623 ASBO orders, with 818 on the 10 -17 year old age group across England and Wales. The latest breach statistics from 1/6/00 to 31/12/02 indicate a breach rate of 36%. Some may say that this is a sign of failure because the breach rate is so high. Others would recognise that occasional misbehaviour by one person who breaches an order is a massive improvement upon virtually constant misbehaviour often by large groups. Breach of an order is not a failure if it is sentenced effectively and the community are protected.

The criminal process on breach includes determination of bail during adjournments, and all penalties excluding a conditional discharge e.g. compensation, curfews with electronic tagging. It extends to 5 years custody at Crown Court, subject to the usual limitations on youths. The Magistrates Court Sentencing Guidelines give custody as the entry point for breach of an ASBO.

7.3.7. Other actions in relation to anti-social behaviour

There are a number of new actions which are directed at anti-social behaviour:

- **Fixed penalty notices** at either £40 or £80 depending on seriousness level for offences such as being drunk and disorderly and throwing fireworks. The amount increases by a half and is registered as a fine if the fixed penalty is unpaid.

- **Environment penalty notices** issued by local authority employees, community support officers and also persons accredited under a community safety scheme e.g. throwing litter, dog-fouling. If the penalty is not paid, the local authority can prosecute the perpetrator for the original offence.

- **Dispersal of intimidating groups** in areas which a senior police officer, with local authority agreement, has designated as an area where there is persistent anti-social behaviour and a problem with groups causing intimidation. The details of the designated area must be published. In such areas, the police and community support officers have the power to disperse groups where their presence or behaviour has resulted, or is likely to result in a member of the public being harassed, intimidated, alarmed or distressed. The individuals are then excluded from the area for up to 24 hours. Refusal to disperse constitutes an offence.

- **Acceptable Behaviour Contract** is a written agreement between the individual and their local authority, youth inclusion support panel, landlord or the police. It can be used for any age as an agreement which may have both negative prohibitions and also positive actions e.g. to attend school regularly and other agencies may be involved in providing support to keep the agreement. Although the agreement is not legally binding, it may be cited in court in any subsequent ASBO proceedings.

- **Parenting contracts** offer a method for agencies to work with parents on a voluntary basis in a structured way. The contract is between the parent and either school, Local Education Authority or youth offending teams as appropriate. A formal parenting order is likely to be applied for if the contract is breached.

- **DPPOs** (Designated Public Places Order). DPPOs are available in areas which have experienced alcohol-related disorder or nuisance. Over 90 areas across the country have now introduced controlled drinking zones ranging from small areas to city-wide. It is not an offence as such to consume alcohol within the designated area but the police have power to control the consumption within that place and they can require people to stop and confiscate the alcohol. Failure to comply with the police request can be dealt with by way of a fixed penalty notice or prosecution for the offence which carries a level 2 fine. Some areas have established 'wet areas' out of the public eye so that drinking is taken away from town centres and children's playgrounds.

- **Noise interventions** continue as before e.g. power of entry for the local authority to enter a dwelling to remove any equipment causing the noise; noise abatement notices which carry a level 5 fine on failure to comply. The additional power is the issue of a warning notice from local authority in respect of noise at night followed by prosecution or fixed penalty (£100 at March 2004).

7.4.   Drugs and crime

7.4.1   Criminal Justice Interventions Programme (CJIP)

This is a Home Office programme which has been live since April 2003 and is due to run for three years. Its aim is to make the most of the opportunities provided by the Criminal Justice System to get drug misusing offenders into treatment and out of crime and, solve the underlying problem of offending to feed drug habits. It involves the police, prisons, probation, Department of Health, National Treatment Agency, Drug Action Teams, treatment services, housing and employment services and the courts. An essential objective of the programme is to ensure that there is delivery of an end-to-end system for drug misusing offenders with effective partnership and case management. CJIP was initially rolled out in the 30 areas with the highest levels of acquisitive crime and nation wide elements are being phased in across England and Wales.

The process begins at the point of charge for specific 'trigger' offences e.g. possess class A drug, theft, burglary, by drug testing. The screening test normally involves a swab under the tongue and the results are known immediately - positive or negative for heroin and crack/cocaine. Failure to supply a sample is an offence carrying up to three months imprisonment. The results can lead to prompt referrals for treatment on a voluntary basis. Additionally, the court may consider a positive test to be material to bail and sentence. In West Yorkshire 70% + of tested defendants have provided positive tests during 2003. During 2004/5 drug testing on charge will become operational in more than 120 custody suites.

Some form of arrest referral, with or without drug testing has been available in all police areas since 2002. Under CJIP, new elements are being added to the basic arrest referral process to create an Enhanced Arrest Referral. These extend the role of the drugs worker beyond simple assessment and referral to include a basic level of treatment service which will bridge the gap between referral and entry into treatment, the phase at which people are at risk of being lost from the system. The Criminal Justice Act carries provision, when put into effect, for restrictions on bail for those who are tested positively and then refuse to undergo assessment or follow-up.

So far as sentencing is concerned, CJIP aims for increased use of Drug Treatment and Testing Orders (DTTO), and CJIP staff will work closely with the DTTO teams to re-engage offenders on the programme and provide support if the order is revoked.

The two key elements of CJIP are through-care through the whole criminal justice process, and then aftercare at the end of a period in custody or community sentence. It will target drug using offenders at all stages of the system and will build upon work undertaken within prisons and on community based programmes. This will mean picking up offenders who are released after periods of remand or short term sentences and those who complete their community sentences or who drop out.

The Prime Minister, Tony Blair said, 'The Criminal Justice Interventions Programme aims to stop the destructive cycle of drugs and crime and stop the 'revolving door' between offending and prison. Everybody wins. Drug users get help through treatment support, and communities suffer less from the scourge of related crime'.

7.4.2.   Basic information on the most commonly used drugs

Heroin, cocaine and ecstasy are all class A drugs, carrying a maximum of 7 years imprisonment for possession and carrying a maximum of life imprisonment for supplying.

(a) Heroin (Smack, Brown, H, Junk, Skag)

A pain-killing drug made from the opium poppy. Street heroin is usually brown, rather than pure white powder.

*   Methods
    It can be smoked (inhaled), sniffed or injected. Inhaling ('chasing the dragon') involves placing the heroin on a piece of tinfoil and gently heating. It forms an oil which runs in lines on the foil leaving a trail of black residue. As it evaporates the resulting smoke is inhaled through a tinfoil tube. Injecting involves mixing street heroin with water and citric acid in a spoon and heated. The solution is then drawn up in a syringe, often using a cigarette filter to filter out impurities. It can then be injected into a vein. This causes damage to veins and the risk of infections e.g. HIV, hepatitis.

*   Effects
    It is sedative drug and very easy to become addicted to. It relaxes the brain and slows down the heart and breathing. The user feels

physically and mentally calm. Blood vessels dilate giving a feeling of warmth. It can be detected in urine for up to three days.

- Problems
  Tolerance develops to opiates so that if someone is in search of repeated euphoria then the dose must be increased or they change their method of administration to the more intense and immediate experience through injection. However there comes a point when no further increases can restore the positive effects of the drug and it is taken just to 'feel normal'. High doses can cause drowsiness. Excessive doses produce stupor and coma. Overdose can cause respiratory failure. Withdrawal symptoms include sweats, chills, cramps and a runny nose. Such symptoms will normally fade after about ten days but the loss of well-being can last for several months.

- Cost
  £20 to £30 for quarter/half of a gram depending on where it is sold. An addict might use a quarter of a gram per day.

(b) Cocaine (Charlie, Coke, Snow) and Crack (Rock, Freebase, Base, Wash, Stone)

Cocaine is a stimulant white powder derived from the coca plant. Crack cocaine is made by chemically altering cocaine powder to form crystals or rocks.

- Methods
  Cocaine powder is usually sniffed up the nose, and it can also be injected (sometimes with heroin). Crack is smoked.

- Effects
  A sudden increase in heart rate, blood pressure and breathing, leading to alertness, exhilaration and feelings of well-being and confidence. When cocaine is sniffed, the effects come on gradually and peak after about 15-30 minutes, for up to an hour in total so the dose may have to be repeated to maintain the effect. It can be detected in urine for up to three days.

- Problems
  Users may develop a strong psychological dependence on the grandiose feelings of physical and mental well-being and are tempted to step up the dose. Large doses or a 'spree' over a few hours can lead to extreme agitation, anxiety and perhaps hallucination. The after-effects of cocaine use include fatigue and depression. Repeated sniffing damages the membranes in the nose. Excessive use can cause an epileptic fit, a stroke or

a heart attack. With chronic, frequent use, a state of mind similar to paranoid psychosis can develop.

- Cost

Cocaine powder £20 to £25 for half a gram. The purer the cocaine, the higher the price. A 'rock' of crack can cost £5 to £20.

(c) Ecstasy or MDMA (E)

MethylenDioxyMethylAmphetamine!

- Methods

This is almost always swallowed as a tablet.

- Effects

Ecstasy is a stimulant which produces a relaxed, euphoric state. It takes effect 20 to 40 minutes after taking a tablet with little rushes of exhilaration which can be accompanied by nausea. The peak effect is 60 to 90 minutes after taking the drug - sensations are enhanced, music sounds better, inhibitions reduce.

- Problems

Taking real ecstasy will cause a rise in body temperature and together with the hot environment of a club, energetic dancing and not drinking water, an ecstasy-induced heat stroke can occur and a number of deaths have occurred. Users often feel 'down' a few days after taking MDMA, caused partly by MDMA's action on the brain, lack of sleep and a suppressed appetite. It is not addictive but the drug can often take on great importance in people's lives and users may move on to other drugs.

- Cost

£2 to £5 for a tablet. One or two tablets as a normal dose during a night/day of dance/clubbing.

(d) Ampetamines (Speed, Whizz, Dexies)

Amphetamines are synthetic stimulant drugs which come as powder, tablets or more rarely as a paste and are class B drugs.

- Methods

May be smoked, sniffed, swallowed, dabbed on the tongue, dissolved in soft drinks, or injected.

- Effects

Arousal is similar to an adrenaline rush in the face of an emergency or stress. Breathing and heart rate speed up and appetite and the need for sleep reduces. Sensations of alertness, confidence and well-being and increased levels of energy and stamina. The effects of a single dose last about three hours and leave the user feeling tired. Amphetamines can be detected in urine for up to four days.

- Problems

Increase of the dose to produce the same effect and craving for the drug can become compulsive. There can be an unpleasant 'comedown' with users feeling tired, lethargic and depressed. Loss of appetite can result in weight loss and susceptibility to infections. Excessive use can cause mental health problems such as paranoia and psychosis.

- Cost

£5 to £10 per gram for amphetamine powder.

(e) Cannabis (Pot, dope, blow, draw, smoke, puff)

Cannabis is derived from the cannabis plant and is now a class C drug. The most important ingredients are concentrated in 'resin' which is exuded mainly at the tops of the plant. 'Hash' is the commonest from of cannabis in the UK, which is resin, scraped or rubbed from the plant and then compressed into brown blocks. 'Herbal' cannabis (grass, marihuana, ganja, weed), is a less strong preparation of the dried plant material. Less common is cannabis oil (hash oil), which is generally prepared by percolating a solvent through the resin. Cannabis with a very high content is known as 'skunk' or 'northern lights'.

- Methods

Most commonly smoked with tobacco in a 'joint'. Pipes, bottles, hot knives, buckets and bongs are used to smoke the drug. Alternatively it can be swallowed, usually by eating it in cakes.

- Effects

In small quantities, users find cannabis both relaxing and stimulating. The senses are enhanced and users often find that it makes them hungry. It is often used in groups as it increases sociability, talkativeness, and brings a greater appreciation of sensory experiences including sound, colour and taste. The effects start gradually a few minutes after smoking and may last up to an hour with low doses and for several hours with high doses. When the effect wears off the user may feel tired. It can be an effective relief for certain conditions e.g. multiple sclerosis. It can be detected in urine for up to 3 or 4 weeks among heavy regular users.

- Problems

In larger quantities or with stronger types, it can cause nausea, hallucinations, anxiety and panic attacks. Smoking cannabis can make throat, chest and lung problems worse. If smoked with tobacco, the nicotine in the tobacco is addictive and causes cancer. It is dangerous to operate machinery whilst under the influence and it can affect short-term memory. Generally it is not viewed as being physically addictive, but can be psychologically addictive and may be regarded as a necessary 'social lubricant'.

- Cost

£10 to £20 for an eighth of an ounce which would be sufficient for a week for a regular user but would only be sufficient for one day for a heavy user. Roughly one sixteenth ounce of cannabis resin would be sufficient to make four strong or eight less potent joints.

(f) Alcohol

Alcohol consists chiefly of water and ethyl alcohol (or 'ethanol'), produced by the fermentation of fruits, vegetables or grain. Beer is about one part ethanol to 20 parts water, wine is about twice to four times as strong, and distilled spirits such as whisky, rum and gin consist of almost half ethanol.

- Effects

Alcohol is absorbed into the bloodstream and starts to have an effect within 5 to 10 minutes, lasting up to several hours. The effect depends on its strength, how quickly it is drunk, whether there is food in the stomach, and the body weight and mood of the drinker, and how much the person is used to drinking. After an equivalent of 2 pints of beer, most people would feel less inhibited and more relaxed. Emotional reactions range from jovial to aggressive and mental and physical functioning is reduced. After another 2 pints, drinkers generally become rather unco-ordinated, slur their words and emotional reactions become highly exaggerated and variable. More drink may result in staggering, double vision and unconsciousness.

- Problems

Alcohol supplies calories but no other dietary essentials so heavy drinking encourages obesity with its attendant dangers. Dietary deficiencies allied with stomach and liver disorders can result in incapacitating brain damage.

Excessive drinking commonly aggravates family, personal and financial problems.

Between 1988 and 2001 the number of women drinking more than the recommended limit of 14 units rose by more than 50%. 3 in 5 men and 1 in 5 women drink well over the maximum safe drinking limit. Some 18 to 25 year olds are now regularly drinking 5 times the daily limit and 'getting drunk' is commonly regarded as 'having a good night'.

The British Crime Survey shows that only 16% of violent acts by strangers are prompted by other drugs, as opposed to 53% which are prompted by alcohol.

• Cost

Compared to other drugs, alcohol often costs more in terms of units of consumption. As little as £1.50 of cannabis resin can make a potent enough joint to last 2 or 3 smokers an hour or so of intoxication. A pint of strong lager in comparison may cost up to £2.50 for one person lasting at most for half an hour of drinking. An ecstasy user may spend £10 for a whole night of clubbing which is the equivalent of 3 or 4 pints of beer.

(HIT drugs training and consultancy (in part) : www.hit.org.uk)

7.4.3.   Drug treatment by court order

The spectrum of maximum penalties for possession and supply of drugs range from possession of a class C drug e.g. cannabis, carrying a maximum of 2 years, through to supply of a class A drug e.g. heroin, cocaine, ecstasy with a maximum of life imprisonment. When a custodial sentence is imposed, the Prison Service will deal with drug treatment as part of the prison regime. Whilst progress is often made within the prison, the return to the community and drug-using circles presents enormous challenges for drug users.

Sentencing in the community band may include a Community Rehabilitation Order which may include a requirement to reside in a hostel (which could provide some support and encouragement to address drug-related problems), or attend the 'Addressing Substance Related Offending' (ASRO) programme. The ASRO programme does not include treatment and requires some level of stability in order to actively engage with the inter-active group work - it relates to alcohol and other drugs.

The principal court tool to provide treatment rather than punishment for drug offenders is the Drug Treatment and Testing Order.

7.4.4.   Drug Treatment and Testing Order (DTTO)
See also at 2.8.11.

The purpose of the DTTO is to 'break the link between drug use and crime'. Suitability for the order rests upon the offence seriousness falling high in the community band as the restriction on liberty is high and will usually begin with 5 days per week for 20 hours per week. For the same reason, the court must be satisfied that the defendant is susceptible to treatment, but it is probable that there will have been failures to comply with previous drug schemes simply due to the very nature of addiction. In practical terms the court is looking for 'motivation potential' rather than expecting real evidence of motivation at the outset. Is there optimism that this time may be different and that the order will at the very least reduce offending to fund the habit for a time at least?

The treatment element will include various elements such as attendance on probation programmes e.g. ASRO (above); individual discussions to attain targets set by the monthly court reviews, and substitute drugs may be offered in the short term. Some courts have a specialist panel for making DTTOs (6%) and others have a DTTO review panel (42%) which deals with the monthly review hearings when the order has been made in a normal court list. Magistrates who sit on the monthly review hearings may find it helpful to have some awareness of the most common alternative substances which are prescribed during treatment.

- **Methadone**

This is the most commonly prescribed drug (class A) for heroin users. It is usually prescribed as a liquid. It is a much longer-acting drug than heroin. Users will normally take it once a day. It can give feelings of well-being, less intense than heroin but longer lasting. It takes about 4 days from the start of the treatment to build up in the system and the risk during this period is that fatal overdoses can occur if methadone is taken with other downer-type drugs such as heroin, alcohol and tranquillisers. The main difference from heroin is that it is free and legal on prescription and it may be prescribed safely for years.

- **Subutex (buprenorphine)**

This is a long-acting opiate which is taken as a pill which dissolves under the tongue. It is taken once a day to start with and then once treatment is stable, reduces to once every 2 or 3 days. There has to be a gap of at least 12 hours since the last heroin or 24/36 hours since the last methadone or there will be an instant and severe withdrawal. Subutex does not usually give a strong opiate effect - more like just 'feeling normal'. This is helpful for those who have not been using for a long period or find that methadone slows them down. Withdrawal from subutex is usually less severe than from heroin or methadone.

- **Britlofex (Lofexidine)**

This drug does not have any heroin-like effects. It helps to reduce the symptoms of withdrawal, and is used for those who are able to cope with a rapid detoxification. It does not help with anxiety or sleeplessness.

- **Nalorex (Naltrexone)**

This drug works by sticking to, and blocking all of the opiate receptors in the brain. It basically means that taking heroin and other opiates will have no effect. There has to be a gap of 10 days since the last methadone/heroin or instant withdrawal will follow. There may well be side effects of anxiety, stomach upsets and sleeplessness. There is a high risk of overdose if the user stops taking the nalorex and starts using opiates again as tolerance will have been lost and the opiate receptors are made more sensitive by the nalorex.

A recent survey in West Yorkshire of 56 DTTO participants at the 6 month stage revealed that their self-reported criminal activity had fallen by an average of 70% and their general health problems had reduced significantly. At the start of the order their average weekly spend on drugs was £200 per week. None of them were earning or claiming this amount. It is perhaps safe to speculate that they will have stolen goods valued at least 3 or 4 times more than the £200 cash which they secured to buy the drugs? That involves a lot of property and victims.

7.4.5. Prison Service Drug Strategy Programme

This strategy for prisoners aims to reduce the supply of illegal drugs into prisons through a range of supply reduction initiatives and to reduce the demand for drugs amongst prisoners by effective treatment interventions in prison. Examples are reducing dependence through detoxification; providing drug rehabilitation and support and mandatory and voluntary drug testing programmes to encourage prisoners to remain drug-free. Since the strategy was introduced in 1995, the level of positive mandatory drug tests has halved from 24.4% in 1997 to 11.7% in January 2003.

7.5. Domestic Violence

7.5.1. Statistics and features of domestic violence

- Domestic violence accounts for nearly one quarter of all recorded violent crime.
- Every year around 120 women and 30 men are killed by a current or former partner.
  (Safety and Justice, Home Office 2003).
- Approximately 1 in 4 women will experience some form of domestic violence in their lifetime.
- 81% of victims were women and 19% were men in 2001/2.
- Every minute in the UK, the police receive a call from a member of the public for assistance in respect of domestic violence. Less than 1 in 3 domestic incidents are reported at all. (British Crime Survey, 2000).
- Domestic violence is the single most quoted reason for people becoming homeless.
  (Shelter, 2002).

There are various features which make domestic violence different to any other type of violence. It will very often form a pattern of repeat offending and it is probable that a victim has been abused on a number of occasions before notifying the police. The parties know each other and their strengths and weaknesses and may well still love each other. This unique knowledge and power brings enhanced opportunity and planning, and intimate knowledge of vulnerability. There are rarely any other witnesses as the offence is usually committed in the privacy of the home (which should be a place of safety), and the victim is reluctant to involve children as witnesses. The injuries may be purposely inflicted on parts of the body which are not visible to the public.

The controlling behaviour of violence is likely to be accompanied by other abuse across the range of behaviours including verbal, emotional, sexual, using the children, blaming, stalking, preventing financial/social independence. The impact on the victim therefore can extend far beyond physical injury, to isolation, exhaustion, loss of self esteem, desperation, illness, psychological dysfunction and drug/alcohol dependency to get through the day. Children in the family will almost certainly be affected by the violence, ranging from trauma and truancy to self-harm and negative attitudes for life.

The court should always be alert to domestic violence so that realistic concerns can be explored and dealt with during a remand period, and so that appropriate sentencing objectives are identified when selecting penalty.

7.5.2. Bail in domestic violence cases

In determining bail, it is important to recognise that the proceedings are inquisitorial and the bench are entitled to ask questions to determine level of risk. Strict rules of evidence do not apply. For instance, evidence of police call outs to the home are not previous convictions and are not necessarily the 'fault' of the defendant, but they do demonstrate that the couple are not living peaceably. An existing domestic injunction is relevant because it does not seem to be stopping the problem. The strength of evidence should be assessed as with any bail decision with a determination of whether witnesses may require protection through bail conditions or a remand in custody in order to preserve the evidence to statement and court hearing.

Four aspects regarding bail conditions may usefully be considered if the relevant exceptions are made out.

(i)   'No contact' with the victim and any other known witnesses, and not to make contact indirectly or through 3rd parties.

(ii)   A 'keep out' area for the victim and children so that they are protected from any physical approach by the defendant within that area. A hundred yards is derisory. The defendant will be well aware of the day to day movements of the victim and children and he can easily make contact outside of the school, place of work or local shops. For the critical bail period - only a few weeks at the most - the victim desperately needs the protection to go about her normal daily life within the area of school/work/shops as defined on a plan. More realistically this will be a good half mile or mile of the home. It may well be necessary to include some exceptions, e.g. except to visit doctor by appointment, except to travel by car directly to and from work along X road. Around 50% of domestic violence cases are withdrawn or discontinued on the instigation of the victim. This is one aspect of bail which can help to avoid retraction of statements caused by unwelcome approach, cajoling and threats.

(iii)   A reside/live and sleep address for the defendant so that the victim is aware of where he is living so that she knows where to avoid. Applications to vary a bail address would then be controlled by the court. This is relevant if the defendant sought to move to an address which would require additional controls, e.g. move to his parents who look after the children on days of the week. It also gives the court and the agencies notice of any variation to return back to the victim's home, so that checks can be made that the return is genuinely welcome and also put support mechanisms in place prior to any return, e.g. help line phone numbers, cocoon police watch.

(iv)   A timed and dated visit to the home in order to collect belongings.

It is sometimes suggested that conditions should include contact arrangements with the children 'as arranged through solicitors'. This creates several difficulties. Predominantly, contact is a matter for application to the family courts and the criteria is based upon the welfare of the child, rather than upon any 'right' of a parent to see a child. The criminal court, particularly on the limited information available on a remand application, will not be able to assess child welfare and protection issues. The victim does not necessarily have a solicitor and why should she have to hire a solicitor at this point simply to assist the defendant? If an application is made to the family court, then that is a different matter. The reality is that mothers will be the first to arrange contact of their own volition if they feel that it is safe and appropriate.

At the close of a pronouncement on bail conditions, it is helpful in domestic cases to emphasise that the conditions can only be varied formally by the court and breach of conditions may of course result in a remand in custody. This may reduce the regular breach of condition cases where the defendant states that the victim instigated contact and he responded because he had failed to grasp the seriousness of breaching the bail condition.

7.5.3.   Trial of domestic violence cases

At trial, every effort should be made to reduce the obvious tensions. There are now significant efforts to build prosecution cases without putting even more pressure on the victim to be a witness. This may be achieved by using evidence of what the arresting police officer saw and heard, photographs of the scene and the injuries, 999 calls, but the reality is that the victim's evidence is usually necessary. She may sometimes welcome the issue of a witness summons to require her attendance and the police are likely to explore this option, to reduce the impact of unwelcome cajoling to drop the case. Separate waiting areas, use of video evidence if the children are giving evidence, screens possibly for the victim, full support by the witness service, intervention by the chairman to prevent witness bullying and breaks in the proceedings when emotions run high.

7.5.4. Sentencing domestic violence cases

So far as sentence is concerned, the Sentencing Guidelines list 'abuse of trust (domestic setting)' as an aggravating feature for assault. Aggravating - not mitigating, as sometimes suggested! Similarly, self-induced intoxication is not mitigation or any form of excuse for drunken violence. Always ask whether there is a victim personal statement as this may provide helpful information.

The sentencing objectives of a domestic violence offence are likely to focus upon prevention, protection and/or rehabilitation, rather than 'one off' punishment which may well exacerbate matters e.g. fine, community punishment, short prison sentence. A full pre-sentence report will normally be necessary in order to provide a full risk assessment for the family as a whole and an independent description of the defendant's attitude to the offence and the relationship. A community rehabilitation order with a requirement to attend a domestic violence programme may well be appropriate. Where such efforts have been made in the past and failed, it may be necessary to ensure protection by long term custody and commit to the Crown Court for sentence where this is available.

When the parties live apart, it may be appropriate to make an ancillary binding over order directed to protect the victim. This could assist also in protection following release from a custodial penalty, bearing in mind that there is no licence protection on sentences up to 12 months. If the binding over order is breached, forfeiture of the recognisance will depend upon finances and the circumstances of the relationship at the time.

Whilst compensation may be well deserved, the issue is that the order may well be paid either from a joint family purse or it may deprive the children and be used as an acrimonious tool.

Many victims are clear that they want the court to impose a sentence which allows the relationship to continue but makes the violence stop - or at least reduce. If they feel that the legal process is effective, they will have no hesitation in reporting again.

7.5.5. Special courts or special cases?

Special domestic violence courts have been created in some areas - often with attendance in court of voluntary agencies and/or police domestic violence co-ordinators to support any victims who chose to attend court. Aims of specialist courts vary, but include expedition of trials by express service of evidence, or a dedicated officer to notify the victim of the outcome of the case e.g. whether the defendant has been granted bail to return home or not. All areas now have some form of inter-agency liaison to build a smooth passage from reporting the case to the police right through to attendance at court as a witness. Inter-agency information - sharing is improving so that victims do not have to repeat their story several times to different agencies.

Whilst 'special courts' are useful, the fact is that domestic violence cases are generated every day in any crime list. From the court viewpoint, the critical issue of bail must be determined and cannot be adjourned to a specialist court. The Crown Prosecution Service, police and Witness Service must ensure that the victim is supported and protected so far as practicable, and is made aware of what has happened in court - whatever the day of the week. The crucial hours are the first hours after the incident to set the case on course for an effective outcome. Everyone involved in the process must be aware of this. Domestic violence is a special case in any list.

7.6.   Truancy

7.6.1.   Facts and figures

- There are approximately 50,000 'truants' from school per day in England and Wales - 8 million lost school days in a year.
- In 2002/03 the total absences in maintained primary schools was 5.81%, and 8.28% in maintained secondary schools (http://www.dfes.gov.uk/rsgateway/DB/SFR/ accessed 24.2.04).
- Most absences are 'authorised'. The decision to prosecute is made on the basis of 'unauthorised' absence, which is the definition of 'truancy'. It is important to recognise that 'authorised absence' is absence with permission from the head teacher or other authorised representative of the school, and there are wide variations in the level of scrutiny in respect of 'excuses' for failing to attend school.
- National prosecutions rise from 3% of pupils at Year 1 to 32% of pupils in year 10, with the significant rise beginning at year 7 at the transition from primary to secondary school.
- Prosecutions against 'father only' accounted for 7% and against 'mother only' for 47%.
  (National Foundation for Educational Research)

There is some evidence of a link between truancy and crime.

- Two-thirds of those of school age sentenced in court had either been excluded or were known to be missing a significant amount of schooling through truancy (Misspent Youth1998).
- Provisional results from female prisons for 2001/2 showed that the proportion whose results were low (level one and below) was 74.3% in writing and 70.6% in numeracy.

7.6.2. Truancy sweeps

The police have a statutory power to pick up truants found in public places and return them to school or a designated place e.g. community centre to check out information given. 'Sweeps' are conducted with Education Welfare Officers (EWOs), and children and young people of school age can be stopped and questioned if suspected of truancy. The officers will then assess whether there is a reasonable excuse for absence, or take steps to re-integrate into school. In a recent truancy sweep in Leeds city centre, 90 children during one week were questioned who did not have authorisation to be absent from school. Some were returned to school on the same day. Two thirds of the children were actually with a parent. Follow-up action, particularly where children are with parents who are condoning unauthorised absence may be necessary. Parents of unaccompanied children are notified and a home visit will normally follow.

7.6.3. Fast track prosecutions

Most authorities now pursue a 12 week 'fast -track' procedure, at least in respect of some target schools/pupils. This will normally follow the following process, with the aim of each stage securing a satisfactory return to school:

Weeks 1 - 5
1. School identifies pupils falling below their target attendance figure e.g. 85% (secondary) or 90% (primary) attendance level, and make contact to re-establish attendance.
2. Education Welfare Officer (EWO) involvement with at least one home visit to identify 'needs'. Social Services will only be drawn into the situation if the EWO believes that there is a likelihood of 'significant harm' or risk to the child, probably via the designated child protection teacher. This compares to identification of 'needs', which may only be referred to Social Services if the parent/carer consents. Without consent, the EWO effectively takes on a pivotal role to address any 'needs' which are impacting upon school attendance so far as practicable.

Weeks 5 - 8

8. School Attendance Panel convened by the school with a teacher, EWO and any other agencies deemed appropriate. Parent and child are invited to attend. School governors may be involved at this stage, and in some areas, there may be designated 'attendance governors'. An action plan signed by local education authority, school and parent/carer to tackle problems with phased processes and support e.g. to address bullying. A voluntary parenting contract may be agreed at this stage which may well include an attendance target for the child.

9. School communication continues. EWO makes at least one more home visit with continued family dialogue and 'brokering' for the school.

Weeks 8 - 16

10. Local Education Attendance Panel convened with a formal invitation and warning letter sent to parent/carer. Action plan agreed. Other agencies may be involved in the plan, e.g. Youth Offending Team providing voluntary parenting classes; 'Sure Start' for the under 8s; 'Connexions' for the over 13s; quality assurance representative.

11. At week 12, consideration of court action, with an information being laid by week 16 and summons issued to parent(s) to attend court.

7.6.4.   Criminal offences

There are now two offences, with the option of imprisonment on the aggravated offence which basically requires proof that the parent is condoning the absence.

- s. 444 (1) Education Act 1996 - if a child of compulsory school age, who is a registered pupil at a school, fails to attend regularly at the school, his parent is guilty of an offence, punishable by a fine of up to £1000.
- s.444 (1A) Education Act 1996 - if in the above circumstances the parent knows that his child is failing to attend regularly at the school and fails without reasonable justification to cause him to do so, he is guilty of an offence punishable by a fine of £2,500 and/or 3 months imprisonment. Magistrates Court Sentencing Guidelines entry point = Community penalty.

Note that the child must be a registered pupil for a prosecution to be launched. Many children are not registered to attend a school. This may be legitimate as parents have the right to arrange for their children to be educated out of school, provided that the local education authority consider this to be suitable and therefore do not serve a school attendance order on the parent. This is known as Education Otherwise (parental choice).

7.6.5. Education Supervision Orders

The local education authority must consider this order before moving to prosecution, and the court may direct that it is considered on conviction for the above offences. It may be made whenever there is a failure to comply with a school attendance order or failure to attend school regularly. It is made in the family proceedings court and the supervisor (usually the Education Welfare Officer) must advise, assist and befriend, and give directions to the parent and child to secure proper education for the duration of one year. Such applications tend to be made particularly for younger children and where additional needs are identified.

Persistent failure to comply by the parent carries a fine of up to £1000, and persistent failure of the child to comply will result in referral and investigation by the local authority with a view to care proceedings (s.36 Children Act 1989).

7.6.6. Sentencing options and objectives

The options available for both offences are as follows:

- Absolute discharge
- Conditional discharge
- Fine
- Community Rehabilitation Order
- Curfew Order

+ Parenting Order as an ancillary penalty.

The aggravated offence additionally carries imprisonment, and therefore, a Community Punishment Order.

What is likely to be the sentencing objective? Punishment, prevention, protection or rehabilitation? The purpose is obviously to try and get the child back into school so that he can have the benefit of an education. How is this likely to be achieved?

So far as the option of punishment is concerned, it is now open to designated local education officers and teachers, and the police to issue penalty notices (February 2004). The penalty notices form an alternative to prosecution under s.444(1) and enable parents to discharge potential liability for conviction for that offence by paying a penalty of £50 if paid within 28 days, and £100 if paid within 42 days. If the penalty is not paid in full at the end of the 42 day period, the local education authority must withdraw the notice in specified circumstances, or prosecute for the offence. This option is likely to be used where the parent is deemed to be capable of ensuring attendance but is unwilling to do so. A financial penalty may therefore have been tried already to encourage compliance.

Significantly, on a sample of fines cases in West Yorkshire in March/April 2003, only 9% were paid by September 2003, and 45% of the parents were subject to fine default proceedings, including suspended committal.

Since the custodial option became available, one parent has already had two custodial sentences.

The question is whether 'punishment' by the court is likely to be productive for the family concerned, whether it may create resentment and pressure, and whether it is proportionate to the behaviour. Case law guidance on the imposition of custodial sentences highlights offences involving violence or intimidation or other grave crimes, and is clear that other disposals may be 'more appropriate' for 'other categories of offences' (R v. Kefford 2002). The imprisonment of a single parent, in particular, will always engage the children's right to family life under Article 8 and must be a proportionate to the prevention of crime or the rights and freedoms of others. There is the added difficulty with a female that there are less female prisons, more female prisoners than ever, and it is far more difficult to accommodate a woman near to the family (R v. Joanne Mills 2002).

So far as 'prevention of further offending' is concerned, this is unlikely to be assisted by a curfew order or community punishment order on the parent - it may well add to the problems of running the family even more. A community rehabilitation order is geared to the reduction of criminal offending and in a chaotic family there is a high chance of failure to attend appointments and breach action after two failures to attend. Is compliance by the parent really going to get the child to school? Breach of an order under the aggravated offence would carry imprisonment - is this likely to assist?

A conditional discharge? Bearing in mind the lead up action to court proceedings, and the failure to engage on a voluntary basis with the help on offer, is it really appropriate to contemplate an end result of 'nothing'. Perhaps optimism that miraculously the court appearance alone will extinguish long-standing, underlying problems.

Of course every case is different, and every penalty has a value in particular circumstances. However, there is much to be said for a greater and more imaginative use of the ancillary parenting order. Why?

It is interesting that the parent who attends youth court with a child who they have not even registered with a school, or a child who is excluded for bad behaviour, will usually leave the youth court with some measure of parental assistance. This may be in the form of a parenting order, or as part of their child's referral, supervision or action plan. Fines are now becoming increasingly rare in youth court. Supportive, rather than punitive orders are regarded as the first method to try and change behaviour and family lifestyle.

Similarly in the family proceedings court, the welfare of the child is paramount and is at the centre stage for consideration to ensure that there is adequate support, for and by parents and agencies. By comparison, the parent in the adult court who has at least registered a child at a school and their child is rarely involved in criminal proceedings - the starting point is a criminal penalty for the parent. This is surely an anomaly between the court jurisdictions?

7.6.7.   Parenting orders

So how can the adult court attach similar values and purpose? The parenting order is ancillary to prosecution cases, but it can be attached to any penalty, including an absolute or conditional discharge so that it essentially forms the main outcome. This is the current focus in Leeds both from the EWO viewpoint and as a primary consideration when parent(s) attend court.

Parenting orders are not necessarily a series of parent craft classes. They are not solely available through youth offending teams alongside parents of criminals. They can be focussed on one problem alone, e.g. failing to attend school, with one to one support by the education welfare officer. There are 2 features to the order:

(i)   Compliance for up to 12 months with such requirements as are notified in the order.

Example:

To take reasonable steps to ensure attendance in accordance with instructions of responsible officer.

It is very difficult for any parent to physically ensure attendance of an older child. There is a limit. Realistically they can be made responsible 'to take reasonable steps' as suggested or facilitated by the officer. This could be action to get the child up in the morning and send off to school with bus pass in hand, rather than just sleeping through school departure time and then going shopping together. Ringing the school to report genuine sickness, rather than just keeping the child at home to look after younger siblings. Arranging to obtain school uniform before the start of term rather than using the excuse that the uniform has not been obtained. This would be the difference between being culpable or not in subsequent proceedings.

(ii)   Attend guidance/counselling sessions for a concurrent period of up to 3 months. The limitation to attend no more than once per week has recently been deleted to allow for residential courses where necessary (unlikely in the school attendance scenario).

Example:

To attend three fixed appointments with the responsible officer at .... on .....

The sessions will provide guidance and monitor whether the parent is complying with the requirement. It will also be helpful to assess the impact of actions agreed by the school, e.g. moving the child to a different class.

Whilst breach of the order carries a fine of £1,000, the reality is that breach is not worth pursuing if the child is now attending school satisfactorily and if not, then further proceedings will no doubt follow for the non-attendance. Next time around, the aggravated offence may be appropriate.

At a first hearing, the picture may well be a catalogue of family 'needs' which parent has failed to engage upon solving. At the court hearing, the support moves from voluntary to court ordered, which is a different situation - often with little change in actual resources required. At a subsequent hearing, the court have the assurance that even court ordered support has failed to draw parental input into their child's education. A community based option has at least been tried.

(As a separate power, from February 2004, the local education authority may apply for a parenting order to be made in respect of parents of a child who is excluded from school for serious misbehaviour).

7.7. Living on state benefits - types, amounts and assessing court payments

7.7.1. Contribution based Job Seekers Allowance

The claimant must be actively seeking work. The allowance relies on a person's contribution record and it is a fixed single person rate regardless of a person's circumstances or savings. However it is only payable for a period of 26 weeks. A defendant over 25 would have a weekly benefit of £55.65. This may be their only income, but they may also have considerable savings.

7.7.2. Income based Job Seekers Allowance

The claimant must be actively seeking work. This allowance is not based on contributions and there are more restrictions on who can claim, namely:

- Those with savings of over £8,000 if under 60, or £12,000 if over 60 cannot claim at all.
- Those with a partner who is working more than 24 hours, or who themselves are working more than 16 hours per week cannot claim at all.

The basic scale rates are set dependent predominantly on a person's age, although there are increases for dependants.

Examples:

- *Young people aged 16 to 18 will only be able to claim benefit if they can demonstrate why they are 'estranged' from their family, and if they are not found to be entitled, their only recourse is a discretionary severe hardship payment.*

- *A person aged 18-24 receives £11.60 per week less benefit than a person aged 25 or older even though he has the same bills to pay.*

- *If a couple are both aged 18 or over, they will receive £87.30 per week, whereas if one of them is under 18, the couple will only receive £44.05.*

Job Seekers Allowance can be sanctioned for a number of reasons, e.g. failing to attend an appointment - particularly problematic for drug users with chaotic lifestyles. An initial sanction will mean no benefit for 2 weeks, a second sanction extends the period to 4 weeks and a third sanction means that a person will not receive benefit for 26 weeks.

7.7.3. Income Support

The claimant does not have to show that he is available for work. The biggest group of claimants are single parents and those who are sick. Whilst they have to attend periodic interviews in order to get benefit, they do not have to sign on fortnightly. The rules about savings are the same as for Job Seekers Allowance.

From April 2004 all child elements of income support and job seekers allowance will be paid together with child benefit as the child tax credit.

Example:

S is a single parent aged 28, with a child aged 3. She receives £5 per week from the child's father and child benefit of £16.50. She owns her own property.

Child tax credit:		
Family element	*£10.45*	
Child aged 3	*£31.25*	
Total	*£41.70*	
Income support for self:		
IS Adult rate	*£55.65*	
Total weekly income	*£55.65*	*(IS)*
	£41.70	*(child tax credit)*
	£16.50	*(child benefit)*
	£5.00	*(maintenance)*
	————	
	£118.85	
	————	

From this she will have to pay gas, electricity, phone, water rates. She will be entitled to either mortgage interest which is paid directly to the lender, or Housing Benefit to cover rent, and also, council tax benefit, free school meals, prescriptions, dental and optical treatment. A number of local authorities also run schemes whereby leisure facilities are offered a reduced cost too, e.g. swimming baths.

7.7.4. Incapacity benefit

Incapacity Benefit relies on contributions in the same way as contribution based Job Seekers Allowance. A defendant may describe himself as 'being on the sick' but could be in receipt of either Income Support or Incapacity Benefit. The difference is significant because defendants on Incapacity Benefit lose maximum, full entitlement to passport benefits, so will not qualify for rent/mortgage interest and full council tax benefit. Additionally debts including fines cannot be deducted.

There are 3 levels of Incapacity Benefit, depending upon how long a person has been unfit for work. For a single person these rates are:

Week 1 - 28	£55.90
Week 29 - 52	£66.15
Week 53 onwards	£74.15

7.7.5. The poverty trap

When a single person returns to paid work he is allowed to keep £5 of his wages, or £10 if he is part of a couple. The remainder is taken off their benefit pound for pound.

Example:

J is aged 26 and in receipt of Job Seekers Allowance of £55.65 per week. He finds a part time job of 10 hours per week and is paid £45. He is allowed to keep £5 under JSA rules and only £40 is deducted from his benefit. He therefore has £45 wages + the balance of his JSA of £15.65. He is £5 per week better off than before.

J is offered full-time employment. This would mean coming off JSA altogether and also losing his passport benefits. The resulting new outgoings e.g. rent/council tax, plus travel to work would almost certainly mean that he would be worse off.

Passport benefits are paid in full to people in receipt of Income Based Job Seekers Allowance and Income Support. This would include having rent paid via housing benefit and council tax paid via council tax benefit; free prescriptions; dental treatment; school meals. There is also access to Community Care Grants. Although these are discretionary, they may cover essential 'one off' items such as fridge, cooker, bed etc.

7.7.6. Deductions from benefits for fines

Deductions may be made at the rate of £2.80 per week from Income Support or Job Seekers Allowance or Pension Credit. For a single claimant over 25, a single deduction is 5% of his basic scale rate. Only one deduction can be made at any one time for a fine or group of fines which are all applied for at one time. Other applications can be made and stacked at the Department of Work and Pensions. This would arise when a new fine is imposed at a time when there is already an existing deduction. It may be appropriate to consider an alternative disposal if the existing fines are already extending beyond 12 months repayment period. Such options include the new option of disqualification as a penalty in its own right for the multiple traffic offender. A curfew or community rehabilitation order is available even for non-imprisonable offences. This may be appropriate, for instance, if the fine is in default (as opposed to a consent deduction) because this demonstrates a failure to respond to a financial penalty which may escalate seriousness out of the fines band. If such an order is breached and revoked though, the original offence will be back before the court - and it still will not carry imprisonment!

Deductions in relation to housing costs, fuel charges, water charges and council tax take higher priority than deductions for fines and the application for deduction for a fine will not be considered in cases where there are already 3 deductions in place. (Less than 3% of those in receipt of relevant benefits actually have 3 debt deductions - March 2004).

The court must now apply for an attachment of benefit order in respect of fines if there is default unless it is inappropriate or impractical to do so. An attachment may be applied for at the point of imposition if the defendant is not a defaulter, provided that he consents to the application being made.

BIBLIOGRAPHY

Ashcroft, P. et al. (1999). *Human Rights and the Courts: Bringing Justice Home.* Winchester: Waterside Press.

Audit Commission Update (1998). *Misspent Youth '98.* Abingdon: Audit Commission Publications.

Card, R., and Ward, R. (1998). *The Crime and Disorder Act 1998: a Practitioner's Guide.* Bristol: Jordans.

Carr, A. P. and Turner, A. J. (eds.) (2003). *Stone's Justices' Manual 2003.* 135th ed. 3 vols. London: LexisNexis UK.

Criminal Justice System (2004). *Working Together for Justice.* London: CJS / Home Office / CPS / Department of Constitutional Affairs.

Department for Education and Skills (2003). *Ensuring Regular School Attendance: Guidance on the Legal Measures Available to Secure Regular School Attendance.* Nottingham: DfES Publications.

Elliot, C. and Quinn, F. (1998). *English Legal System.* 2nd ed. London: Longman.

Goring, R. (ed.) (1994). *Dictionary of Beliefs and Religions.* Edinburgh: Larousse.

Haynes, M. E. (1988). *Effective Meeting Skills.* London: Kogan Page.

Home Office (1999). *Statistics on Race and the Criminal Justice System: a Home Office Publication under s.95 of the Criminal Justice Act 1991.* London: Home Office Research and Statistics Directorate.

Home Office (2002). *Statistics on Women and the Criminal Justice System: a Home Office Publication under s.95 of the Criminal Justice Act 1991.* London: Home Office Research and Statistics Directorate.

Honey, P. (1998). *Improve Your People Skills.* London: Institute of Personnel Management.

ISDD (1999). *Drug Abuse Briefing: a Guide to the Non-medical Use of Drugs in Britain.* London: Institute for the Study of Drug Dependence.

Judicial Studies Board (1998). *Magistrates Bench Handbook: a Manual for Lay Magistrates.* London: Judicial Studies Board.

Judicial Studies Board (1999). *Race and the Courts: a Short Practical Guide for Judges.* London: Judicial Studies Board.

Judicial Studies Board (2001). *Equality before the Courts: a Short Practical Guide for Judges.* London: Judicial Studies Board.

Judicial Studies Board (2003). *Domestic Violence: an Ordinary Crime: Training Manual on Domestic Violence Prepared by the JSB for Use in the Magistrates' Courts.* London: Judicial Studies Board.

Judicial Studies Board (2003). *Adult Court Bench Book.* London: Judicial Studies Board.

Judicial Studies Board (2003). *Magistrates National Training Initiative Handbook: MNTI 2.* London: Judicial Studies Board.

Justices' Clerks' Society (2000). *Fair Treatment Pack. London: Justices' Clerks' Society.* Winchester: Waterside Press.

Leng, R., Taylor, R., and Wasik, M. (1998). *Blackstone's Guide to the Crime and Disorder Act 1998.* London: Blackstone Press Limited.

Magistrates Association. *Magistrate.* (The journal of the Magistrates Association, ISSN 0024-9920). London: Magistrates Association.

Moore, T. G. (ed.) (2000). *Anthony & Berryman's Magistrates' Courts Guide 2001.* London: Butterworths.

NACRO Race and Criminal Justice Unit (1998). *Equal Treatment Training for Lay Magistrates: Training Materials.* London: Judicial Studies Board.

Weller, P. (ed.) (1993). *Religions in the UK: a Multi-faith Directory.* Derby: University of Derby.

USEFUL WEBSITES

Criminal Justice System Online
www.cjsonline.gov.uk

Crown Prosecution Service
www.cps.gov.uk

Department of Constitutional Affairs
www.dca.gov.uk

Home Office
www.homeoffice.gov.uk

HM Prison Service
www.hmprisonservice.gov.uk

Judicial Studies Board
www.jsboard.co.uk

Magistrates Association.
www.magistrates-association.org.uk

Magistrates' Court
www.courtservice.gov.uk

National Probation Service
www.probation.homeoffice.gov.uk

National Statistics Online - Census 2001
www.statistics.gov.uk/census2001

Victim Support
www.victimsupport.org.uk

Witness Service
www.victimsupport.org.uk/services/witness_services.html

Youth Justice Board
www.youth-justice-board.gov.uk

APPENDIX 1
Summary of general competences - MNTI 2

Permission was not given by the Judicial Studies Board to publish the full competence framework as an appendix - hence the summary. See Judicial Studies Board (2003). Magistrates' National Training Initiative Handbook: MNTI 2 for full reference.

Competence 1 - Managing yourself
Competence 2 - Working as a member of a team
Competence 3 - Making judicial decisions

Element	Performance criteria (summarised)	'Needs to knows' (summarised) and key reference pages
Competence 1 - Managing yourself		
1.1.a	Obtaining and reading relevant paperwork	Use of Adult Bench Book, Checklists, Sentencing and MOT Guidelines - 178 Pre-court briefing - 200
1.1.b	Agreeing roles and responsibilities	Delegation - 202 Reporting restrictions - 170
1.1.c	Checking any conflict of interest	Disqualification and bias - 169 Human Rights Act - Article 6 – 169
1.1.d	Discussion with legal adviser and colleagues, issues including case management	Case management - 214 Role of the legal adviser - 24 Role of other main agencies - 16
1.2.a	Focussing attention and demonstrating communication in the court room	Communication - 179 Attentive listening in court - 179 Relationship winger/chairmen - 202, 228
1.2.b	Taking accurate notes and asking questions via the chairman	Note-taking - 180 Questioning in court - 183
1.2.c 1.2.d	Identifying requirements of court users and acting in a dignified and impartial manner	Understanding special needs of court users/ potential for disadvantage - 158 Judicial oath - 146 Human Rights Act - Article 6 - 169

1.3.a	Assessing own performance against competence framework, seeking feedback and identifying own learning needs	Post court reviews - 188, 241 Feedback - 188, 241 Self assessment - 197 Preferred learning styles - 197 Range of learning information - 178
1.3.b	Adapting and developing own performance and keeping resource material up to date	
Competence 2 - Working as a member of a team		
2.1.a	Expressing own views clearly	Behaving assertively - 187
2.1.b	Questioning views of colleagues to clarify issues	Questions in the retiring room - 186 Types of questions - 206
2.1.c	Giving equal consideration to colleagues, including listening attentively	Listening (retiring room) - 185 Discussion through structure - 185 Listening strategies - 231
2.1.d	Using non-discriminatory language Challenging stereotyping	Diversity and fair treatment issues - 147 Non-discriminatory language - 156, 159, 161, 163, 164 Challenging comments – 166
2.2.a	Building supportive, constructive relationships with others in the team	Effective communication in a team - 185 Sharing ideas, being non-judgemental - assertiveness – 197
2.2b	Being receptive to advice of legal adviser	Role of Justices' Clerk.- 24 Role of legal adviser - 24 Communication with legal adviser – 188

Competence 3 - Making judicial decisions		
3.1a	Agreeing most appropriate structure for decision-making and applying correct principles	Bail - 27 Mode of trial - 43 Verdict - 52 Sentencing and options - 60 Enforcement of court orders - community (80), fines (118) Human rights – 168
3.1.b 3.1.c	Sifting and clarifying information Analysing information within the relevant structure	Doctrine of precedent/higher courts - 9 Difference of civil and criminal proceedings - 10 Beyond reasonable doubt - 10,54 Balance of probabilities - 10,54 Inquisitorial approach - 214 Presumption of innocence - 48 Consistent approach to decision making - Structure - bail (36), verdict (52), sentencing (60)
3.1.d 3.1.e	Identifying outcomes that flow from the use of the structure Assisting in formulation of reasons and pronouncements	Structured approach - bail (36), verdict (52), sentencing (60) Sentencing 'totality' - 63 Bail 'proportionality' - 33 Pronouncements - 178, 236 Reasons - verdict (52), sentence (63)
3.2.a 3.2.b	Identifying and setting aside prejudices Challenging any bias or prejudice	Prejudice - 164 Discrimination - 163 Labelling - stereotyping - 164 Stereotyping - 164 Cultural differences - 146 Making the challenge - 166 Non-verbal communication - 179,185, 226 Admissible/ inadmissible evidence – 53

APPENDIX 2
Summary of chairmanship competence - MNTI 2

Permission was not given by the Judicial Studies Board to publish the full competence framework as an appendix - hence the summary. See Judicial Studies Board (2003). Magistrates' National Training Initiative Handbook: MNTI 2 for full reference.

Competence 4 - 'Managing judicial decision making.

Element	Performance criteria (copied in full)	'Need to knows' (headings summarised only) and key reference pages
4.1.a	Identifying issues for clarification prior to each court session and establishing the relevant structures and processes to facilitate routine applications and procedures	Pre-court briefing - 200 Bail - 27 Mode of trial - 43 Verdict - 52 Trial procedure - 212 Sentencing and options - 60 Enforcement of orders - 80 (community), 118 (fines) Human rights - 168 Precedent and the higher courts - 9 Order of civil and criminal proceedings and standard and burden of proof - 10 Facts that could disqualify a magistrate from hearing a case and potential bias – 169
4.1.b	Agreeing with the legal adviser respective roles and responsibilities and maintaining these	Pre-court briefing - 200 Agreeing speaking roles - 201 Practice direction on the role of the legal adviser – 24
4.1.c	Reviewing the day's sitting with the legal adviser	Post-court review - purpose and content - 188, 241 Feedback skills - 188, 241

4.2.a	Ensuring that the purpose and framework of the hearing is established and maintained from the outset by giving appropriate directions, setting realistic timetables, seeking explanations from participants for failure to comply with directions and taking appropriate action	Case management - 214 Role of chairman in ensuring that cases proceed effectively - 214 Inquisitorial approach - 214 Gathering information - 205 Effective questioning techniques - 205 Attentive listening - 179 Making directions - 221 Local and national case management protocols - 246 (national)
4.2.b	Giving clear instructions to participants through-out the proceedings and checking that all those involved understand what is happening in the court room and any decisions that have been made	Running commentary - 204 Diversity and fair treatment issues - 147 Requirements of those who are vulnerable, unrepresented or who have special needs are met - 158
4.2.c	Addressing those in court fluently, clearly and audibly at all times	Projecting voice in a clear, logical way - 236 Formulating and delivering pronouncement – 236
4.2.d	Encouraging participants at the hearing to contribute constructively and dealing assertively with any inappropriate, inaccurate or unhelpful contributions by restricting representations, speeches and discussions and dealing promptly with any behaviour that is or may disrupt the functioning of the court	Gathering information - 205 Dealing with unrepresented defendant - 208 Control of proceedings and maintaining relevance - 208 Contempt of court procedures - 223 Maintaining dignity - 225 Challenging stereotyping and discriminatory comments - 166
4.3.a	Asking colleagues to take responsibility for key tasks	Delegation of tasks - 202

4.3.b	Facilitating discussion by focusing on the structure, identifying and summarising key issues, intervening promptly when disagreement is preventing constructive discussion and progressing and exploring areas of disagreement in order to achieve a resolution	Managing decision-making process - 228 How to summarise key points accurately - 228 Ensuing full participation - 228 Techniques for managing disagreement and potential conflict - 233 Structured approach - bail (36), verdict (52), sentencing (60)
4.3.c	Agreeing the decision, reasons and pronouncement to be given in court	Formulating reasons - verdict (52), sentence (63) Identifying the appropriate pronouncement - 178
4.3.d	Reviewing the day's sitting with your magistrate colleagues and/or the legal adviser and seeking, receiving and giving feedback	Post-sitting review - 200 Objective feedback with view to minimising conflict - 188, 241
4.4.a	Assessing your own performance against the competence framework. Regularly seeking feedback and identifying your learning and development needs on a continuous basis	Using feedback to assess own competence - 188, 241 Preferred learning styles and selecting appropriate methods to meet your own learning needs - 197
4.4.b	Adapting and developing your own performance in light of changes to law, practice, procedure, research and other developments. Keeping your own resource materials (e.g. bench guide, handbooks, guidelines) up to date.	Range of source materials - 178 Current issues - 243

Summary of general competences - MNTI 1

All competences are covered with the exception of local (L), outdated (O/D) or non-specific issues (N/S). Key reference pages are provided.

Competence 1
The structure of the Judicial System
House of Lords - 9
Appeal Court - 9
High Court - 9
Civil Division - 9
County Court - 10
Criminal Division - 9
Magistrates' Court - 10, 12
Appeals - 14
European Court of Justice - 15
European Convention - 15
Criminal Justice System
Home Office - 16
Lord Chancellor's Department - 16
Police - 16
Prison - 17
Probation - 17
Crown Prosecution Service - 16
Prosecuting Agencies - 18
Legal profession - 19
Variety of legislation - 13
Civil cases in the Magistrates' Court
Community safety legislation - 19
General licensing (O/D)
Local authorities - 18
Other agencies - 18
18 - 25 Local community omitted (L)
26. Crime statistics - 13
Bench
27. Magistrates' Courts Committee - 20, 193
28. Local Advisory Committee - 21

Competence 2
Basic law and procedure
How proceedings initiated
Laying an information - 20
Issuing a summons - 20
Issuing a warrant - 20
Community safety - 19
TV licences - 19
General licenses (O/D)
Sequence of events - 46
Prosecution outline - 47
Prosecution case - 48
No case to answer - 50
Defence case - 50
Verdict - 52
Mitigation - 56
Sentence decisions - 60
Rules of evidence
Sequence of questions - 46
Tests of evidence/burden of proof - 54
Hearsay evidence - 54
Civil and criminal differences - 10
Police - 16
Crown Prosecution Service - 16
Other agencies - 18
Prosecutor - 18
Defence - 19
Witnesses - 46
Case management
24, Statutory time limits - 42
Court diary (NS)
Case in court for the first time - 44
Uncontested traffic matters - 111
Initial decisions
Adjournments - 214

Competence 3
Think and act judicially

Competence 4
Work as a member of a team

Summary of chairmanship competences - MNTI 1

Competence 5
Managing people and processes
Leading the team

1 - 4	Consulting wingers on the bench - 226
5.	Structured decision making - 36, 52, 60
6.	Getting discussion started - 228
7.	Consulting - 228, 232
8.	Listening actively - 231
9.	Purposeful and relevant - 228
10.	Speaking for the bench - 233
11.	Legal adviser - 201
12.	Delegating tasks - 202
13.	Wingers to prompt - 203
14.	Full participation - 232

Legal advisers' role

5 - 21	Relationship - 24, 201
22.	Pre-court briefing - 200
23 - 25	Relationship - 24, 201
26.	Post-court review - 241

Routine procedures

27.	Adjournments - 214
	Bail - 27
	Trial - 46, 212
	Sentence and options - 60
28.	Identifying elements of charge - 228
29.	Evidence - 53
30 - 34	Structure to sentence - 60
	Sentencing options - 65
	Consulting legal adviser - 24
35.	Ensuring defendant understands (NS)
36.	Correct order of proceedings - 208, 212

Competence 6
Adult Chairmanship
Communication

1 - 8.	Clear pronouncements - 236
9 - 11.	Listening - 231
12 - 14.	Questioning - 205

APPENDIX 5
Adult Court - Sentencing options menu

Increase of seriousness and restriction of liberty ➡				
Inexpedient to punish		'Serious enough'	'So serious'	Too serious
Absolute Discharge **Conditional Discharge** +	**Compensation** **Fine** **Disquaify** **1 day detention** +	**Community penalties:** • **Attendance Centre** • **Community Punishment** • **Community Rehabilitation** • **Community Punishment and Rehabilitation** (Combination Order) • **Curfew** • **Drug Treatment and Testing** + *Combinations for single offence Examples:* *CPO + Curfew.* *CRO including Curfew.* *CRO + CPO = Combination (ICCP programme).* *Fines and ancillary penalties (below) can also be added.*	**Custody** +	**Commit to Crown Court**

++ ANCILLARY PENALTIES - always seek representations first - check proportionate (see over)

Ancillary Penalties

Penalty	Key points
Anti-Social Behaviour Order	Caused or likely to cause harassment, alarm or distress and order is necessary. 'Must not' requirements. Minimum of 2 years.
Binding Over Order	Future breach of peace apprehended. Amount and period to reflect seriousness of behaviour.
Compensation	Damage, injury, loss, or terror and distress.
Exclusion from licensed premises	Violence or threats of violence in licensed premises. 3 months to 2 years.
Re-test or test disqualification	Endorseable offence and concern for safety of other road users. 'L' plates and passenger, or driver is committing offence of driving whilst disqualified instead of just driving other than in accordance with licence.
Disqualification	Also as a stand-alone penalty since 2004.
Endorsement	Penalty points allocated to most serious on the occasion, or reasons given for separate points. 12 points = disqualify.
Football banning order	Relevant offences only + believe order will help prevent violence/disorder at designated matches. Minimum 3 years.
Restraining order	Only to offences under Protection from Harassment Act 1997 offences. Specific requirements. 'Until further order' maximum.
Sexual offences prevention order (May 2004)	Relevant offences only - necessary to protect public or members of public from serious sexual harm.
Sex offender notification requirement	Relevant offences only - report details to police within 3 days. Period depends on sentence. Replaces registration in May 2004.
Parenting order	Child is convicted, ASBO, Sex Offender Order. Non-school attendance cases. Up to12 months with counselling/guidance sessions.
Costs	Proportionate but not necessarily less than any fine imposed.
Forfeiture of property	Statutory powers e.g. drugs, offensive weapon.

APPENDIX 6 - FINES CALCULATOR

ANNUAL SALARY	2080	2340	2600	2860	3120	3380	3640	3900	4160	4420	4680	4940	5200	5460	5720	5980
MONTHLY	173	195	217	238	260	282	303	325	347	368	390	412	433	455	477	498
WEEKLY	40	45	50	55	60	65	70	75	80	85	90	95	100	105	110	115
BAND A	20	23	25	28	30	33	35	38	40	43	45	48	50	53	55	58
A(with credit)	13	15	17	18	20	22	23	25	27	28	30	32	33	35	37	38
BAND B	40	45	50	55	60	65	70	75	80	85	90	95	100	105	110	115
B(with credit)	27	30	33	37	40	43	47	50	53	57	60	63	67	70	73	77
BAND C	60	68	75	83	90	98	105	113	120	128	135	143	150	158	165	173
C(with credit)	40	45	50	55	60	65	70	75	80	85	90	95	100	105	110	115

ANNUAL SALARY	6240	6500	6760	7020	7280	7540	7800	8320	8840	9360	9880	10400	10920	11440	11960	12480
MONTHLY	520	542	563	585	607	628	650	693	737	780	823	867	910	963	997	1040
WEEKLY	120	125	130	135	140	145	150	160	170	180	190	200	210	220	230	240
BAND A	60	63	65	68	70	73	75	80	85	90	95	100	105	110	115	120
A(with credit)	40	42	43	45	47	48	50	53	57	60	63	67	70	73	77	80
BAND B	120	125	130	135	140	145	150	160	170	180	190	200	210	220	230	240
B(with credit)	80	83	87	90	93	97	100	107	113	120	127	133	140	147	153	160
BAND C	180	188	195	203	210	218	225	240	255	277	285	300	315	330	345	360
C(with credit)	120	125	130	135	140	145	150	160	170	180	190	200	210	220	230	240

*Credit figure quoted as one third.

Acknowledgement to J.W.C. Cook, J.P, Leeds.

293

INDEX

NOTES

NOTES

NOTES